GRINGO JUSTICE

Gringo Justice

Alfredo Mirandé

University of Notre Dame Press
Notre Dame, Indiana

Library of Congress Cataloging-in-Publication Data

Mirandé, Alfredo.
  Gringo justice.

  Bibliography: p.
  Includes index.
  1. Discrimination in criminal justice
administration—United States.   2. Mexican Americans.
I. Title.
HV9950.M57   1987   364.3'468073   86-40580
ISBN 0-268-01012-9

Manufactured in the United States of America

Para El Futuro—"Los Chilpayates"

Gamin
Vita
Armando
Raúl
Michele
Ayala
Lucía
Alejandro

Contents

Preface   ix

Acknowledgments   xi

1. A Legacy of Conflict   1

2. *Mi Casa Es Su Casa:*   Displacement from the Land   27

3. Vigilantes, Bandits, and Revolutionaries   50

4. The Border and the Law   100

5. *La Placa:*   The Police   146

6. Gangs or Barrio Warriors?   183

7. A Theoretical Perspective on Gringo Justice   216

Notes   237

Bibliography   241

Index   259

Preface

This book deals with an important but neglected area of study—the experience of Chicanos before the legal and judicial system. Other works have addressed specific topics such as social bandits, the Texas Rangers, the zoot-suit riots of the 1940s, and contemporary Chicano gangs, but this work attempts to trace the relationship of Chicanos to the legal and judicial system from 1848 to the present. Although my training is in sociology, I am convinced that the contemporary situation cannot be divorced from its historical context. Historians may well be critical of my treatment of materials, but my intent is to provide a historical context, not to write a history of Chicanos.

Titles such as *Law, Justice, and the Chicano* and *Chicanos and the Legal and Judicial System* were considered and discarded because they implied that the American legal and judicial system had been just and equitable in its treatment of Chicanos. The title *Gringo Justice* seemed to more accurately capture the reality of the Chicano experience before the American tribunals. An underlying premise of the present work is that since the end of the war between Mexico and the United States, displaced Mexicans, or Chicanos, have been subjected to prejudicial and discriminatory treatment—a double standard of justice that applied one system to Anglo-Americans and another to Chicanos. A related premise is that while there have been obvious differences between undocumented Mexican nationals who enter the United States and American citizens of Mexican descent, there are also important commonalities between them. Racism knows no borders. All too often Mexicans on both sides of the border were labeled as "greasers" and members of an inferior, mongrel, treacherous, and innately criminal race.

A final caveat is in order. Those who believe that academic scholarship is a value-free process where one arrives at objective observations and detached conclusions will not be pleased with *Gringo Justice*. As a Chicano scholar, it is my contention that it is neither possible nor desirable to be

indifferent towards racism or the unequal system of justice that has prevailed. On the other hand, I do not wish to suggest that a Chicano has never
committed a crime or perpetrated an injustice. Every racial/ethnic group
has its share of good and bad persons; its saints and sinners. The issue
is not one of individual differences, but, rather, of collective experiences.
The point is that subsequent to the American takeover, Chicanos were
displaced politically and economically and subjected to an alien, inherently unequal legal and judicial system which placed them at a distinct disadvantage, and functioned to maintain their subordinate status.

Until very recently, historical and social science depictions of *la raza*
were written by members of the dominant group. Since I do not believe
that value-free scholarship is possible, my intent is simply to join a number
of Chicano scholars who have started to tell the other side of the story.
I do take comfort in the knowledge that truth and justice are ultimately
on the side of the oppressed and only the oppressor finds it necessary to
distort history so that it will conform to and justify the socially created order.

Acknowledgments

In the limited space available it is only possible to acknowledge a few of the individuals who contributed to the completion of this book. I introduced a class on the Chicano and the Law at the University of California, Riverside (UCR) during the fall quarter of 1975. The class came on the heels of two major disturbances in August involving residents of the barrio of Casa Blanca and the Riverside police. For approximately nine months I served on a "blue ribbon" City Council committee that sought to mediate the conflict and tension between barrio residents and police. I am very grateful to the students in this initial class for their efforts in carrying out an extensive survey of community attitudes toward the police and making the results available to the committee. A large number of students have taken the Chicano and the Law class in subsequent years and stimulated my ideas on the topic. Some of the individuals who deserve special recognition are Jorge Cruz Hernández, Ernesto "Neto" Medrano, and Enrique López. Javier "Guero" López, Anna Larios, Catherine "La Carrie" Parsons, Josefina "Josie" Canchola, and Larry Peña are to be commended for reading the entire manuscript and providing invaluable comments and suggestions. I would also like to thank David V. Baker for his critique of the last chapter.

For a period of approximately six years a group of UCR students and I taught a Chicano Issues class at the California Rehabilitation Center (CRC) in Norco, California, as part of the Chicano Studies Community Internship Program. While I would like to thank each and every student who participated, Richard Alvarado, Gudelia Davila, Mary Figueroa, Irene Howard, Mary Lou López, Julio Espinosa, Diana Váldez, Gilbert Cadena, Elba Quintanilla, Carmen Arreola, Blas Coyazo, and Julio Vigoreaux should be singled out for their contribution to the CRC program. Although we were "teaching" the class, as it turned out we received much more than we gave and learned a great deal in the process. *Muchas gracias a los carnales de MAYO de CRC*, especially Gilbert "Beto" Ruiz, Mike "Pecas" Ortega, Ben Hernández, Juan Salcido, Ricardo López, and Jeronimo Ulloa.

I received a Rockefeller Foundation Postdoctoral Fellowship and was in residence at the Stanford Center for Chicano Research (SCCR) in 1985-86. The staff and faculty at SCCR provided a warm and intellectually stimulating environment for my research. Gerald "El Jerry" López of the Stanford Law School read the entire manuscript and made some important suggestions for revision. The Research Committee of the Academic Senate at the University of California, Riverside, provided financial support for the project. During the 1984-85 academic year, I received a National Research Council Postdoctoral Fellowship and was in residence at the national office of the Mexican American Legal Defense and Education Fund (MALDEF) in San Francisco. I would like to thank Mike Baller for giving me access to the MALDEF files on police abuse.

Valuable assistance was provided by staff at the Bancroft Library in Berkeley, the Eugene C. Barker History Center at the University of Texas at Austin, the Texas State Archives in Austin, and the Special Collections of the Green Library at Stanford University. I am most grateful to Josie Tamayo and Gil Nava, staff members of the Tómas Rivera Library at UCR for their unwavering support and assistance. Nancy Rettig typed and proofread the bibliography under adverse circumstances. I am indebted to Clara Dean who not only typed the entire manuscript but corrected my many errors. Finally, I would like to acknowledge residents of the barrio of Casa Blanca for extending their hands in friendship and being a continuous source of strength, encouragement, and inspiration.

1

A Legacy of Conflict

INTRODUCTION

In 1970 the U.S. Commission on Civil Rights issued a landmark report that to date is the most far-reaching and comprehensive study of Chicanos and the legal and judicial system. It concluded:

> Mexican-American citizens are subject to unduly harsh treatment by law enforcement officers . . . they are often arrested on insufficient grounds, receive physical and verbal abuse and penalties which are disproportionately severe. We have found them to be deprived of proper use of bail and adequate representation by counsel. They are substantially underrepresented on grand and petit juries and excluded from full participation in law enforcement agencies, especially in supervisory positions. (p. iii)

The commission set forth eighteen recommendations on the federal and state levels designed to rectify many of these problems and to assist Chicanos[1] in obtaining equal opportunity before the law. It also pointed to the existence of a double standard of justice for Anglos and Chicanos.

Although public awareness of the problem has been increasing, little has been done to implement these recommendations (Castro 1974, p. 49). Nearly a decade after the Civil Rights Commission Report, the Mexican American Legal Defense and Education Fund (MALDEF) complained of police violence and abuse against Chicanos, gathering information on over one hundred cases and focusing on fifty-six that were thoroughly documented. It noted that in the preceding two years alone, law enforcement officers had killed at least thirty-two Hispanics (MALDEF 1978a and b; National Hispanic Conference on Law Enforcement 1980, p. 62). MALDEF (1978a) concluded on the basis of its investigation that official

1

violence against Chicanos has reached epidemic proportions in the Southwest and "that this violence was a severe, widespread and, for Mexican-Americans, highly emotional phenomenon." Widespread patterns of police abuse and mistreatment of Chicanos have also been documented by Armando Morales (1972) in *Ando Sangrando* (I Am Bleeding), a detailed study of the 1970-1971 East Los Angeles riots, and by the National Hispanic Conference on Law Enforcement and Criminal Justice (1980). In *Gunpowder Justice* (1979), Samora, Bernal, and Peña provide extensive documentation of abuses perpetrated by the Texas Rangers. Other works have focused on specific topics, such as Chicano "social bandits" (Castillo and Camarillo 1973; Vigil 1974), Chicano gangs (Moore 1978), and *mexicano* resistance to Anglo-American domination (Rosenbaum 1981).

These are welcome additions to a neglected area, but it is significant that a single comprehensive scholarly assessment of the Chicano and the legal and judicial system has yet to appear. The present work seeks to fill this void by placing this issue within a broad social-historical framework.

A number of excellent histories of Chicanos are available and, although *Gringo Justice* draws from these treatises, it is not intended to be a historical work. A basic premise of the present volume is that the contemporary situation cannot be divorced from its historical context. Much of the current criminological and sociological literature is, unfortunately, ahistorical. This work seeks to link contemporary social science theories with the historical reality of the Chicano population.

A related premise is that the experiences of Chicanos before the legal and judicial system are a direct result of their overall social, economic, and political status in society. Thus, the material covered here extends well beyond what is found in conventional criminological and sociological literature. The American invasion of Mexico and the Treaty of Guadalupe Hidalgo, which marked the end of hostilities between the two nations and provided extensive guarantees for displaced Mexican citizens, meant that from the onset Chicanos occupied a unique position relative to American society and its judicial system. Despite the many guarantees of the treaty, an alien culture, language, and legal and judicial system were subsequently imposed, and a variety of legal and extralegal mechanisms were used to depose them from their land and other possessions. The end result was the emergence of a double standard of justice: one system applied to the Anglo-American and another to the Chicano. It is this system of gringo justice that is the focus of this book.

This chapter is an introduction and historical overview of Chicanos and the legal and judicial system. After tracing the legacy of conflict and the significance of the Treaty of Guadalupe Hidalgo, the evolution of the image of Chicanos as *bandidos*, criminals, is considered. Subsequent chapters address more specific issues such as the displacement of Chicanos from the land, vigilantism and social banditry, immigration law and the Border Patrol, police harassment and abuse, Chicano youth gangs, and prevailing criminological and sociological theories. The concluding chapter presents a Chicano perspective on gringo justice.

LOS GUEROS MALVADOS

At the time of the Mexican-American War "Meskins" were viewed largely as a despicable, inferior, and subhuman race.[2] This attitude provided a ready-made justification or rationale not only for the many atrocities perpetrated against them but also for the acquisition of a vast and rich area of land. The Mexican, after all, was racially, culturally, linguistically, and religiously inferior and lacked the technological sophistication to develop the area (see De León 1983, chapter 1).

Walter Prescott Webb, a staunch supporter of the Texas Rangers, for example, noted that "Without disparagement it may be said that there is a cruel streak in the Mexican nature . . . this cruelty . . . doubtless should be attributed partly to the Indian blood" (Webb 1965, p. 14). Stephen Austin, often termed sympathetic toward the Mexican in Texas, was certainly not free of bias, as revealed by the contents of a letter he wrote to the Honorable L. F. Linn:

> A war of extermination is raging in Texas . . . a war of barbarism and of despotic principles, waged by the mongrel Spanish-Indian and Negro race against civilization and the Anglo-American race.
>
> For fifteen years I have been laboring like a slave to Americanize Texas . . . to form a nucleous around which my native countrymen could collect and grow into a solid body that would forever be a barrier of safety to the southwestern frontier, and especially to the outlet of the western world . . . the mouth of the Mississippi . . . and which would be a beacon-light to the Mexicans in their search for liberty . . . . But the Anglo-American foundation, the nucleous of

republicanism, is to be broken up, and its place supplied by a population of Indians, Mexicans, and *renegados*, all mixed together, and all the *natural enemies of white men and civilization* . . . . Oh! Spirit of our fathers, where are you? Just and omnipotent God, where is thy influence? Where is the fatherly care and protection of a wise and watchful government. (Austin 1926, vol. III, pp. 345-47)

One eyewitness, reporting on the discovery of gold in California in 1848, was similarly negative toward nonwhites, both men and women. He remarked that "the men are generally lazy, fond of riding, dancing, and gambling . . . . The women will gamble as well as the men. The men are mostly addicted to liquor. The women are, or may be generally considered, handsome, with dark, fascinating eyes and good features; the better kind very courteous, but, in general, indolent; they dress rich and costly, are addicted to fandangoing and gallantry, but not much coquetry" (McMurtrie 1943, p. 4). In 1864 George L. Robertson described "greasers" as the "lowest," most "contemptible, despicable people on earth" (Robertson 1864).

The American takeover of the Southwest proved to be much more than a political and military victory; it was a racial and cultural triumph as well. In *They Called Them Greasers*, Arnoldo De León argues that although racism was not *the* cause of the Texas revolt, it was undoubtedly "*very* prominent as a promoting and underlying cause" (De León 1983, p. 12). Most whites had never encountered Mexicans before, but their Elizabethan and Puritan heritage predisposed them to view Mexicans as a contemptuous, inferior, and barbaric race. "Mexicanos were doubly suspect, as heirs to Catholicism and as descendants of Spaniards, Indians, and Africans" (ibid., p. 4). Antipathy toward Spain and the Roman Catholic Church was deep-seated. The Mexican aborigines, on the other hand, were conceived by the English as "degenerate creatures—un-Christian, uncivilized, and racially impure" (ibid., p. 5). Despite all the talk of oppression, the Texas revolt appears, in the end, to have been motivated by racism and white supremacy. "For Anglo-Texans to have accepted anything other than 'white supremacy and civilization' was to submit to Mexican domination and to admit that Americans were willing to become like Mexicans" (ibid., p. 13). Anglos could co-exist with the *criollo* elite and were attracted to Mexican women, especially upper-class women who were considered "white," but most Mexicans were either *mestizos* or descendants of Tlascalan Indians who played an important part in Spanish colonization of northern Mexico and were considered non-white (Tijerina 1977, pp. 10-12).

These negative racial attitudes were more formally articulated and legitimated through the concept of Manifest Destiny, which decreed that the superior Anglo-Saxon race was predestined by God to rule over the entire hemisphere. Violence and hatred directed at Mexicans could be justified because they were an indolent, heathen, barbaric, and violent people. The American takeover of the land was seen as "rescuing" it from its primitive status. "Order and discipline had to be rescued from the wilds in the name of civilization and Christianity . . . . To allow an inverse order and a concomitant surrender of themselves and their liberties to primitive things was to allow chaos to continue when God's will was to impose Christian order" (De León 1983, pp. 1-2).

Even though Mexicans were technically Christians, they were Catholic and adhered to a brand of Catholicism considered "pagan" and therefore inferior (Grebler, Moore, and Guzman 1970, p. 450). E. C. Orozco argues, moreover:

> When Anglo-Americans describe the manner by which religious liberty came to be achieved by Anglo-American "pioneers" in the Southwest and how religious privileges in the country came to be shared on an equal basis, their reference is to the spiritual exercise of republican protestantism. In other words, to the secular and natural religion of the United States and not to Christianity *per se*. (Orozco 1980, p. 46)

The doctrine of republican Protestantism also "mandated and compelled 'melting down' religious and ethnic differences for the presumed good of the whole" (ibid., p. 80). Thus, both the acquisition of more than half of Mexico (in exchange for $15 million) and the destruction of Mexican culture were decreed by divine imperative.

This legacy of conflict preceded the North American invasion of Mexico and continued long after it ended. Without doubt it was most strongly manifested in Texas. To the Anglo-Texan settlers "Mexicans were lazy, shiftless, jealous, cowardly, bigoted, superstitious, backward, and immoral. To the Mexicans, on the other hand, the Texans were 'los diablos Tejanos': arrogant, overbearing, aggressive, conniving, rude, unreliable, and dishonest" (McWilliams 1968, p. 99). The Anglos considered themselves superior to the Mexicans, but to the Mexicans they were seen as "full of brag, bluster, and spreading chauvinism" (ibid.).

These cultural and ideological differences were substantial and created tension and conflict between the two groups. The American settlers were white, Protestant, English-speaking, and strong supporters of self-government. The Mexicans, on the other hand, were Indian or Mestizo, Catholic, and committed to a highly centralized government (ibid., p. 100). In addition, most of the Anglo settlers were from the South and supported slavery, whereas Mexico had recently outlawed slavery.

Given these antagonisms and the contemptuous attitude toward the Mexican, it is not surprising that Anglo settlers typically disregarded Mexican laws. The first Anglo settlers consisted of filibustering expeditions that forcefully fought their way into Texas. Hayden Edwards, involved in a conflict over disputed territory, attempted to evict settlers rather than subject the dispute to adjudication by Mexican authorities (Acuña 1981, p. 4). When Mexico ordered him to leave the territory, he and two hundred of his supporters took the town of Nacogdoches on December 21, 1826, proclaiming it the Republic of Fredonia (ibid.). Although the rebellion was quickly quelled, it became a symbol of American disdain for Mexican law and authority.

Fearing possible annexation of its sparsely settled northern territories, Spain, and subsequently Mexico, encouraged colonization by liberalizing its colonization laws to include Anglo-American settlers (Tijerina 1977, p. 3). In 1821 Moses Austin obtained an *empresario* (colonist) land grant, permitting him to bring in three hundred Spanish families from Florida. Austin died before he could accomplish this mission but his son was awarded a comparable grant from the Mexican government in 1823 (Meier and Rivera 1972, p. 58). This signaled the beginning of an Anglo influx and eventually twenty such *empresario* grants were awarded. Under conditions of the grant all settlers were required to be of good moral character, to be Catholic or to convert to Catholicism, and to swear allegiance to Mexico. Austin, however, was one of the few *empresarios* who made an effort to honor the terms of the agreement. Most of the settlers did not recognize the authority of the Mexican government and ignored or disregarded Mexican customs and laws.

Texas functioned as a self-governed province until 1824 when the new Mexican constitution declared it a department within the newly created state of Coahuila y Tejas (Tijerina 1977, p. 3). In 1825, the state of Coahuila y Tejas passed its own colonization law, which served to implement Mexican federal law (ibid.). Anglo settlers who had legally colonized in Texas numbered around 1,800 in 1825; by 1830 there were 4,248 Anglo colonists in the area (ibid., p. 4). By 1830 Anglos outnumbered Mexicans in Texas by more than five to one. Many of them were not legal settlers but illegal aliens from the South who sought to develop cotton cultivation and to import slaves. Mexico, anticipating that the United States would move to annex Texas, began to take measures to stem the tide of illegal aliens. In 1829 slavery was abolished by executive decree. Following intense protest by Anglo-Texans, the decree was quickly suspended, but on April 6, 1830, Mexico passed a law that prohibited the importation of slaves and attempted to severely restrict Anglo settlement (ibid.). Another law set up customhouses and presidios along the border (Meier and Rivera 1972, p. 59). Mexican soldiers were also sent to Texas to enforce Mexican laws, including laws pertaining to immigration.

Disturbances occurred in 1832 and 1833, and by 1835 the Texas revolt was in full swing. The revolt placed *tejanos* in a precarious position and forced them to choose sides (Tijerina 1977, p. 318). José Erasmo Seguín was a leading *tejano* "statesman" and in 1824 served as the Texas representative in the national congress in Mexico City. His son, Juan N. Seguín, however, joined the Anglo insurgents but "soon found himself a foreigner in his native land" (ibid.). As he hid on his ranch, he saw it pillaged by Mexican troops and burned by Anglo forces on different days. "Fernando de León of Victoria, who had contributed generously to the Texas forces, was arrested by a Mexican general in 1836 and again by an Anglo commander in 1837—each time for conspiring with the enemy" (ibid.).

Despite victories at the Alamo and Goliad, Santa Anna was soundly defeated at San Jacinto on April 21, 1837. By signing the Treaty of Velasco, Santa Anna agreed to Texas independence in exchange for his freedom. The treaty, however, was not recognized by Mexico. Texas eventually obtained de facto independence; annexation to the United States did not come until 1845. The Texas revolt set the stage for an all-out war between the two nations. Mexico, fearing total annexation, broke off diplomatic relations with the United States.

Anglo contempt of the Mexican during the Mexican period grew into even more open hatred and hostility following Texas independence. Racial tension was exacerbated not only by economic and cultural conflicts but also by deeply ingrained racist attitudes. Many of the Anglo migrants to Texas were from the South and racist attitudes were transferred to the "swarthy" dark-skinned Mexican. A Chattanooga journalist in San Angelo noted that "Mexicans were a race of mongrels" and "dark to the point of blackness" (*San Angelo Standard* 1889, p. 1). De León writes:

> From the Southern and frontier-oriented culture they had acquired a certain repulsion for dark-skinned people and a distaste for miscegenation . . . . By conditioning, they were predisposed to react intolerantly to people they found different from themselves but similar to those they considered as enemies and as inferiors. (De León 1983, p. 6)

Mexicans were viewed as primitive, inferior, and an impediment to progress. In a letter to his wife dated September 11, 1849, Thomas B. Eastland described the town of El Paso Del Norte:

> A poor, miserable, dirty town, badly built, containing a population of some 5,000 Mexicans, and a few foreigners—the greater portion of the former are *Peons* or slaves, and as miserable a set of looking *greasers*, as you would see, nowhere else in the wild but in this land of *"God and Liberty."* (Eastland 1939, p. 125)

In short, "backwardness was equated with Mexicanness" (ibid., p. 20). Anti-Mexican attitudes were so intense that some Mexican *tejanos* were quick to dissociate themselves from the *mexicano* who was considered separate and inferior. Members of the small landed elite who had managed to retain their land following the American takeover were considered "Spanish" or "Castilian" (i.e., "white") by American pioneers, whereas Mexican workers were "half-breeds" or "Indians" (Montejano 1982, p. 12). As the Mexican ranch society was displaced during the twentieth century, however, the distinction blurred and they simply became "Mexicans." Thus, the loss of economic and political power resulted in the "darkening" of the Mexican (ibid.).

During the course of the Mexican-American War numerous atrocities were committed against Mexicans. The American army was composed largely of patriotic volunteers (McWilliams 1968, p. 102) and many of them considered the Mexican to be less than human. These troops proceeded to murder, rob, and to rape mothers and daughters (ibid.). These abuses were bitterly resented by the Mexicans as evidenced by an article appearing in a Mexican newspaper of the time that described the troops as a "horde of banditti, of drunkards, of fornicators . . . vandals vomited from hell, monsters who bid defiance to the laws of nature . . . shameless, daring, ignorant, ragged, bad-smelling, long-bearded men with hats turned up at the brim, thirsty with the desire to appropriate our riches and our beautiful damsels" (ibid., p. 103).

Even in defeat, Mexico expressed great concern for the welfare of the *mexicanos* left behind in the territories which were to be acquired by the United States. *Los Olvidados* (the "Forgotten Ones") were not totally forgotten. "As late as 1943 maps were still used in Mexican schools which designated the old Spanish borderlands as 'territory temporarily in the hands of the United States' " (ibid.). Mexico also took great care to assure that the property and rights of its citizens were duly protected. Such explicit provisions were negotiated prior to the signing of the Treaty of Guadalupe Hidalgo.

THE TREATY OF GUADALUPE HIDALGO

It can be safely said that no document is more important for the Chicano people than the Treaty of Guadalupe Hidalgo. The treaty meant that, except for American Indians, Chicanos are the only racial-ethnic group to be incorporated by conquest. Like American Indians, they are also the only group to have their rights specifically guaranteed by treaty (McWilliams 1968, p. 103).

The Treaty of Guadalupe Hidalgo was officially agreed upon by Mexico on February 2, 1848, recognizing the Rio Grande as the border with Texas and ceding territory that today is California, New Mexico, Nevada, and parts of Colorado, Arizona, and Utah.

Nicholas Trist had been sent as an emissary to negotiate the peace settlement, but President Polk had previously ordered Trist to break off negotiations and return to the United States. Trist angered Polk by ignoring the order and negotiating the treaty. Polk wanted more territory for less money and was initially incensed with the treaty, but he reluctantly submitted it to Congress for ratification. In a sense, Mexico was fortunate because many in the United States wanted to acquire all of Mexico.

Under provisions of the treaty, Mexicans had one year to decide whether to return to Mexico or remain (Article VIII). Those who stayed would be considered American citizens and entitled to the enjoyment of all rights thereof. The articles that specifically protected the rights of displaced Mexicans were numbers VIII, IX and X (Bevans 1972, pp. 796-98). Article VIII stipulated that the property of Mexican citizens who remained in the occupied territory would be "inviolably respected." Article IX further guaranteed them the enjoyment of all rights as citizens according to the principles of the Constitution, including the right to the free exercise of their religion. Even more extensive guarantees were found in Article X, which recognized the validity of all land grants issued by the Mexican government. The Articles as amended by the Senate read as follows:

ARTICLE VIII

Mexicans now established in territories previously belonging to Mexico, and which remain for the future within the limits of the United States, as defined by the present Treaty, shall be free to continue where they now reside, or to remove at any time to the Mexican Republic, retaining the property which they possess in the said territories, or disposing thereof and removing the proceeds wherever they please; without their being subjected, on this account, to any contribution, tax or charge whatever.

Those who shall prefer to remain in the said territories, may either retain the title and rights of Mexican citizens, or acquire those of citizens of the United States. But, they shall be under the obligation to make their election within one year from the date of the exchange of ratifications of this treaty: and those who shall remain in the said territories, after the expiration of that year, without having declared their intention to retain the character of Mexicans, shall be considered to have elected to become citizens of the United States.

In the said territories, property of every kind, now belonging to Mexicans not established there, shall be inviolably respected. The present owners, the heirs of these, and all Mexicans who may hereafter acquire said property by contract, shall enjoy with respect to it, guaranties equally ample as if the same belonged to citizens of the United States.

ARTICLE IX

The Mexicans who, in the territories aforesaid, shall not preserve the character of citizens of the Mexican Republic, conformably with what is stipulated in the preceding article, shall be incorporated into the Union of the United States and be admitted, at the proper time (to be judged of by the Congress of the United States) to the enjoyment of all the rights of citizens of the United States according to the principles of the Constitution; and in the mean time shall be maintained and protected in the free enjoyment of their liberty and property, and secured in the free exercise of their religion without restriction.

ARTICLE X [stricken by the U.S. Senate]

All grants of land made by the Mexican Government or by the competent authorities, in territories previously appertaining to Mexico, and remaining for the future within the limits of the United States, shall be respected as valid, to the same extent that the same grants would be valid, if the said territories had remained within the limits of Mexico. But the grantees of lands in Texas, put in possession thereof, who, by reason of the circumstances of the country since the beginning of the troubles between Texas and the Mexican Government, may have been prevented from fulfilling all the conditions of their grants, shall be under the obligation to fulfill the said conditions within the periods limited in the same respectively; such periods to be now counted from the date of the exchange of ratifications of this treaty: in default of which the said grants shall not be obligatory upon the State of Texas, in virtue of the stipulations contained in this Article.

The foregoing stipulation in regard to grantees of land in Texas, is extended to all grantees of land in the territories aforesaid, elsewhere than in Texas, put in possession under such grants; and, in default of the fulfillment of the conditions of any such grant, within the new period, which, as is above stipulated, begins with the day of the exchange of ratifications of this treaty, the same shall be null and void.

The Mexican Government declares that no grant whatever of lands in Texas has been made since the second day of March one thousand eight hundred and thirty-six; and that no grant whatever of lands in any of the territories aforesaid has been made since the thirteenth day of May one thousand eight hundred and forty-six.

It should be noted that the Senate significantly altered Article IX and completely omitted Article X from the treaty. Article IX was amended and a lengthy set of conditions reduced to a single paragraph. A comparison of the original and the amended versions shows that the phrase "shall be incorporated into the Union of the United States, and admitted as soon as possible" in the original text was altered to read "at the proper time (to be judged of by the Congress)." In addition the two paragraphs spelling out the specific rights of the Catholic Church and the guarantees protecting church property were deleted.

The omission of Article X was especially significant, for it was this article that in effect protected "all prior and pending titles to property of every description" (Perrigo 1971, p. 176). It specifically declared valid all land grants issued by the Mexican government or competent authorities prior to March 2, 1836, in Texas, and May 13, 1846, in all other territories.

Once ratified by the United States (March 16, 1848), there was concern that Mexico would refuse ratification because of the amendments and deletions introduced by the Senate. The delicate task of obtaining ratification was delegated to Ambrose H. Sevier, senator from Arkansas and chairman of the Senate Committee on Foreign Relations, and Nathan Clifford, Maine Attorney General. The two commissioners were given lengthy and explicit instructions, which indicated that they were not sent to Mexico to negotiate a new treaty or to change the treaty that had been ratified:

> Your whole duty will then consist in using every honorable effort to obtain from the Mexican Government a ratification of the Treaty in the form in which it has been ratified by the Senate, and this with the least practicable delay.
>
> For this purpose it may and most probably will become necessary, that you should explain to the Mexican Minister for Foreign Affairs, or to other authorized agents of the Mexican Government, the reasons which have influenced the Senate in adopting their several amendments to the Treaty. (Miller 1937, p. 374)

The instructions revealed that the United States would be willing to make minor concessions in order to obtain peace with Mexico, but under no circumstances would it be acceptable to reinstate Article X:

> Neither the President nor the Senate of the United States can ever consent to ratify any Treaty containing the tenth article of the Treaty of Guadalupe Hidalgo in favor of grantees of land in Texas or elsewhere. The Government of the United States does not possess the power to carry such an article into execution; and if they did, it would be highly unjust and inexpedient. (Ibid., p. 375)

Should Mexican authorities prove reluctant to ratify the treaty, they were to be reminded that war would be resumed and that "the Mexican Government can never again expect to make peace on terms so favorable" (ibid., p. 376). At the same time that strong pressure was to be applied, the commissioners were cautioned to treat the Mexicans with care and respect:

> The Mexicans are a sensitive and suspicious people. They are now humbled in their own estimation by our brilliant and repeated victories. Their jealousy ought to be allayed by treating them, in all

intercourse, with marked respect. All the external forms of civility to which the Spanish race attach such peculiar importance, ought to be strictly observed by you. (Ibid.)

Vigorous protests by Mexico over the Senate amendments and deletion of Article X led to issuance of the Protocol of Querétaro, signed by the United States commissioners and Mexican representatives on May 26, 1848. The Protocol affirmed:

FIRST.

The American Government by suppressing the IXth article of the Treaty of Guadalupe and substituting the IIId article of the Treaty of Louisiana did not intend to diminish in any way what was agreed upon by the aforesaid article IXth in favor of the inhabitants of the territories ceded by Mexico. Its understanding [is] that all of that agreement is contained in the IIId article of the Treaty of Louisiana. In consequence, all the privileges and guarantees, civil, political and religious, which would have been possessed by the inhabitants of the ceded territories, if the IXth article of the Treaty had been retained, will be enjoyed by them without any difference under the article which has been substituted.

SECOND.

The American Government by suppressing the Xth article of the Treaty of Guadalupe did not in any way intend to annul the grants of lands made by Mexico in the ceded territories. These grants, notwithstanding the suppression of the article of the Treaty, preserve the legal value which they may possess; and the grantees may cause their legitimate titles to be acknowledged before the american tribunals.

Conformably to the law of the United-States, legitimate titles to every description of property, personal and real, existing in the ceded territories, are those which were legitimate titles under the Mexican law in California and New Mexico up to the 13th of May 1.846, and in Texas up to the 2d March 1.836.

THIRD.

The Government of the United States by suppressing the concluding paragraph of article XIIth of the Treaty, did not intend to deprive the Mexican Republic of the free and unrestrained faculty of ceding, conveying or transferring at any time (as it may judge best) the sum of the twelfe millions of dollars which the same Government of the United States is to deliver in the places designated by the amended article.

And these explanations having been accepted by the Minister of Foreign Affairs of the Mexican Republic, he declared in name of his Government that with the understanding conveyed by them, the same Government would proceed to ratify the Treaty of Guadalupe as modified by the Senate and Government of the United States. In testimony of which their Excellencies the aforesaid Commissioners and the Minister have signed and sealed in quintuplicate the present protocol.

[Seal]   A. H. Sevier

[Seal]   Nathan Clifford

[Seal]   Luis de la Rosa

(Miller 1937, pp. 381-82)

The Treaty was ratified by Mexico and ratifications were exchanged at Querétaro on May 30, entering into force on that date. Ironically, the Treaty of Guadalupe Hidalgo was officially proclaimed by the president of the United States on July 4, 1848.

Controversy over the treaty, however, was to continue long after its adoption. President Polk, it will be recalled, was displeased with the agreement negotiated by Nicholas P. Trist. Trist's authority to negotiate on behalf of the United States had been revoked in October 1847, several months prior to the signing of the treaty. President Polk and some members of the Senate argued, therefore, that the treaty itself was "utterly void and ineffectual." But in a sense Polk wanted to "have his cake and eat it too," arguing that the treaty was invalid and at the same time submitting it to the Senate for ratification.

Polk's motives in seeking ratification at this time were clear. Opposition to the war was growing and he feared that Congress would not grant either men or money to carry on the war (ibid., p. 247). A majority of the House of Representatives opposed the administration and, according to Polk, "they have falsely charged: that the war was brought on and is continued by me with a view to the conquest of Mexico" (ibid.). In the end, he feared losing the provinces of New Mexico and, especially, Upper California, which had already been ceded by the treaty. Polk explained in his diary that, "I adverted to the immense value of Upper California;

and concluded by saying that if I were now to reject my own terms, as offered in April last, I did not see how it was possible for my administration to be sustained" (ibid.).

In the final analysis, Polk acceded to the treaty not because it was deemed an honorable or equitable resolution to the conflict but because it was practical and politically expedient. By significantly altering Article IX and deleting Article X, while reassuring Mexico via the Protocol of Querétaro that the property rights as well as the civil, political, and religious guaranties of the inhabitants of the ceded territories would be protected, the United States unlawfully acquired a land rich in natural resources, constituting one-third of the territory of the United States and larger than any European nation with the exception of the Soviet Union (Steiner 1970, p. 57).

According to Hunter Miller, editor of *Treaties and Other International Acts of the United States of America*, the signing of the protocol by Sevier and Clifford was both "ill advised" and "unnecessary":

> The protocol was not in any legal sense part of the Treaty of Guadalupe Hidalgo or obligatory as an international act; on this point the two Governments were in accord in the latest of the official exchanges on the subject (July 13 and September 3 and 4, 1849; quoted above). That the protocol did correctly interpret the treaty was maintained on the one part and denied on the other . . . the protocol, strictly speaking, did not, and did not purport to, interpret or construe a treaty text, for none existed for interpretation or construction; all that the protocol did in its item "Second" (particularly in the second paragraph thereof) was to record the opinion of the two American lawyers who signed it on the law of their country regarding titles to land in Texas and in California and New Mexico. (Miller 1937, p. 405)

For Mexico, the protocol was an integral part of the treaty and binding, but the United States argued that it in no way altered the original terms of the agreement and had no binding effect. So much confusion arose that there was concern in Congress that the protocol may have had the effect of "abrogating the Mexican Treaty" (ibid., p. 383). Armando Rendon (1972, p. 77) argues, however, that the protocol is valid *only* if the treaty is valid, and if the treaty and protocol are valid, the United States has failed to adhere to its most basic conditions.[3] On the other hand, if the treaty and the protocol are not valid, the hostilities between the United States and Mexico have not ceased, and by its unlawful possession of seven southwestern states the United States is in violation of international law.

The treaty thus afforded rights to Chicanos that extended well beyond their constitutional guarantees. "In other words, besides the rights and duties of American citizenship, they [the Mexicans] would have some special privileges derived from their previous customs in language, law, and religion." But Guadalupe Hidalgo differed from treaties between tribal nations and the United States in that neither the sovereignty of Chicanos as a nation nor their right to occupy land as a people were recognized. Individual land titles were to be respected ostensibly, but the wording of the protocol cast doubt on the validity of these titles (ibid., p. 78). The protocol stated that these grants "preserve the legal value which they *may* possess; and the grantees *may* cause their *legitimate* titles to be acknowledged before the American tribunals" (emphasis added).

Not surprisingly, Chicanos did not fare very well before such American tribunals. Within two decades most were landless. Since the Mexican-American War, the treaty has been largely ignored and its provisions have not been adhered to by the United States. Chicanos have been exploited economically, politically, and culturally, and much violence has been perpetrated against them. At the same time that the legal and judicial system has worked to advance the interests of the dominant society and to maintain Chicanos in a subordinate position, Chicanos have been depicted as a lawless and violent people.

In retrospect it is clear that the United States has failed to honor the agreement and to live up to the ideals espoused in the Introduction to the Treaty of Guadalupe Hidalgo:

> In the name of Almighty God:
>
> The United States of America, and the United Mexican States, animated by a sincere desire to put an end to the calamities of the war which unhappily exists between the two Republics, and to establish upon a solid basis relations of peace and friendship, which shall confer reciprocal benefits upon the citizens of both, and assure the concord, harmony and mutual confidence, wherein the two peoples should live, as good neighbours, have for that purpose appointed their respective Plenipotentiaries: that is to say, the President of the United States has appointed Nicholas P. Trist, a citizen of the United States, and the President of the Mexican Republic has appointed Don Luis Gonzaga Cuevas, Don Bernardo Couto, and Don

Miguel Atristain, citizens of the said Republic; who, after a reciprocal communication of their respective full powers, have, under the protection of Almighty God, the author of Peace, arranged, agreed upon, and signed the following

Treaty of Peace, Friendship, Limits and Settlement between the United States of America and the Mexican Republic.

EVOLUTION OF THE *BANDIDO* IMAGE

Chicanos have typically been victims of police abuse and injustice, but they have been portrayed as a violent and criminally prone people. The image of the Mexican throughout history, in fact, has been that of a ruthless, bloodthirsty, and treacherous outlaw (De León 1983, p. 75; Trujillo 1974; Martínez 1969). Although taking various forms such as the "greasy *bandido*" of the Old West, the zoot-suit or pachuco gangs of the 1940s (see chapter 5, below), or contemporary "lowriders" and youth gang members, the image persists, nonetheless. Even today there is much more media and public interest in issues such as Chicano gang violence and criminality than in police abuse or denial of equal protection of the law (see chapter 6, below). Media portrayals are especially significant, for they help to shape and reinforce public conceptions of Chicanos which are held not only by members of the dominant society, but by Chicanos themselves.

The Treaty of Guadalupe Hidalgo may have ended the war between Mexico and the United States, but it also marked the beginning of hostilities between Anglo-Americans and Chicanos, displaced Mexicans who now found themselves within the territorial boundaries of the United States. As legal and extralegal mechanisms were used to take land and power away from the Chicano, the police, military, and Border Patrol were employed to maintain them in a subordinate position. The "*bandido* image*" emerged as Chicanos responded to such injustices and to lawlessness on the part of the dominant society. If an Anglo took the law into his own hands, he was generally labeled a hero or a revolutionary, but a Chicano who engaged in lawlessness was somehow a bandit (see chapter 3, below).[4] It is precisely because Chicanos did not passively accept exploitation that they became *bandidos*. Force was thus integral not only to the acquisition of Mexico's northern territories by the United States but to the political, economic, and social displacement of the Chicano.

In the aftermath of the Mexican-American War, treaty provisions designed to protect land and water rights and the cultural and religious autonomy of Mexican citizens were not honored. The legal and judicial system, rather than serving as an objective and impartial institution, became a vehicle for advancing the interests of Anglo-Americans. In a word, justice became a mockery for Chicanos, inviting the interpretation that it meant "just us."

Yet, ironically, it was the Mexican who was accused of perpetrating crimes against American citizens. In response to the establishment of a commission sent by the president of the United States to investigate robberies allegedly committed by Mexicans and Indians, the Mexican government set up its own commission in 1873 to carry out an independent evaluation of these charges. The work of the Mexican Border Commission was impressive. It visited all of the towns and many ranchos along a 450-mile stretch of the border, culled archives, and interviewed nearly three hundred witnesses. In the end, the various reports and appendices covered 17,688 pages (Comisión pesquisidora de la frontera del norte 1875, p. ix). The commission concluded:

> The complaints of the Texans are groundless, inasmuch as the cattle stealing done among them is not the work of any residents in the adjoining country, but of Indians belonging to the United States, and their own outlaws disguised as Indians. If either of the two nations can complain of Indian and other depredations—as it is now demonstrated—it is Mexico, some of whose entire States have been ruined by Indians and banditti from the United States, who still depredate there to a certain extent, robbing horses and perpetrating other outrages. The origin of those evils on both banks of the river, it is clearly proved, consists, in a great measure, in the encouragement given to the Indians for plunder by the traffic carried on with them ever since 1835, tolerated and consented by the American authorities. (pp. iii-iv)

Many Chicanos were compelled to go outside the law to defend rights and property that should have been legitimately theirs. Mexican "social bandits" such as Joaquín Murieta, Tiburcio Vásquez, Catarino Garza, and Gregorio Cortez, for example, challenged the dominant order (see chapter 3, below). Labeled *bandidos* and bloodthirsty outlaws by Anglo society, they became heroes to their own people—men who were respected and admired, and whose exploits were romanticized and idealized in *corridos* (ballads).

The mythology surrounding Chicano banditry may well have served as a justification for the many injustices and atrocities committed against innocent persons. More often than not, the Mexican was the victim of injustice. In the California Mother Lode, for example, there was massive retaliation for crimes said to have been committed by Mexican bandits:

> Three hundred armed miners assembled on Sunday, January 23rd, and commenced a systematic search for the bandits.... The posse fanned out over the countryside and in their fear and exasperation, burned Mexicans' houses, took away their arms and told them to leave. The entire Mexican population was driven from San Andreas and the forks of the Calaveras River. Everywhere there were excited groups of men scouring the hills and valleys. (Secrest 1967b, p. 14)

In addition to individual and somewhat "primitive" forms of social protest, numerous organized revolts took place. In 1859 Juan "Cheno" Cortina led an army into Brownsville, occupying the city and proclaiming it the Republic of the Rio Grande (Goldfinch 1949). In New Mexico *Las Gorras Blancas* (White Caps) emerged in the early 1890s as a response to the Anglo land grab that threatened the traditional pastoral way of life of the region (Schlesinger 1971; Rosenbaum 1973, 1981). This secret organization terrorized residents of Las Vegas through nocturnal raids, fence cutting, and other disruptive activities.

Even more ambitious was the drafting of *El Plan de San Diego*, a revolutionary call to arms for Chicanos in 1915 (Rocha 1981; Gómez-Quiñones 1970; Harris and Sadler 1978; Cumberland 1954; Pierce 1917). Although originating in South Texas, *El Plan* outlined a military revolt that would lead to the creation of an independent nation in the territory acquired by the United States during the Mexican War (see chapter 3).

More recently, Reies López Tijerina and *La Alianza Federal de Mercedes* (The Federal Alliance of Land Grants) called for the return of land grants to those persons whose protection was guaranteed by the Treaty of Guadalupe Hidalgo. Initially they pursued constitutional means to return the land, but López Tijerina later advocated any means necessary for its reinstatement. In 1966 *La Alianza* took two forest rangers into custody for trespassing in the Kit Carson National Forest. The following year it attempted a citizen's arrest of the local district attorney for violating constitutional rights and interfering with local organizational activities in the famous *Tierra Amarilla* courthouse raid (U.S. Commission on Civil Rights 1970, p. 14).

Even more impressive than the number and variety of Chicano

rebellions has been the intensity of response elicited by them. Such protests typically have been quelled by the massive force of the military and the police. During the Mexican Revolution (1911-1918), for example, there was much tension and conflict along the border as Anglo residents expressed fear of raids and invasions from Mexico, and Chicano uprisings such as *El Plan de San Diego*. There was some basis for these fears. However:

> the Anglos' actual suffering and hardships paled beside the horrors that they inflicted upon the Hispanic population. In their hysteria over the bandit attacks, the Anglo residents turned to vigilante action, and a bloodbath that claimed from two hundred to three hundred Hispanic lives ensued. (Anders 1982, p. 224)

It has been estimated that between 1915 and 1917 some five thousand Mexicans were killed in South Texas, whereas only sixty-two American civilians and sixty-four soldiers were killed (Webb 1965, p. 478; Montejano 1982, p. 80).

For the Chicano people the Texas Rangers, *los rinches*, are the epitome of police abuse and brutality (see, chapter 3, below). Given that the Rangers committed numerous abuses, violated the civil liberties of Chicanos, and killed Chicanos and Indians at will, one cannot escape the conclusion that images of the Anglo Ranger and the Mexican *bandido* not only evolved along parallel lines but were in fact mutually reinforcing mythologies. If the "Meskin" could be successfully depicted as a bloodthirsty subhuman species, then those delegated the task of exterminating these despicable creatures were not murderers, but heroes to be honored and respected. According to Arnoldo De León, the Rangers "became a corps that enjoyed the tacit sanction of the white community to do to Mexicans in the name of the law what others did extralegally" (1983, pp. 75-76).

Throughout the history of the Southwest, then, the Rangers have served as a fairly accurate barometer of Anglo prejudice and hostility toward the Mexican. Anti-Mexican feeling has been especially intense when the United States has been at war and hostile attitudes toward foreigners have flourished. On the eve of World War I, George Marvin recorded:

> The killing of Mexicans...through the border in these last four years is almost incredible.... Some rangers have degenerated into common man-killers. There is no penalty for killing, for no jury along the border would ever convict a white man for shooting a Mexican.... Reading over the Secret Service records makes you feel almost as

though there were an open game season on Mexicans along the
border. (McWilliams 1968, p. 112)

The tacit acceptance of police abuse continues, as evidenced by a 1977
case in which three Houston policemen received one-year prison sentences
for the murder of a Chicano Vietnam veteran, José Campos Torres. More
recently, a U.S. Border Patrol agent shot a 13-year old boy who was allegedly throwing rocks at the agent across the international border. The Mexican Consulate General Javier Escobar denounced the shooting as "a brutal,
unjustified action and a very serious violation of the Mexican border" (San
Francisco Chronicle, 1985, p. 12).

Without doubt the economic, political, and legal exploitation of the
Chicano has been facilitated by the proximity of the border and the
availability of an unlimited pool of labor that can be manipulated and
exploited by American industry and agriculture (see chapter 4, below). The
demand for Mexican labor has intensified during times of economic expansion, or when there has been a shortage of American labor as in World
Wars I and II. The supply of Mexican labor has been likened to a "faucet"
that can be readily turned "on" or "off," depending on prevailing economic
conditions. During the Great Depression, for example, thousands of Mexicans were deported or "repatriated" and their civil rights wantonly
violated. A reign of terror ensued in Chicano neighborhoods as they were
cordoned off and raided.

Although Mexican labor was very much in demand during World
War II, antiforeign sentiment was strong and the Mexican became a very
visible symbol of the so-called foreign element in the United States. Perhaps
it is not coincidental that the first shipment of braceros, or temporary contract laborers, would arrive in Los Angeles in the summer of 1942 in the
midst of a "crime wave," attributed by the press and law enforcement to
Mexican zoot-suiters or gangsters (see chapters 5 and 6).[5]

The 1950s also proved to be a period of intense and open political
repression. The threat of "communism" and foreign "subversion" provided
a ready-made rationale for muting political protest and intimidating
Chicano communities. Under "Operation Wetback," millions were
deported and, once again, a reign of terror prevailed. As Carey McWilliams
astutely observed:

The viciousness of the present roundup consists in the fact that once
such a campaign has been decreed, there is only one way to carry
it into effect; namely, to make systematic house-to-house raids in every

Mexican settlement in the state. In the course of these raids, it is inevitable that some long-time resident Mexicans will be picked up....
The mere announcement that the Immigration Service is conducting a roundup of this character operates, of course, to spread fear and panic throughout the Mexican settlements. Many of the long resident entrants have married American citizens and have Americanborn children. (1949, p. 19)

Confrontations with the legal and judicial system continued into the 1960s and 1970s to the present. Although the 1970-1971 Los Angeles riots did not draw the national attention of Kent State, thirty-five persons were shot by police in the January 31, 1971, confrontation alone (see chapter 5, below). These incidents were erroneously termed the "East Los Angeles Riots" by the mass media, the police, and the public at large. Just as it would have been more accurate to term the zoot-suit riots the "U.S. Servicemen's riots" or "government riots," so it is more accurate to refer to these incidents as the "Los Angeles police riots." The media presented them largely as unprovoked eruptions by the Mexican-American community.

These were not isolated incidents: encounters with police are commonplace in the barrios of the Southwest. Many of them go unnoticed and receive little publicity or are dismissed as isolated incidents, but they reflect escalating Chicano-police conflict. Barrios remain ethnic enclaves, physically and socially isolated from Anglo society, and in contemporary society the police bear much of the burden for enforcing this isolation—that is, for keeping Chicanos in their place. Given this isolation, the mass media assume an increasingly important role in shaping and maintaining public images of Chicanos.

The wanton killing of Mexicans along the border is not a distant phenomenon but one that continues today. One of the most blatant incidents was the infamous Hannigan case, which occurred in the summer of 1976 on the ranch of George Hannigan near Douglas, Arizona (see Associated Press 1976; Bell Blawis 1977; Law 1977; Negri 1977; El Paso Times 1976a and 1976b). Hannigan and his two sons (aged 22 and 17) forcefully detained three undocumented Mexicans who were looking for work. After stripping, stabbing, and burning them with hot pokers, they were dragged across the desert. They also pretended to hang one of the Mexicans and shot another. George Hannigan died before the case went to trial, but his sons were acquitted, despite public outcry on both sides of the border.

Many beatings and killings of Chicanos today, moreover, rather than being carried out by vigilante groups or *los rinches*, are being perpetrated by rank-and-file law enforcement officers and U.S. Border Patrol agents. This is a serious, perhaps endemic, problem reflective not only of the attitudes of individual officers but of departmental policies and procedures that, directly or indirectly, encourage such abuses.

Thus, images of Chicanos as criminal, violent, and lawless have persisted well into the twentieth century, in the face of widespread patterns of abuse and lawlessness perpetrated against them, and a double standard of justice. The double standard that emerged was not an arbitrary or random occurrence but one intended to systematically maintain the subordination of the Chicano. Inasmuch as economic and political power was held by Anglo-Americans, the legal and judicial system, rather than striving for justice and impartiality, became a vehicle for advancing the interests of the dominant group.

Cultural conflict and racist ideologies also worked to perpetuate the view of Chicanos as an inferior, almost subhuman, people. The stereotype of the Chicano as a lazy, bloodthirsty, and deranged outlaw, after all, had its counterpart in the thrifty, moderate, pious, and law-abiding Anglo-American. In addition, because Chicanos lacked the power to create and shape images of themselves, atrocities could be committed against them with relative impunity.

In the twentieth century, force and coercion continue to play a prominent part in maintaining Chicano subordination, but more insidious methods have also evolved. Such methods are extremely important and difficult to counteract, for they create the illusion of equality while maintaining the subordination of the group.

One mechanism of indirect control is co-optation: elevating to positions of power token representatives of the oppressed group who do not really represent the interests of that group. These are the "Uncle Toms" or "Tio Tacos." A second technique is gerrymandering, and yet another is that of "divide and conquer" (Barrera et al. 1972, p. 489). A very important but relatively unexplored technique is the mobilization of bias. The concept will be discussed more fully in subsequent chapters but, briefly, it involves the manipulation of symbols in such a way that they perpetuate myths about the inferiority of the group (ibid., p. 490). Because Chicanos lack power over the schools, the media, and other agents of socialization, most prevalent images of them are externally induced.

The mobilization of bias is not a totally new phenomenon but one that is exacerbated by the proliferation and pervasiveness of the mass media as well as other external impersonal agents of socialization. The mobilization of bias is a broad and inclusive process that shapes many images, but the focus here will be on how the mobilization of bias has propagated the image of the Chicano as criminal and lawless. It will be contended that the mobilization of bias is an effective, if subtle, mechanism of control: by depicting the Chicano as violent and criminal, emphasis is shifted away from the exploitation and subordination of Chicanos toward problems and inadequacies within the barrio. The ideology becomes an insidious way of blaming victims for their own oppression while giving tacit approval and legitimation to police abuse. Such abuse is no longer viewed as abuse but rather as badly needed enforcement of the law.

It is argued, moreover, that the effects of the mobilization of bias are most intensified when Chicanos internalize and espouse such negative images. In addition to being economically and politically exploited and subjected to a double standard of justice, Chicanos today are subjected to cultural control. This often leads them to internalize negative images and to blame Chicanos themselves for their subordination. When they began to internalize and espouse such negative images, the mobilization of bias has come full circle.

A PERSPECTIVE ON GRINGO JUSTICE

The perspective on gringo justice presented here is not intended as a definitive statement, but rather a preliminary formulation that will be expanded and developed more fully in subsequent chapters. Given that so little has been done in the area, a full-blown theory may be premature, but demonstrating the need for such a formulation is surely an essential first step in its development. Before summarizing the basic tenets of the perspective, its theoretical underpinnings and rationale will be outlined.

THEORETICAL UNDERPINNINGS OF THE PERSPECTIVE

1. The image of Chicanos as criminals or bandits has persisted since the initial contact between Anglo settlers and Mexicans on the frontier.

2. There is a need to develop viable theoretical perspectives on gringo justice that not only reject the notion that Chicanos are somehow more criminal or violence-prone but are sensitive to the nuances of Chicano culture and firmly grounded in a Chicano worldview.

3. Traditional sociological and criminological theories are inadequate for understanding either the evolution of the *bandido* image or the relationship of Chicanos to the legal and judicial system.

4. Because the ultimate goal of traditional theories is to explain Chicano violence and criminality, they inevitably attribute the *bandido* image to some defect in the Chicano, not to the dominant society.

5. Emergent theories in Chicano scholarship have been more positive, but they have focused almost exclusively on political economy and largely ignored the legal and judicial system, whereas works that have concentrated on the legal and judicial system have been primarily descriptive and almost devoid of theory.

6. Theories that characterize Chicanos as criminal, delinquent, or violent are not benign but pernicious and must be actively resisted and rejected, even when they are ostensibly sympathetic, for they ultimately work to control Chicanos and maintain their subordinate status.

BASIC TENETS OF THE PERSPECTIVE

1. The criminalization of the Chicano resulted not from their being more criminal or violent but from a clash between conflicting and competing cultures, worldviews, and economic, political, and judicial systems.

2. In the aftermath of the North American invasion and the acquisition of Mexico's northern territories, Chicanos were rendered landless and displaced politically and economically, but they became a vital source of cheap and dependent labor for the developing capitalistic system.

3. Chicanos were labeled as *bandidos* because they actively resisted Anglo encroachment and domination but lacked the power to shape images of criminality or to articulate sociological/

criminological theories. The *bandido* image served to reinforce or legitimate their economic, political, and legal exploitation.

4. As Chicanos were displaced economically and politically, they became increasingly concentrated in ethnically and residentially homogeneous neighborhoods or barrios. Barrioization made it possible to maintain a constant supply of cheap labor without contaminating Anglo society, while keeping Chicanos in a subordinate and dependent position.

5. Conflict with law enforcement intensified during the twentieth century. With growing barrioization the police assumed an increasingly important role in maintaining Chicanos under control and enforcing the social and physical isolation of the barrio.

6. Although Chicanos are essentially a landless people not integrated into the American melting pot, barrios are a symbolic land base and an important source of identity and pride.

7. So-called gangs or barrio youth groups may have negative manifestations, but they are not inherently deviant or criminal, and they provide an essential sense of identity, self-worth, and pride for their members that is afforded other youth by more socially acceptable groupings.

2

Mi Casa Es Su Casa:
Displacement from the Land

INTRODUCTION

Although Mexico had lost the war, much of the land was still under the control of individual Mexican families. The decades immediately following the North American invasion were critical, for it was in this period that Chicanos were to be displaced from the land and rendered economically and politically dependent.

Nowhere did the downfall come more quickly or dramatically than in California. The discovery of gold came on January 24, 1848, only nine days before the end of the war. The gold rush brought with it a massive influx of Anglos so that the Chicano population was very quickly outnumbered. According to Leonard Pitt:

> After a century of slow population growth, during which the arrival of twenty-five *cholos* or fifty Americans seemed a momentous occasion, suddenly and without warning California faced one of the swiftest, largest, and most varied folk migrations of all time. More newcomers now arrived each day in California than had formerly come in a decade. Briefly told, the story of the Californians in the gold rush is their encounter with 100,000 newcomers in the single year of 1849—80,000 Yankees, 8,000 Mexicans, 5,000 South Americans, and several thousand miscellaneous Europeans. (Pitt 1966, p. 52)

By 1850 even the Mexican *cholos*[6] outnumbered the fifteen thousand native Californios and, overall, the Californios were outnumbered by a ratio of between ten and fifteen to one (ibid., p. 53).

27

Members of the native California elite considered themselves Spanish, or white, and thereby racially, culturally, and morally superior to the *indio* or the *mestizo*. Eager to establish their identity, they began calling themselves *Californios*, instead of *españoles* or *mexicanos*, seeking to be distinguished not only from "low-life" Mexicans but from the many other newly arrived Latin Americans. Yet, Anglos did not typically acknowledge differences either between native born *Californios* and Mexican immigrants or among Latin Americans, and considered them all simply as "greasers." Antiforeign sentiment in the mines was directed largely against Latin Americans but by 1854 most of the Sonoran and Chilean miners had returned to their native land (Wright 1940, pp. 326-27). Significantly, the majority of *chilenos* who remained "worked in the Southern mines, where they could associate with the Spanish-speaking Mexican" (ibid.).

This antipathy was intensified by the fact that most of the desirable land was controlled by a small number of Californio families, constituting less than three percent of the total population (Griswold del Castillo 1979, p. 31). There was also extensive competition in the mines where Mexicans and other Latin Americans had made significant strides and often held the most desirable claims. Not only were Mexicans driven from the mines, but by 1880 they lost title to much of the land in California and throughout the Southwest.

DECLINE OF THE PASTORAL ECONOMY

The American takeover of the Southwest entailed not only the imposition of an alien culture and language but the ascendancy of a new economic order as the pastoral Mexican economy yielded to American capitalism. Within much of California, especially the north, the change was quickly effected: the Mexican population was greatly outnumbered and lost economic control. But in some areas to the south, such as Santa Barbara, the ranchero class remained firmly entrenched during the 1850s and well into the 1860s.

The secularization of the missions and the transformation of the economy of Mexico's northern territories were completed long before the war between Mexico and the United States. Under the Secularization Proclamation of 1834, the missions were to be dismantled and brought under secular control. Secularization had a profound impact on Mexican California society and set the stage for the period that has been termed the golden age of the ranchos (1834-1846). Not only did mission secularization bring an end to "the economic and political influence of the mission padres" but it "radically changed the system of land tenure and land disposal in California" (Camarillo 1979, p. 9). During this period, land ownership became increasingly concentrated in the holdings of a few families who were awarded large land grants by the Mexican government.

Southern California remained a Mexican stronghold even after the war of 1846. The assessor of San Diego County wrote in 1855 that "large quantities of arable and grazing land are held under Mexican or Spanish titles, and occupied by rancheros of the ancient order of shepherds and herdsmen" (Cleland 1941, p. 72). During the 1850s and late 1860s the ranchero class owned much of the land and controlled the pastoral economy. *Mexicanos*, consequently, were able to retain control of the political scene, the judicial system, and the schools. In Santa Barbara, for example, council minutes were recorded in Spanish; English language instruction was not available until 1858; Mexican juries seldom convicted Mexican defendants (Camarillo 1979, pp. 14-25). An exasperated Anglo attorney, Charles Huse, concluded that "it would be better to close the doors of the Courthouse. It makes no difference what the testimony is, if the criminal is Spanish or Californian, he is always set free by a jury of 'native sons' " (Huse 1977, p. 110).

However, as the Anglo population expanded, so did it gain in political power. Loss of political control by the *Californios* went hand in hand with economic and occupational displacement. In 1873 the ranchero class no longer controlled the economy and was supplanted by an emergent professional and merchant class that was basically non-Mexican.

By the 1880s the Mexican pueblo of Santa Barbara had been transformed into an American city. Americanization set in motion the barrioization of the Chicano or, in other words, "the formation of residentially and socially segregated Chicano barrios or neighborhoods" (Camarillo 1979, p. 53). The process was something more than simply segregation; it intertwined economic, social, and demographic forces. Barrioization virtually eliminated Chicanos from the social and political life of the community at large; through isolation Chicanos became almost invisible, if not nonexistent. Conversely, for Chicanos, homogeneous neighborhoods provided security and protection from American influence. It enabled them to retain traditional Mexican culture and customs intact within the boundaries of modern American cities.

The economic position of Chicanos declined throughout the Southwest as the pastoral Mexican economy was supplanted by American capitalism. Nonetheless, there were differences in how quickly displacement occurred. Within southern California, for example, the ranchero class was much less firmly entrenched in Los Angeles than in Santa Barbara and it was easily toppled. Richard Griswold del Castillo observed that in Los Angeles "the process of property disenfranchisement was well under way before the 1860s" (1979, p. 47). Whereas in 1850, 61 percent of Chicano heads of household owned land valued at more than $100, by 1860 only 29 percent owned this much land (ibid., p. 46). By 1870 less than 25 percent of the Chicano heads of household owned property and at a value of about half of that owned in 1850. Finally, in 1880 the only Chicano families that owned land were recent arrivals to Los Angeles who had not been landowners prior to 1850 (ibid., p. 49). Thus, a new propertied class had replaced the old Californio social order.

A very similar pattern was found in San Diego. Almost all land was held by *mexicanos* in 1850, but within a decade the *ricos* or *gente de razón* had lost most of their wealth. By 1860 they controlled less than 30 percent of the total value of real estate (García 1976, p. 70). With the rise of commerce, Mexican feudal society gave way to an expansionist capitalistic system.

The death knell for the golden age of the ranchos came with the economic depression of the 1860s. In 1861 the sagging cattle industry was decimated by a series of natural disasters, including rainstorms and floods followed by a severe three-year drought:

> For many ranching families, 1864 meant the end of solvency; their names generally went on the delinquent tax list and stayed there until they had sold their property . . . . Before the catastrophe, practically all land parcels worth more than $10,000 had still been in the hands of old families; by 1870, these families held barely one-quarter. A mean and brassy sky thus eventually did in the south of California what lawyers and squatters had accomplished in the north—the forced breakup of baronial holdings, their transfer to new owners, and the rise of a way of life other than ranching. (Pitt 1966, pp 247-48; see also Cleland 1941, pp 157-83)

Whereas the cattle counties of southern California remained under Mexican control during the 1850s and early 1860s, the northern ranchos were almost instantly destroyed. Squatters, speculators, and unscrupulous lawyers who sought to acquire land through legal and extralegal means were aided in their efforts by the legislature and passage of congressional bills such as the Land Act of 1851, which encouraged squatters to challenge the validity of Spanish and Mexican land grants and abrogated provisions of the Treaty of Guadalupe Hidalgo.

By 1856 a massive change in landownership had taken place and much of the land was now in Yankee hands. The feeling of betrayal was common among Californios who lost their land. Juan Bandini, a prominent landowner in southern California remarked:

Of the lands mentioned some have been in the quiet possession of the proprietors and their families for forty or fifty years. On them they have reared themselves homes—they have enclosed and cultivated fields—there they and their children were born—and there they lived in peace and comparative plenty. But now—our inheritance is turned to strangers—our houses to aliens. We have drunken our water for money—our wood is sold unto us. Our necks are under persecution—we labor and have no rest. (García 1976, p. 71).

The pattern of political repression and economic displacement was repeated throughout the Southwest. Within Texas, Mexicans or *tejanos* constituted a small and relatively insignificant group, except for South Texas, which remained heavily Mexican. *Tejanos* made up only 10 percent of the population of Texas in 1840 and 6 percent in 1860.

The process of displacement, moreover, had started long before the North American invasion. During the Texas revolt many *tejanos* were forcibly driven from their lands (Nance 1963, vol. 1, p. 547) and the Treaty of Velasco simply intensified the expansionist fever. "Much of the Hispano population was driven out of Bexar [County] and took refuge along the Rio Grande or beyond" (Meining 1969, p. 46). As in California, legal and extralegal means were used to deprive Mexicans of their land. A favorite target of squatters was the *Expíritu Santo* grant, a 260,000-acre parcel along the northern bank of the Rio Grande.

Many Mexicans, especially those with small landholdings, had their land taken away by force or intimidation. Even apologist Texas historian, Walter Prescott Webb, recognized the existence of a dual standard of justice so that " 'One law applied to them [Mexicans], and another, far less rigorous, to the political leaders and to the prominent Americans' " (Fehrenbach 1968, pp. 509-10). A Mexican who killed an American was usually hanged, but Anglos injured and killed Mexicans with little fear of reprisal (ibid., p. 510). Although the lower classes were more likely to be victims of Anglo abuse and violence, the Mexican upper classes grew increasingly weary of the imposition of Anglo authority and the double standard of justice. In South Texas:

> Families who had lost their land accused the Anglo purchasers of intimidation, violence, and fraud. Although the courts held out the promise of redress for these grievances, all too often this alien legal system not only invalidated the land claims of the Hispanic proprietors but also overwhelmed them with ruinous lawyers' fees. (Anders 1982, p. xiv)

Economic displacement came more slowly in the predominantly Mexican counties of South Texas: some rancheros retained title to their land. Although Americans arrived in the Lower Rio Grande Valley in the 1820s, their presence was not really felt until the occupation of the Trans-Nueces region by United States troops during the war with Mexico (ibid., xiv-xv). At the time of annexation, the class structure consisted of a landed Mexican elite or *hacendados*, an Anglo mercantile class, a group of independent but poor Mexican ranchers, and a class of Mexican *peones* or peasants (Montejano 1982, p. 9). During the war, the United States army had introduced the steamboat as a vehicle for transporting supplies and troops. By 1852 Charles Stillman, Mifflin Kenedy, and Richard King monopolized the lucrative steam trade market with northern Mexico. Brownsville emerged as a dominant trade center (Anders 1982, p. xiii). These Anglo entrepreneurs reaped enormous profits from both legal trade and smuggling, and were able to utilize their profits to establish vast cattle empires during the 1850s. While the cattle barons fenced off large tracts of land, introduced large-scale sheep raising, and organized drives, the area remained heavily Mexican. Anglo businessmen often acquired large tracts of land by marrying into wealthy Mexican families, but they adopted local customs and lifestyle. Although many rancheros were displaced, the feudalistic economic order prevailed:

> The cattle *hacienda* remained the dominant social and economic institution of the region, and the relations that bound the Anglo patron with his Mexican workers remained paternalistic, patriarchal, and permanent. (Montejano 1982, p. 10)

The *patrón* exercised almost complete control over his *peones*, and despite the economic exploitation inherent in the system, social relations were characterized by permanence and stability:

> Responsibility as well as power defined the rancher's social role. He
> provided the laborers with living quarters and other necessities, pro-
> tected them from Indian and bandit raids, offered fatherly advice,
> and sponsored fiestas, weddings, and funerals. (Anders 1982, p. xii)

The *patrón* provided a certain amount of security and protection in
exchange for labor and loyalty.

By the turn of the century, however, the development of commer-
cialized farming had brought with it the demise not only of Mexican ranch
society but the paternalistic relationship between ranchero and worker.
Commercial farming required a temporary and disposable work force so
that ties between employers and workers, rather than being personal
and permanent, were contractual, impersonal, and transitory. David
Montejano argues that this transformation had a critical impact on relationships between Anglos and Mexicans, and led to the eventual implementation of a segregated economic and social order. In the modern period,
Mexicans became an inferior people: the division of labor in the emergent
farm economy was organized largely along racial lines (Montejano 1982,
p. 12). The farmers were Anglo and the laborers were Mexican. The
organization of work had important consequences: "The impersonal temporary relations on the commercial farm basically made exclusionary institutions and policies a necessary means of controlling 'strange' Mexicans"
(ibid., p. 13).

This economic transformation occurred in South Texas and
throughout the Southwest. By the end of the nineteenth century, Chicanos
had not only lost most of their land but had emerged as the primary source
of cheap, dependent labor for the expanding capitalistic system, occupying the least desirable, most menial, lowest paying jobs. Mechanization
and modernization also brought displacement from agricultural occupations. Chicanos, in other words, went from working within a pastoral
economy, as ranchers or laborers, to working as an urban proletariat. In
San Diego, in 1860, for example, 30.5 percent of Chicanos were employed as
ranchers or farmers, 39.1 percent as skilled laborers, and only 15.9 percent as unskilled laborers (Camarillo 1979, p. 128). By 1880, however, less
than 2 percent were in pastoral/ranching occupations, and 80.9 percent
were unskilled workers (ibid., p. 133). Santa Barbara followed a similar
pattern with 24.3 percent working in ranching or farming, 9.9 percent as
skilled laborers, and 47.9 percent as unskilled laborers in 1860. But by
1880 only 4.7 percent were ranchers or farmers, 3.1 percent skilled workers,
and 79.7 percent unskilled workers (ibid.).

In a relatively brief span Chicanos went from being part of a feudal order that was internally stratified to being a colonial labor force and, eventually, an urban proletariat not fully integrated into the modern economic order (see Barrera 1979). This economic subordination was so extensive that Raul Fernandez (1977) proposes that the Mexican-American War and the American takeover of the Southwest should be seen more as a clash between competing and conflicting economic systems than as a military victory or cultural conflict. It marked the victory of a modern capitalistic system over a traditional feudal order, which he argues occurred in three distinct stages (1977, pp. 6-12).

The first stage of capitalistic expansion began in 1848 and extended to the turn of the century. It signified the defeat of a more "backward" economic system by a more "advanced" one. The Treaty of Guadalupe Hidalgo thus simply formally recognized the victory of capitalism over feudalism. "After the War of 1848, the battle moved from the economic sphere to the political and judicial levels" (ibid., p. 7). In subsequent decades, Mexicans lost their land as a result of legal and coercive extralegal mechanisms with both Mexican and Anglo landowners, giving way to a rising entrepreneural class.

The second stage brought on the development of capitalism and the emergence of demand for a cheap labor force needed for its expansion in the Southwest. Much of this labor was provided by Mexican immigration which began in the 1880s and increased very rapidly during the twentieth century.

The present stage, according to Fernandez, is one where the legal border is, "in *some* ways, a fiction, and has been left behind by the advance of the integration process." With the rise of multinational corporations, the economy of border towns is being "increasingly shaped by the presence of American industry" (ibid., p. 11), and the United States-Mexican border can no longer be understood in isolation from economic forces and the dependent/independent relationship between the Mexican and the American economies (see chapter 4).

IMPOSITION OF AN ALIEN LEGAL SYSTEM

Chicanos were at a clear disadvantage in the economic competition not only because their pastoral, feudal economy was being supplanted by the emergent capitalistic order, but because they were also confronted with a different language and an alien legal system.

Under Spanish and Mexican law, land could be owned either individually or collectively, and held in common by an entire village or community. Two basic types of land grants were awarded by the Spanish colonial and Mexican governments: private land grants given to individuals, and communal land awarded to the heads of ten or more families.[7] A significant difference between this system and American legal tradition is that land was never granted in fee simple with complete right of private ownership (Knowlton 1980, p. 13). Land use and ownership, in other words, was conditional and could be revoked if the conditions were not met or, perhaps, for some other reason:

> Petitioners for a community land grant usually stated in their petition that they were poor men without farming or grazing lands to support their families and that they had found an area of empty unclaimed land that would meet their needs without harming any nearby Indian tribe or other third party. (Ibid.)

Each family was generally awarded sufficient land for its use, and a portion of the land was set aside for future settlers. All other tracts, such as water, forests, and mountains, were granted to the entire village as an *ejido*. Because natural resources were held in common by the village, each family had open access to them (ibid.).

This land grant system can be traced directly to the Spanish law for colonization and is itself derived from Roman law:

> When Spain was regaining the land she had lost from the Moors, the towns were strategically important as strongholds against the enemy, as well as colonizing centers. Because of this importance, the crown frequently granted ownership to areas of land surrounding the towns to be governed according to a city charter whose articles were drawn specifically for the needs of that town or district. This charter comprised to a large extent local custom rather than a national body of codified law. Under the sixteenth-century Castilian monarchs, numerous laws were passed to protect the common lands of the towns against usurpation of the nobility, municipal officials and ordinary citizens. (Westphall 1983, p. 9)

Each family was given a parcel of land *(solar)* for a house and another parcel or parcels *(suertes)* for cultivation, in addition to having the right to use common land and resources. Individual allotments were owned outright after a specified period of time, normally four or five years, and could be sold (ibid., p. 10). Ownership, however, was not inalienable. If land was not cultivated for two years, it reverted to the crown. In short, land grants "constituted simply a permission to use the land, in perpetuity, upon certain conditions" (McBride 1923, p. 109). Unallotted land and community land also could not be sold.

In New Mexico community land grants were the norm in the mountain valleys and the foothills of the Sangre de Cristo Mountains, whereas the large individual land grants, devoted mostly to ranching, were found primarily in the eastern and southern plains and the broad river valleys (Knowlton 1980, p. 13). In time, village communities developed on private grants but their pattern of land use was similar to that of communal grants in the sense that only the land that was cultivated was considered private property and all other land and natural resources were held in common (ibid.).

However, even common lands were differentiated by their use:

> The common lands of community grants were classified according to use. The *debesa* was pasture land, and the *monte* (grove) was used principally for gathering wood and natural foods. The *ejido* was located just outside the town and was used variously for recreation, as a threshing floor, as a garbage dump, or as a pound for stray cattle. The *propio* was a class of town land the income from which was used to defray municipal expenses. In due time the institution of community grants was transplanted to New Mexico, where common lands, while theoretically retaining the aforementioned classifications, were customarily referred to simply as *ejidos*.
>
>   In Spain both the ungranted crown lands—*tierras realengas*—and the common lands of areas that had been granted to communities in fee and full ownership were broadly classified as public domain, but the community lands possessed some qualities of private property so only the *tierras realengas* of the sovereign were truly public domain. Even if only the usufruct (use) to community lands had been granted, and not its fee-simple ownership, that type of usufruct is perpetual under normal circumstances. Either way, the land was strictly set aside for the common use of the citizens, present and future, of that community and no other. (Westphall 1983, p. 10)

The Anglo-American system of land tenure stood in direct contrast and in many ways conflicted with the Hispanic system (Van Ness and Van Ness 1980, p. 8). The Anglo-American system was essentially fee simple in that it had no limitations as to any class of heirs or restrictions on the sale of the property (ibid.). It was also formal and rigid. The earth's surface was plotted on an imaginary grid, which was then symbolically represented on a map:

> The physical features of the land are then correlated with it through surveying and cartography. Obviously this grid must be completely rigid, and to achieve precision, it is defined astrally, with overtly assigned relationships to quite arbitrary points on the earth's surface. This system is specifically not defined terrestrially by earthly landmarks, except as such landmarks have first been located astrally. Through this system of reckoning, land becomes a precisely measurable entity, divisible into parcels which may be located exactly on a map. An additional refinement is that rights are not denoted by direct reference to the land but rather to a piece of the official survey plat. It is to this piece of the map that the legal description in a title refers, since this system assures one that the relationship between the map and the terrestrial surface is a permanent one. (Ibid.)

Such a meticulous system of land tenure was critical to the emergent capitalistic economy, for it clearly facilitated the market exchange of the land and its resources (ibid.).

The *hispano* system, on the other hand, was much more informal and relied heavily on terrestrial landmarks and nearby landholders to describe property. The governor and *alcaldes mayores* played a key role in the process of awarding land grants. Once a petition for land was received by the governor, he instructed the local *alcalde* to investigate the petition and make sure there were no competing claims or objections to the claim (Westphall 1983, p. 17). The *alcalde's* written report to the governor was to include a sketch map of the grant. If the governor approved the grant, he had a title of possession drawn up, which set the limits of the grant. This was followed by a ceremony of possession:

> The Spanish custom of conveying title to land, later followed in essential details by Mexico, incorporated the idea that there could be no valid vesting of title to real estate without a personal delivery by the authorized official. Thus it was that the local alcalde, with two witnesses or a notary, accompanied the grantees to the site of the grant and showed them the prescribed boundaries. The grantees then performed such ceremonial acts as pulling up weeds, scattering earth,

throwing stones, and other acts of possession while giving thanks to
God and the king, or to the nation during the Mexican period. This
act of possession was followed by delivery of a written document
detailing the method of delivery, the boundaries of the grant, and
the sovereign's reasons for donating the land. (Ibid., p. 18)

The written document described the land by reference to natural
features and/or neighboring landowners, and at best only included a sketch
map of the land (Van Ness and Van Ness 1980, p. 9). Even more critical
was the fact that subsequent transactions were typically not recorded. Under
hispano and Mexican law such transfers could be negotiated by a simple
verbal agreement. Social and political considerations, such as social class,
kinship, and community membership, took precedence over economic factors in land transactions (ibid., p. 8). The vastness of the territory also
made it difficult to observe many legal technicalities. Hence agreements
were more often enforced by informal community sanctions than by the
formal apparatus of the law (ibid., p. 10).

As a result of these differences in land tenure, many *mexicanos* had
no formal written confirmation of ownership for either individual or communal holdings. This placed them at a great disadvantage before the Anglo-
American tribunals. As land was contested by the representatives of commercial interests in the new economic order, "their lack of knowledge of
the workings of the Anglo-American land tenure system, its courts, and
adversary form of legal proceedings also contributed to their plight" (ibid.).

Many attorneys took unfair advantage. Leonard Pitt, for example,
notes:

> Since most Californios scarcely understood English, much less the
> technical language of the courts, they had to depend greatly on their
> attorneys, whom they usually paid in land itself and only rarely in
> cash. Sad to say, of the fifty or so attorneys who specialized in claim
> law in the 1850s, most were shysters who lacked not only honesty
> but also knowledge and experience. (Pitt 1966, p. 91)

The actions of unscrupulous lawyers, speculators, and ordinary squatters
were actively aided and abetted by passage of repressive legislation. The
Land Act of 1851, for example, placed the burden of proof on the owners
to demonstrate the validity of their titles *(Statutes at Large* 1851, pp.
631-34). William Gwinn, well known for being strongly anti-Mexican, introduced the bill in the United States Congress and openly admitted that his
intent was to encourage squatters and force Mexicans off the land (García

1976, p. 70). The bill established a three-person Board of Land Commissioners who were to decide on the validity of land titles brought before them and would be "governed by the Treaty of Guadaloupe *[sic]* Hidalgo, the law of nations, ... the principles of equity, and the decisions of the Supreme Court of the United States, so far as they are applicable" (*Statutes at Large* 1851, p. 633). Decisions of the board could be appealed to the district court and, if necessary, the Supreme Court of the United States. Decisions in favor of the claimant were appealed by the United States to the U.S. District Court (Huse 1977, p. 248). The massiveness of the ensuing land grab was unanticipated, even by Gwinn.

The social and political climate of California openly encouraged squatters. In order to "protect" a claimant's property, it was necessary to undergo the equivalent of six separate trials (Huse 1977, p. 248). "Many rancheros were utterly ruined by squatters and the cost of litigation with the Government" (ibid.). The war with Mexico exacerbated hostility toward the Mexican and appeared to affirm Anglo superiority.

In 1849 there was great resentment over the fact that land was inequitably distributed so that some two hundred California families owned some 14 million acres of rich land (Pitt 1966, p. 86). This was deemed "unfair" by newly arrived Americans. The Land Act, moreover, reinforced the belief that many of the Mexican titles were not legitimate and encouraged individuals to challenge their validity.

The board met from January 1852 to March 1855. It was unfamiliar with *hispano* traditions of land usage, and proceedings were in English. The hearings proved disastrous for Chicanos. Out of 813 claims, 521 were confirmed, 19 discontinued, and 273 were rejected (ibid., p. 79). However, 417 of the 521 claims that were confirmed were subsequently appealed. In the end, about 75 percent of the grants were confirmed, but it proved to be a long and, in many cases, expensive process. On the average it took 17 years to validate a land title, and even confirmation did not necessarily secure the land:

> It was severe hardship for owners of land under grants from Mexico, that they should be required to sue the government of the United States (which ought to have protected—not persecuted them), or lose their land; but this hardship was rendered much more severe by the peculiar circumstances under which the suits had to be tried. The trials were to be had in San Francisco at a time when the expenses of traveling and of living in San Francisco were very great, and the fees of lawyers enormous. The prosecution of the suits required a

study of the laws of Mexico, in regard to the disposition of the public lands, and this study had, of course, to be paid for by the clients. In many cases the claimants had to come to San Francisco from remote parts of the State; having three hundred miles to travel, bringing their witnesses with them at their own expense. The witnesses were nearly all native Californians, and it was necessary to employ interpreters at high prices. (Hittell 1858, pp. 444-45)

Although most Mexican land titles were confirmed, the process proved disastrous for many landowners who were forced to borrow or to sell part of their land in order to pay off their lawyers and court costs. In a letter dated April 5, 1852, for example, Josiah Merritt wrote to Manuel Castro informing him that a rancho he had previously sold was sold again in order to settle taxes. He also urged Castro to come to San Francisco to present his titles before the land commissioners for confirmation.

Graham has lost the Rancho you sold him. He sold for the taxes and I expect you will have some difficulty with him. His son bought it. The Commissioners to settle land titles are sitting in San Francisco and a number of titles have been presented so that you have to prove the signatures to the Government and those from whom the titles were derived. It would be well for you to come up as soon as you can as you have all the title papers. (Manuel Castro Papers, #136, April 5, 1852)

The board adjourned in 1855. By 1856 a massive change in landownership had been effected in California.

A similar pattern was observed in New Mexico and southern Colorado. The Treaty of Guadalupe Hidalgo recognized land titles of Mexicans residing in the territory as valid and declared all other property part of the public domain. Congress established the office of surveyor-general of the territory of New Mexico in 1854 and gave it the mandate of "ascertaining the origin, nature, character, and extent of all claims to lands under the laws, usages, and customs of Spain and Mexico" (Van Ness and Van Ness 1980, p. 10). The surveyor-general was to arrive at a recommendation and submit it to the secretary of the interior who would present it to Congress for adjudication. As in California, however, the process proved to be difficult, prolonged, and expensive (ibid.). Not only did the surveyor-general's office lack the resources and personnel to adequately process claims, but:

The expense of filing a claim and successfully seeing it through to confirmation was beyond the means of most Hispanic communities and individuals, for it meant hiring attorneys and often even securing a Congressional lobbyist in Washington. Many Hispanos found that their only avenue to meet these expenses was to agree to deed one-third or more of the land confirmed to the attorneys to pay their fees. Thus, ironically, winning recognition of their land rights generally meant losing a large part of their holdings. (Ibid.)

Very few claims were confirmed by this process and those confirmed generally involved cases where large business interests had acquired the rights to Chicano grants (ibid.).

On March 3, 1891, Congress established the Court of Private Claims (*Statutes at Large* 1891, pp. 854-62). Section 8 of the act proved to be very questionable in that it "permitted" but did not require that "any person or corporation claiming lands ... under a title derived from the Spanish or Mexican Government that was complete and perfect at the date when the United States acquired sovereignty therein," to bring such a claim to the court for confirmation (ibid., p. 857). Although supporters of the bill argued that submission of claims was voluntary and that only imperfect or incomplete claims were required to be submitted, critics maintained that it was, in effect, mandatory and the only way a person could be sure that there were no adverse existing claims and secure a clear title from the United States (Westphall 1983, p. 241). Critics of the bill also asked how one would determine if a claim was perfect. In truth, it was impossible to know whether a claim was perfect without submitting it for confirmation (ibid.).

Under Section 9, the decision could be appealed within six months to the United States Supreme Court, which had the authority to retry the case not only with regard to issues of fact but also issues of law (*Statutes at Large* 1891, p. 858). Section 10 stipulated that after confirmation was finalized, the clerk of the court was to notify the commissioner of the General Land Office. The commissioner, in turn, would have the land surveyed and the cost would be absorbed by the United States. However, upon completion, the claimant had to pay one-half of the cost of the survey before a patent was delivered (ibid., p. 859). In addition, the survey was to be considered a lien against the property, which was enforceable after six months (ibid.). There was strong opposition to this stipulation:

> To many it seemed a direct violation of the provision in Article 8 of the Treaty of Guadalupe Hidalgo guaranteeing that property would

be protected without the imposition of any contribution, tax, or charge. These objectors, likewise, considered it unfair that the United States reserved the right to select the surveyor and to stipulate the amount of his payment. (Westphall 1983, p. 242)

Despite the claim that safeguards would be provided to protect valid claims, Chicanos did not fare very well before the Court of Private Claims. In fact, during its thirteen-year existence it adjudicated over three hundred claims covering some 35 million acres and rejected the bulk of them because of narrow technicalities (Van Ness and Van Ness 1980, p. 10). "The court's record of acreage confirmed (6 percent) relative to earlier Spanish land grant confirmations in Louisiana (100 percent), Florida (90 percent), and California (75 percent), does not stand up on its face" (Westphall 1983, p. 252). These figures constitute an oversimplification, according to Victor Westphall, and the rate of confirmation was probably closer to 30 percent (ibid., p. 254). Although more than 12 million acres were awarded in New Mexico, Westphall concluded after careful analysis that "some eight or nine million more acres of land should have been confirmed by either Congress or the court, or both, to comply fully with the obligation assumed by the United States under the Treaty of Guadalupe Hidalgo" (ibid.). The decisions rendered by the court were most devastating to communal grants because claimants could rarely prove ownership. In the end, less than a dozen communal claims were upheld (Van Ness and Van Ness 1980, p. 10).

In retrospect, it is clear that rather than honoring the Treaty of Guadalupe Hidalgo, the United States cast a shadow over the legality of all land titles held by Mexicans in the newly acquired territories. This proved to be a bonanza for squatters, dishonest lawyers, and wealthy speculators, especially in northern California. By 1853 every ranch in the San Francisco Bay area had a contingent of squatters and by 1856 ranchos in all seven northern counties were infested with nonpaying guests (Pitt 1966, p. 97).

Even more dangerous than squatters, according to Leonard Pitt, were the many lawyers and adventurers who posed either as benefactors or financial advisers to the Californios. Horace Carpentier and two associates, for example, gained the confidence of the Peralta family and promptly proceeded to swindle them out of their 19,000-acre Rancho San Antonio, which was valued at approximately $3 million. Acting as "manager" and "benefactor" for the family, he prepared a lease that was in fact a mortgage against the signer (ibid., p. 98). When Vicente Peralta failed to make payment, Carpentier obtained the Peralta ranch at a sheriff's auction (ibid.). Carpentier proceeded to found the town of Oakland on Rancho San Antonio and became its first mayor, promising to abolish bearbaiting and bullfighting (ibid.).

A favorite scheme of land speculators was to buy interest in several ranches, and graze cattle on the property. Under California law, if one of the owners called for partition of the land, it was to be sold at public auction (Acuña 1981, p. 102). As squatters "swarmed over the land, harassing and intimidating many landowners," officers of the law stood by and did nothing, thereby tacitly condoning these abuses (ibid.). The magnitude of the land grab was overwhelming. In New Mexico alone over seven millions acres of land were acquired by speculators (Westphall 1983, p. 254).

Squatters were aided in their efforts not only by law enforcement, which stood by and permitted their unlawful occupation, but by legislative decree. In California, settlers' advocates supported passage of the Land Act of 1851 because it stipulated that "all lands the claims to which shall not have been presented to the said commissioners within two years" would revert to the public domain (*Statutes at Large* 1851, p. 633). The squatter bill was passed, despite the loud and impassioned plea of Senator Pablo de la Guerra, who remarked that the Californios:

> are the conquered who lay prostrate before the conqueror and ask for his protection in the enjoyment of the little which their fortune has left them. They are the ones who had been sold like sheep— those who were abandoned and sold by Mexico. They do not understand the language which is now spoken in their own country. They have no voice in this Senate, except such as I am now weakly speaking on their behalf. . . . I have seen old men of sixty and seventy years of age weeping like children because they have been cast out of their ancestral home. They have been humiliated and insulted. They have been refused the privilege of taking water from their own wells. They have been refused the privilege of cutting their own firewood. . . . Any impartial party who would examine the law would see that it protects the squatter, and rightly or wrongly displaces the owner of his equal rights—rights which are inviolable according to human or divine law. (*El Clamor Público* 1856, p. 1, my translation)

In the end, however, the United States Supreme Court was to reject only about thirty-two claims covering an area of about seven hundred thousand acres. In sixteen of eighteen cases, involving key property in Marin, Alameda, and Sonoma counties, the court ruled in favor of the original claimants (Pitt 1966, p. 118). But before receiving their patents the Land Office ruled that they were required to survey their land and adjacent land at their own expense (ibid.).

Despite the ruling of the high court, many "settlers" demanded compensation, arguing that they had improved the land and accrued equity with each passing year. Some generous landowners proposed subdividing the land. Mariano Vallejo sold part of Rancho Petaluma at $35 to $50 per acre and was taken up on his offer by several settlers. Yet, the offer of the Castros of Contra Costa to sell eighteen leagues at $100 per acre was bitterly condemned as exorbitant (ibid.).

The arrogance of the squatters was such that they often refused to recognize the legitimacy of Mexican land titles even after they were upheld by the United States Supreme Court. In fact, many felt betrayed by the government and continued their defiance. As could have been predicted:

> Violence attended the final settlements. In 1858, when surveyors tried to draw the lines for lands confirmed to Peña, Fitch, and Berreyesa in Healdsburg, two hundred settlers first ambushed the surveyors, destroying their equipment, and then temporarily drove out the owners as well. A sheriff's posse armed with an ejectment order was no match for the 1,000 gun-carrying settlers who seized Domingo Peralta and held him hostage for a time. José Suñol was killed somewhere on confirmed land, shortly after his family had acquired title. (Ibid., p. 119)

THE ROBBER BARONS

Although the land grab benefited a number of squatters, many were dissatisfied with the land settlement. The land settlement proved unsatisfactory to most settlers and the *Californios* (Ellison 1927, p. 24). In the end, only the speculators and adventurers who reaped huge profits were pleased. In Texas, for example, a small group of unscrupulous men such as Charles Stillman were able to gain economic control and political power by assassination, manipulation, and outright theft:

> A substantial number of newcomers were war veterans who still looked upon Mexicans as the losers. . . . These men did not recognize

Mexican land titles and felt few qualms about taking property from them. Racial and nativist arguments justified their chicanery. At first, Stillman and others feared that the state of Texas would protect Mexican land claims, so they attempted to create their own state. . . . Their plans for secession proved unnecessary because it was soon evident that the state of Texas supported the Anglos' encroachments. (Acuña 1981, pp. 29-30)

Charles Stillman came to the Rio Grande Valley in 1846 and set up a trading post across the river from the city of Matamoros (Fehrenbach 1968, p. 511). With capitalistic expansion and growth in the valley, his business grew and prospered. Stillman had built his trading post on land that belonged to the descendants of Francisco Cavazos and was part of what came to be known after 1848 as the *Espíritu Santo* grant. This 260,000-acre parcel had been granted by the Spanish government to Don José Salvador de la Garza in 1782. Stillman went about acquiring the land through devious means. He called the ownership of the land into question and encouraged hundreds of squatters to settle on the grant. As a result:

A horde of American businessmen, squatters, and ex-soldiers arrived on *Espíritu Santo* lands; many bore headrights, bounty warrants, and Texas veterans' land certificates. There was a general claiming that the land around Brownsville was "vacant," or national land, and thus public land under Texas law by right of conquest. (Ibid.)

Stillman then proceeded to buy out many of the squatters and to acquire other questionable titles (Acuña 1981, p. 30). The Cavazos family took the issue to the courts and on January 15, 1852, their claim was legally upheld. Stillman planned to appeal the decision but offered the family $33,000 for the grant (about 13 cents per acre). Fearing Stillman's political and judicial influence and facing prohibitive court costs, the family accepted the offer. Although title to the land was transferred, the Cavazos family never received the $33,000, because the law firm which represented Stillman had gone bankrupt shortly after the sale (ibid.).

The decline of Mexicans in Texas thus paralleled the decline of the Californios. Within a decade after the signing of the Treaty of Guadalupe Hidalgo, the Texas economy came under Anglo control. An 1860 census showed that out of 263 wealthy Texans, owning property in excess of $100,000, only two were of Mexican origin (Wooster 1967, pp. 171-80).

Another infamous Texas robber baron was Richard King. Born in New York City in 1824, King came to South Texas during the Mexican-American War. Although lionized as a folk hero by apologist historians, he amassed his vast wealth by using brutal and illegal tactics. In 1852, for example, he acquired the *Santa Gertrudis* grant of 15,500 acres for less than two cents per acre (ibid.). The Mexican Border Commission charged in 1873 that he employed cattle rustlers to steal Mexican horses and cattle (Lea 1957, vol. 1, p. 275). King was also accused of sending his men to nearby ranches and branding all unbranded cattle even if they followed cattle with other brands (Comisión pesquisidora de la frontera del Norte 1875, pp. 61-62). The commission singled him out as one of the most serious perpetrators of crimes and depredations along the border:

> One of the proprietors who has distinguished himself most in these depredations is Ricardo King, owner of the estate, Santa Gertrudis, county of Nueces. He has had as chief Tomás Vásquez, accomplice in robberies of Mexican horses, and in the robberies of cattle committed in Texas, and Fernando López, accomplice in the last. He has kept in his rancho this Atilano Alvarado, who is thought to be chief of a party of robbers stationed in Guerrero. They appear also in the dispatches drawn up before the Commission, the dates of which are not very accurate with regard to the robberies in which the individuals have participated who have been in his service. Ricardo King had a large band who ran constantly in all directions of the country marking calves, though they did not belong to him. It is impossible to admit that the people forming that party possessed any sentiments of morality. The laws of Texas offer no energetic remedies for this evil, and are insufficient. (Ibid., p. 105)

One of the most infamous collections of speculators, land grabbers, dishonest lawyers, and swindlers, was the Santa Fe ring. During the 1880s this group gained so much wealth and power that it was said to completely control the New Mexico economy and political system. Some of the most influential members were Thomas B. Catron, Stephen B. Elkins, and Le Baron Bradford Prince, but the ring also included members of the Mexican elite class *(los ricos)* and prominent business leaders and political figures.

Thomas Benton Catron was born in LaFayette County, Missouri, on October 6, 1840.[8] He and his future partner, Stephen Elkins, graduated from the University of Missouri in 1860 (Brayer 1949, p. 167). After serving in the Confederate army and fighting in many battles, he moved to New Mexico with Elkins in 1866. Catron bought a Spanish grammar and taught himself Spanish en route to New Mexico. Although not yet admitted to the bar, he was appointed district attorney in the third judicial district of New Mexico and shortly thereafter became a junior partner in the law firm of Elkins and Catron. In 1873 Elkins was elected territorial delegate and Catron replaced him as United States attorney for the New Mexico territory. He served as a member of the New Mexico legislature for many years and became the leader of the Santa Fe ring after Elkins left New Mexico, amassing a fortune by acquiring interest in at least thirty-four land grants totalling almost six million acres (Westphall 1983, pp. 233-34).

Catron was one of the leading attorneys representing the Maxwell Land Grant Company in its extensive litigation (see Pearson 1961; Keleher 1964). The grant embraced almost two million acres of land, or 2,680 square miles, and was claimed not only by the Utes and Apaches but by Mexicans and American settlers (Keleher 1964, p. xi). It was awarded by the Mexican government in 1841 to Guadalupe Miranda, a citizen of Mexico, and Charles Beaubien, a French-Canadian. When Miranda and Beaubien requested execution of the grant on February 12, 1843, Father Antonio José Martínez, a strong defender of the Chicano people, objected on the grounds that "a part of the land granted to Miranda and Beaubien conflicted with lands claimed by Charles Bent, and that a large portion of the land involved belonged to the people of Taos, and other towns, that such lands had been long known as commons and the people had for generations grazed their livestock on them" (ibid., p. 15). Martínez's request for a stay was successful. Lucien Maxwell bought Miranda's share of the grant in 1858 and part of Beaubien's share. In 1869 Maxwell sold the grant to a British-Dutch consortium, which included members of the Santa Fe ring and Governor Miguel Otero. The Maxwell grant proved extremely troublesome, however, because many squatters moved onto the land after the federal government laid claim to part of the grant.

Catron's close associate, Stephen Benton Elkins, was born in Ohio in 1841. During the Civil War, he fought on the Union side. In 1866 he was elected to the territorial assembly. One year later, at the age of twenty-six, he served as attorney general of New Mexico and in 1868 was appointed United States attorney for the territory. Elkins was president of the First National Bank of Santa Fe and served two terms in the United States Congress. Between 1891 and 1894, he was secretary of war under President Benjamin Harrison.

On the journey from Missouri to New Mexico in 1866, Elkins and Catron had resolved that each would serve in the United States Senate. Elkins married the daughter of Henry Gassaway Davis, U.S. senator from West Virginia, and in 1894 he became senator from that state. Catron, on the other hand, was elected United States senator from New Mexico in 1912 at the age of seventy-one.

In order to enhance the power of the Santa Fe ring, a movement emerged to grant New Mexico statehood. According to historian Ralph Emerson Twitchell, the leader of this movement was Elkins:

> The leading spirit, politically, and most capable of those who controlled in Santa Fe, was elected delegate to Congress. He was possessed of a charming personality, of marked ability, of large acquaintance in the "states," and it was believed that he would succeed. (Twitchell 1963, p. 395)

Although New Mexico did not become a state until 1912, the Santa Fe group continued to exert control and influence for many decades to come. Lawlessness within the territory was rampant and inhibited its admission as a state. When President Hayes appointed Lew Wallace as governor in 1878 he was instructed to "leave no stone unturned in restoring peace and good order in New Mexico" (ibid.). Perhaps what is most disturbing about the prevailing lawlessness and chicanery is that the perpetrators were not common thieves but the leading and most respectable citizens of the territory. This was therefore a classic example of governmental or civic crime and lawlessness.

On April 18, 1887, Justice Miller of the United States Supreme Court delivered the long awaited decision in the case of the United States vs. The Maxwell Land Grant Company. The court held in favor of the Maxwell Land Grant Company, arguing that the grant was confirmed by an Act of Congress on June 21, 1860, and that the courts did not have the power to annul such acts:

> The result is that we are entirely satisfied that the Grant, as confirmed by the action of Congress, is a valid grant; that the survey and the patent issued upon it are entirely free from any fraud on the part of the grantees or on those claiming under them; and that the decision could be no other than that which the learned judge of the circuit court below made, and which this court affirmed. (Cited in Keleher 1964, p. 111)

By reaching this decision the Supreme Court not only uprooted many Indian and Mexican settlers who lived on the land but closed a dark page in New Mexico history. The victory was heralded by *los ricos* and capitalists but not by the many settlers of the 1.7 million acre parcel that stretched across New Mexico and Colorado:

> In the hills and valleys of the immense country that made up the Maxwell Land Grant, when the news of the decision of the Supreme Court had become generally known, there prevailed great disappointment and an atmosphere of gloom and defeat. Many families over a great many years had settled on the Grant in entire good faith, believing that in time their claims would ripen into perfect title and that they would not be molested in their possession of the homesteads and ranches upon which they had made their homes. Now the people were apprehensive, fearful of the next move to be made by the Grant owners, sullen in their resentment. (Ibid. pp. 112-13)

3

Vigilantes, Bandits, and Revolutionaries

INTRODUCTION

One of the most persistent myths in history and social science is that of the passive and docile Mexican-American. The truth, however, is that the history of the Mexican and Chicano people is replete with examples of active resistance to economic, political, and legal oppression (see Rosenbaum 1981). After the North American invasion, Mexico remained concerned with the treatment and welfare of the Mexican inhabitants of the newly occupied territory and insisted on the inclusion of provisions in the Treaty of Guadalupe Hidalgo to protect the land and property rights of Chicanos and safeguard their cultural autonomy. In subsequent years Mexico was to ardently protest violations of the treaty and to insist on equal protection of the law for its displaced citizens. The Mexican Border Commission of 1873, as previously noted, countered the allegations of the American Presidential Commission by noting that it was the Mexican who was typically the victim of banditry and cattle rustling. In response to a program of massive deportation and repatriation during the Depression, Mexican consulates rose in defense of the Mexican community in the United States (see chapter 4). During the 1940s Mexico once again took great care to protect the rights of braceros and bitterly protested the violence perpetrated against Chicanos in the famous zoot-suit riots and the Sleepy Lagoon case.

Mexicans on the United States side of the border were even more vehement in responding to the violation of their rights. Chicanos used every means possible to protect land titles and water rights, but they were at a distinct disadvantage before American tribunals. Those who lacked the

50

resources to seek legal redress were often forced to go outside the law. In fact, the American Southwest in the period following the Mexican-American War was characterized by lawlessness and disorder. What is significant is not that some Chicanos took the law into their own hands, for law-abiders appeared to be the exception rather than the rule, but rather that they were labeled deviant and criminal by the dominant society, whereas Anglo settlers who exceeded the parameters of the law were often treated as heroes. They were admired and respected.

The ruthless robber baron Richard King and his partner in crime Mifflin Kenedy were described by historian T. R. Fehrenbach as "leading merchants" of the region, who "filled a vacuum the native Spanish-speaking ranchers could not fill" (1968, p. 289). Few Mexicans could read or write, and most were unwilling to learn English or familiarize themselves with American institutions, according to Fehrenbach. The political and economic downfall of the Mexican was thus attributed to their deficient or maladaptive culture:

> In the 1850s, the border towns of El Paso and Brownsville, and San Antonio itself, were dominated by a handful of leading merchants or financial men, none of whom were born in Texas or the South. This peculiar politico-social system, in which ethnic Mexicans usually possessed numerical superiority but remained politically inert as individuals, became a lasting feature of south-Texas life. It was a logical outcome to centuries of Hispanic-Mexican tradition, in which the Indian and *mestizo* base were allowed no function in politics, and in which even the Spanish landed elite possessed no initiative beyond being permitted to sit on local municipal councils. Another feature of this developing society was that the American or Americanized newcomers acquired extensive lands; the early entrepreneur, if he stayed, became a rancher. In this way Richard King and Mifflin Kenedy, who with a few others at one time dominated all Texas south of the Nueces from Brownsville, became two of the largest landowners in the South. In the 1850s the nucleus of the immense King Ranch was formed. (Ibid.)

This chapter addresses the issue of why Chicanos and Anglos were labeled "bandits" and "vigilantes," respectively. A basic premise of sociological labeling and conflict theories[9] is that *"social groups create deviance by making rules whose infraction constitutes deviance, and by applying those rules to particular people and labeling them as outsiders"*

(Becker 1966, p. 9). It shifts the focus, therefore, from the "actor" and his/her actions to the "audience" and the process through which behavior is defined as "deviant." Chicanos were termed deviant or criminal not because of their actions but because Anglo-Americans had gained control of the economy, the political order, and the legal and judicial system. Chicanos, in other words, lacked power and control over those agencies, including the police, the courts, newspapers, and books, that shaped public images of criminality and labeled individuals criminal. Until recently, history was written almost exclusively from the perspective of the dominant society. The King Ranch Corporation, as a case in point, commissioned Tom Lea to write a very flattering two-volume work on the King Ranch (1957). From the onset, Lea creates the impression that King was a defender of Chicanos. The dedication, in Spanish, is to all those who were genuine "Kineños" (i.e., Mexican ranch hands on the King Ranch):

> A TODOS AQUELLOS HOMBRES
> KINEÑOS DE VERDAD
> SE DEDICA ESTA OBRA
> EN RECONOCIMIENTO DE LO QUE
> LES DEBE ESTE RANCHO

Throughout the work, King is depicted as a two-fisted and hard-working rancher who, when all is said and done, proved to be a kind and benevolent boss:

> He disciplined his people but he took care of them; he protected them; he never failed to match their faithfulness with his own. He knew the moods of men with rough hands and strong backs. He could humor them. One morning early, the vaqueros around headquarters came to tell the *patrón* that they had a wish just to sit, to enjoy life, as a *patrón* enjoyed life sitting in his house, his fine house. Captain King looked at the brown faces. "*Alal*," he said, "pass in, please." He got chairs and sat them all down in the parlor. After an hour or so, one of the vaqueros got up. "Where are you going?" the *patrón* asked. "Outside, to smoke." "You can smoke right here," the *patrón* said and the vaqueros sat in the parlor until twelve o'clock at noon and then everybody was ready to go to work. (Lea 1957, vol. 1, pp. 349-51)

Lea is also very careful to praise King for his meticulous concern in observing the letter of the law in business transactions. Allegations that King was a robber baron are dismissed as "fables" or "lies." According to Lea:

Every land acquisition King ever made was done through lawyers. They transacted the business. They advised King when he had rights of possession. King bought every piece of land he came to own. He sometimes bought one piece again and again to satisfy multiple claimants. (Ibid., p. 330)

The effects of such portrayals are insidious not only because they transform Richard King from an unscrupulous robber baron into a law-abiding model of virtue but because they create the illusion that he was loved and respected by his Mexican *peones*. This reinforces the view that the issue of banditry somehow transcended race. The "good Mexicans" were the Kineños who loved and respected their *patrón*. King did hire Mexican ranch hands and they were involved in stealing cattle from other ranches, but it was King who controlled the purse strings and who dictated the actions of his men.

According to sociological labeling and conflict theories, language plays a critical part in the process of social control. Depending on one's vantage point, a person might be variously described as a robber baron and thief or as an enterprising and law-abiding merchant. The term "settler," for example, connotes that one has a bona fide right to occupy land, whereas "squatter" has a very negative connotation. Rather than being identified as vigilantes or outlaws, for example, many Anglo-Texans who took the law into their own hands were given legitimacy by use of the term "citizen soldier" (see Nackman 1975). Vigilantes, similarly, are members of a group organized ostensibly to keep order and to punish crime. Yet, vigilante is, in a very real sense, a contradiction in terms, for it is a mechanism that goes outside the law for the express purpose of maintaining order. Vigilantism and social banditry entail essentially the same behavior and differ only in the sense that those in power tend to label the former as positive and law-abiding, and the latter as deviant and criminal. However, not all Chicano dissidents were social bandits. Some were revolutionary leaders who participated in organized revolts against Anglo oppression.

EMERGENCE OF VIGILANTISM

The word "vigilante," ironically, is derived from Spanish and refers to a member of an unauthorized group organized for the express purpose of maintaining order and apprehending criminals. In Spanish, it denotes a watchman or someone watchful or alert to danger or trouble.

Although much violence throughout history has been directed at changing the established order, vigilantism is a unique form of violence. Political violence generally seeks to bring about social change, but vigilantism aims to maintain the established social and political order. It is precisely for this reason that vigilantism has been termed "establishment violence" (Rosenbaum and Sederberg 1976, p. 3). It differs, however, from state or governmental violence in that the state has the legitimate authority to use coercion against individual citizens. Vigilantism is the illegitimate use of coercion or force to maintain the established order or to defend it from subversive elements. Paradoxically, the presence of vigilantism implies that legitimate mechanisms for maintaining order have broken down or proved ineffective, making it necessary for supporters of law and order to take the law into their own hands. As attorney general of California testifying before a congressional hearing on the forcible removal of Japanese-Americans, Earl Warren noted:

> My own belief concerning vigilantism is that the people do not engage in vigilante activities so long as they believe that their Government through its agencies is taking care of their most serious problem. (Brooks 1979, p. 315)

Ted Robert Gurr goes a step further in linking political violence to feelings of "relative deprivation." Relative deprivation occurs to the extent that "value expectations" exceed "value capabilities." "The *value expectations* of a collectivity are the average value positions to which its members believe they are justifiably entitled." The *value capabilities* "are the average value positions its members perceive themselves capable of attaining or maintaining" (Gurr 1970, p. 27). A specific type of relative deprivation identified as operating during vigilantism is *decremental deprivation*. Under these conditions, "a group's value expectations remain relatively constant but value capabilities are perceived to decline" (ibid., p. 46). The more extreme or rapid the decline, the greater is the potential for violence.

It is important to note that these concepts refer to social-psychological states, not to absolute conditions. Hence a group may be experiencing an absolute improvement in material conditions and still experience deprivation. What is critical in identifying such a state of collective consciousness is that members of a group perceive a precipitous drop in its value capabilities, while its value expectations remain fairly constant. There is thus a gap between what a group feels it deserves and what it feels it can attain. According to Gurr, decremental deprivation is more common in traditional societies and in traditional segments of societies undergoing transition. Social banditry, for example, occurred most often in peasant societies of southern Europe (ibid., p. 48).

A basic thesis developed in this chapter is that the prevalence of vigilantism and of violence directed against Mexicans during the nineteenth century was the result not only of economic exploitation and racism but of *decremental deprivation* experienced by American settlers.

VIOLENCE IN THE MINES AND FIELDS

Conditions for violence were ripe in the aftermath of the war between Mexico and the United States. The conquest of Mexico and the acquisition of its northern territory were motivated by "manifest destiny" and the belief that the Anglo-Saxon was superior and was destined to rule over the entire hemisphere. If the Americans thought they were superior prior to the war, the results of the war confirmed this belief. Antagonism toward the Mexican was intensified by the fact that large tracts of land were held by a relatively small group of Mexican families, a pattern deemed unfair by most Americans. Anglo settlers saw the newly acquired territory as a land of opportunity where the common man had a chance of "striking it rich" in the mines or acquiring large tracts of land. Robber barons like Richard King and Charles Stillman served as Horatio Alger models for aspiring settlers. The Mexican residents, on the other hand, were seen as an impediment to progress and modernization. These land-hungry American settlers.

> had been accustomed to small holdings with fixed boundaries, and to them squatting upon uncultivated land was a perfectly respectable American practice in settling new territory. These Americans came to California with the belief that, except for a few settlements confined to the coast, all the land in the territory was public domain, and that, as in the other territories which had been opened to settlement, they might preempt a tract of land by squatter's rights. Hence great was their disappointment when they found thousands of acres of the best lands lying uncultivated and claimed by a small number of landowners under some inchoate loose grant of the benighted Mexican government. (Ellison 1927, pp. 8-9)

The American settlers, moreover, expected that their government would support their claims against Mexican landowners. The fact that many

Mexican titles were upheld by the courts infuriated the settlers. Although large tracts of land were acquired by American companies and isolated individuals, the vast majority of settlers acquired modest tracts.

Conflict and competition were especially intense in the gold fields of California. Most of the Mexican miners in California in 1848 were native Californians and eligible for United States citizenship, according to the Treaty of Guadalupe Hidalgo. "They were quick to point out to any zealous Yankee that they were just as much a citizen as he was, and had just as much right to the riches of the public domain" (Morefield 1955, p. 3). Mexicans from the state of Sonora, moreover, were extremely knowledgeable in mining and were the first teachers of the new arrivals. Once the Americans learned to mine, they began to covet the holdings of Mexicans and Chileans. As nativism grew and intensified, so did resentment toward "foreigners" in the mines.

The Mexicans, on the other hand, saw the violence and antagonism leveled at them as a direct result of the success they enjoyed in mining. They generally believed the reason they were persecuted was that:

> The Sonorans were used to working in mining and consequently found the richest lands and became richer more quickly; that the Mexican Californian—being here on the scene first—was able to take the better lands and was able to learn the mining trade sooner than the Americans; that many of those who came were of criminal or crude social standings;—and finally, that those who came in 1849 to 1850 were "possessed by the terrible fever to obtain gold . . . they wanted to become rich in a moment." (Ibid., p. 6)

The Anglo, on the other hand, countered that foreigners represented unfair competition and were trespassing on public domain. Bayard Taylor, an eyewitness observer, illustrates the prevailing nativist sentiment:

> During the mining season of 1849, more than 15,000 foreigners, mostly Mexicans and Chilenos, came in *armed bands* into the mining district, bidding defiance to all opposition, and finally carrying out of the country some $20,000,000 worth of gold dust, which belonged *by purchase* to the people of the United States. If not excluded by law, they will return and recommence the work of plunder. They may, with as much right, gather the harvest in the valley of the Connecticut, the Ohio, or the Mississippi. (Taylor 1850, pp. 244–45)

A memorial was sent to Congress in 1850 requesting that a customs house be established in San Pedro where, it was alleged, "at least ten thousand

Sonorians generally returning to Mexico pass through Los Angeles on the way to the mines each spring" (Wright 1940, p. 325).

By 1850 the belief that only Americans should be allowed to lay claims was widely accepted and many Mexicans and other *latinos* were forced from their claims. The journal of an American miner, George Enoch Jewett, reveals the antagonism that prevailed. On May 20, 1850, he recorded:

> This morning before day there were about 500 or 600 Americans in Sonoria when we arrived. The Greasers were all quiet but it was reported that some 2000 had been collected to make a stand at Columbia, 3 or 4 mile N.W. of Sonoria. The Yankees were on the way in no time & when they arrived there they found a Mexican flaghoisted, and any quantity of Greasers. They marched into town, pulled down the flag, hoisting the Stars & Stripes, fired a few rounds into the air which had a wonderful effect on the enemy. . . . The leaders were taken and put into jail. This I think is the last time they will attempt to oppose American laws. (George Enoch Jewett's Journal, 1849-50, p. 28)

One month later (July 20, 1850), a mass meeting was held in Sonora by citizens of Tuolumne County in order to protect American lives and property from Mexican *peones*, South American renegades, and British Empire convicts. It was resolved at the meeting that: (1) all foreigners were required to leave the county within fifteen days unless they obtained a permit from the proper authorities; (2) the American citizens of each camp or diggings would select a committee of three which would constitute the "authorities" in that area; (3) the citizens of the county would take it upon themselves to implement the objectives of the meeting; and (4) all foreigners were to turn over their weapons (ibid., p. 29).

Thus, as "foreigners," greasers had no rights and their property could be confiscated at will. Vigilantism, moreover, was not only condoned but legitimized as vigilante leaders became local authorities.

Another American, Charles A. Kirpatrick, even found humor in the exploitation of Mexican miners. Because the Mexicans had been told to "vamoose," Kirpatrick and two of his friends saw no harm in stealing the claim of an old Mexican who had not left in the allotted time:

> We thought there would be no harm in our laying claim to a fine pile of dirt brought down from the dry "diggins" by an old Mexican, so at it we went; but in 15 or 20 minutes here came the old fellow "mad as a hornet" and for sometime we could not tell what

he was going to do. All he could get out of *us* was for him to "vamous." This was indeed poor pay for the loss of his gold, but he took it, pocketed the insult and went to washing the pile himself while we went to work in another place. (Journal of Charles A. Kirpatrick, 1849, p. 38)

When force and intimidation failed, American miners sought to exclude Mexicans by passage of the Foreign Miners' Tax on April 13, 1850. "An Act for the better regulation of the Mines, and the Government of Foreign Miners," imposed a tax of $20 per month in the form of a license on all persons who were not citizens of the United States and were working in the mines of the state (Peterson 1965, p. 48). It also stipulated that license collectors in each county would collect three dollars from each payment as a fee for their services and permitted forcibly removing aliens for failing to pay the tax. The preamble to the Foreign Miners' Tax contained a clear rationale for the tax:

> It pointed out that the mines had brought a multitude of foreigners to California, among whom were a "large portion . . . of desperate characters," that these foreigners took many of the choice locations for mining, that conflicts had broken out to the disturbance of good order and security of the public; and [closed] with the ringing proclamation that "it is the inalienable right in the citizens of this State to enjoy and defend life and liberty, to acquire, possess, and protect property, and to pursue and obtain safety and happiness." (Morefield 1955, pp. 7-8)

Despite its lofty language, the ultimate aim of the tax was to discourage competition from Mexican and Chilean miners. The tax was seldom enforced against anyone other than Mexicans and Chileans, and its intent was clearly to discourage their immigration into California and promote their removal from the mines (Peterson 1965, p. 49).

The Foreign Miners' Tax provided legal sanctioning for the expulsion of Mexicans and other Latin Americans. Their complaints that other foreigners were not being taxed were ignored (Pitt 1966, p. 64). Imposters also posed as collectors and demanded payment. Those who resisted were driven from their claims. When Mexicans refused to pay the tax, one hundred fifty war veterans donned their uniforms, selected a captain, and headed to the town of Sonora to enforce the law. Elsewhere "martial law" ensued:

Next morning, into the diggings marched four hundred Americans—a moving "engine of terror"—heading for Columbia Camp, the foreigners' headquarters. They collected tax money from a few affluent aliens and chased the rest away, with a warning to vacate the mines. One trooper recalls seeing "men, women, and children—all packed up and moving, bag and baggage. Tents were being pulled down, houses and hovels gutted of their contents; mules, horses and jackasses were being hastily packed, while crowds were already in full retreat. . . . " The [American] men liquored up for the road, hoisted the Stars and Stripes to the top of a pine tree, fired off a salute, and headed for home. (Ibid., p. 62)

During the week of rioting and plundering, the camp was burned, dozens of Mexicans were lynched, and most of the Mexicans abandoned their claims.

Yankee nativism was further fueled by the resistance of the foreign miners. The following notice posted and translated into several languages reflects the mood of the foreign miners, for whom the American was the common enemy:

NOTICE: It is time to unite: Frenchmen, Chileans, Peruvians, Mexicans, there is the biggest necessity of putting an end to the vexations of the Americans in California. If you do not intend to allow yourselves to be fleeced by a band of miserable fellows who are repudiated by their own country, then unite and go to the camp of Sonora next Sunday; there will we try to guarantee security for us all, and put a bridle in the mouths of the horde who call themselves citizens of the United States, thereby profaning that country. (Peterson 1965, p. 56)

Vigilante justice prevailed in the mines. The San Francisco Vigilante Committee was established in 1849 and promptly expelled Sonorans from town (Pitt 1966, pp. 64-65). In April of 1849, a group of vigilantes at Sutter's Mill drove away many Mexicans, Chileans, and Peruvians. And a similar incident on July 4 resulted in the killing of foreigners and destruction of their property along the Sacramento River (ibid., p. 56).

Chicanas were not exempted from abuse. "Juanita" of Downieville, California, has the questionable distinction of being the only woman lynched during the gold rush. The lynching of a woman appears to have been a bizarre event indeed, for women were scarce and coveted objects in the mines:

> Miners hacking out the wealth of California Mother Lode treasured a scratched and bent tintype portrait of a woman as they would a solid gold nugget. When a white woman came to the mines, anything could happen as the miners came from miles around just to get a glimpse of her and follow her around. (Secrest 1967a, p. 5)

Why, then, was Juanita hanged? The answer may lie in the fact that she was not a white woman but a Mexican, and therefore considered an inferior and subhuman being.

Although a number of questions concerning the lynching remain unanswered, enough information is available to reconstruct the events preceding her death (see Secrest 1967a; Sinnott 1977). First, it appears from contemporary accounts that the woman's name was probably Josefa, although she is popularly referred to as Juanita. Josefa lived in a small cabin with a slightly built man named José who worked dealing monte in a local saloon (Sinnott 1977, p. 48). It is not clear whether he was her husband or lover, but their relationship was certainly monogamous, and there is no evidence to suggest that she was promiscuous. A visitor to Downieville in the summer of 1851, David Pierce Barstow, described her as "a very comely, quiet creature" who "behaved herself with a great deal of propriety" (Recollections of David Pierce Barstow, 1849-51, p. 7). George Barton, a witness to the trial and lynching claiming to know her well, remarked that "the Mexican woman was a plain person, about 23 or 25 years of age, neat and tidy in dress and person, quiet in demeanor, and like all her race had raven-black hair and a dark complexion, and lived with her husband, or protector, on Main Street" (Secrest 1967a, p. 29). Another resident of Downieville, J. J. McClosky, claimed that she "was about 26 years old, slight in form, with a large, dark, lustrous eye, that flashed at times . . . like a devils [sic] . . . all agreed that her character was good" (ibid.). "She might be called pretty, so far as the style of swarthy Mexican beauty is so considered" (ibid., p. 8). Josefa was considered attractive, for a Mexican.

Whether attractive and of good character or not, Josefa seems to have drawn the attention of a number of miners who were envious of her lover. One man who was said to have been particularly interested and to have pursued her for some time was a popular miner named Fred Cannon, described by eyewitness Alfred Barstow as a prizefighter (Statement of Alfred Barstow, 1849, pp. 1-2). On July 4, 1851, a glorious celebration was held commemorating the second Independence Day since California had become a state. John B. Welles, who later became senator from the state and was a very popular speaker, addressed the crowd and "the men came in from all the outlying districts, and had a high time" (ibid., p. 7). Partying, drinking, and riotous behavior continued into the night. What happened next is disputed, but Cannon and two of his drunken cronies, Lawson and Getzler, found themselves in front of Josefa's cabin. Cannon's account was that he leaned against the door and accidentally fell into the room; Josefa's was that he broke the door down and tried to make advances toward her. Whatever the truth, Cannon put a scarf around his neck, and the drunken miners left the cabin laughing.

The next morning Cannon went with Lawson to obtain some medicine from Dr. Hunter, who happened to live next door to Josefa, and was confronted by the small Mexican who demanded payment for his door. In the ensuing argument, José is said to have refused to fight Cannon, described by Calvin B. McDonald, an eyewitness, as "a giant of a man in stature and strength, weighing about 230 pounds and being well over six feet tall" (Sinnott 1977, p. 48). At this point Josefa, speaking in rapid Spanish, pushed between the two men and asked Cannon to hit her instead. Cannon reputedly called her a whore and other names. José managed to lead her into the house as she yelled at Cannon, daring him to come into the house and call her those names. As the miner rushed the door, the enraged Josefa grabbed a knife from a table and stabbed him in the chest.[10]

Eyewitness David Pierce Barstow felt that the hanging was inevitable because "there was considerable bad feelings toward Mexican gamblers and women generally, and there was no other way but to hang her" (Recollections of David Pierce Barstow, 1849-51, p. 10). Many in the angry, drunken mob wanted to hang them immediately, but it was decided instead, in the words of a crowd leader, to "give 'em a fair trial first—and then hang 'em." Despite the protestations of a lawyer named Thayer, who was beaten and pummeled by the mob, and of Dr. Cyrus D. Aiken, who claimed that Josefa was pregnant and should be spared (Sinnott 1977, p. 49), she was found guilty and sentenced to be hanged in two hours from the Jersey Bridge (Secrest 1967a, p. 24).[11] José was acquitted but told to leave town within twenty-four hours.

Another woman to fall victim to the prevailing lynch-law mentality and the gringo system of justice was Chepita (or Chipita) Rodríguez, the first woman executed in the state of Texas in 1863 (Sutherland 1978, p. 1C). In response to Santa Anna's rise to power, Chepita and her father came to the San Patricio area in 1836 (De León 1983, pp. 80-81). Shortly after her father was killed in a skirmish with Mexican troops advancing toward Goliad, she reputedly became involved with a local cowboy and gave birth to a son, but he abandoned her and took the child with him. Many years later, in 1863, two young men arrived at her cabin along the river. One looked very much like her estranged mate and may well have been her son. The following morning, as his partner lay dead, slain with Chepita's ax, the young man fled, allegedly taking his friend's money (ibid.). Seeking to protect her long lost son, the woman was said to have sought the assistance of a retarded neighbor, Juan Silvera, and to have dumped the body into the river. When the body washed ashore, Chepita and Silvera were arrested.

Anglo residents of the area were outraged and vigilantes demanded that the two culprits be turned over to them. Although there was very little evidence linking her directly to the crime, in October of 1863 she was tried and convicted. Because of her advanced age and the circumstantial nature of the evidence, the jury recommended her to the mercy of the court. The judge, however, ordered her hanged and sentenced Silvera to five years in prison (ibid.). "The case serves as an example of how extreme Anglos were in their persecution of Tejanos suspected of offenses against whites, for Rodríguez's execution was exceptional in the way the law dealt with women in the American West" (ibid., p. 81).

Although the Foreign Miners' Tax was repealed on March 14, 1851, it did not bring an end to the violence in the California mines. Inducements to leave were provided not only by the tax but by the proliferation of mass meetings and the expulsion of greasers from areas where there was trouble or alleged Mexican criminality (see, Journal of Charles A. Kirpatrick, 1849; George Enoch Jewett's Journal, 1849-50).

The resulting mass exodus meant that by September of 1850 between one-half and three-fourths of all the Mexicans had abandoned the southern mines (Morefield 1955, p. 9). The town of Columbia was decimated; only nine or ten men remained during the winter. Ironically, the departure of the Mexican miners—who had numbered around ten thousand in Sonora, California, alone—had a devastating effect on the local economy (ibid.). As the profits of local merchants plunged, they began to call for reduction or elimination of the tax:

> Eight-dollar crowbars in one afternoon dropped to fifty cents; a plot of land worth several thousand dollars went begging "for a few bits."

Out of sheer dollars-and-cents self-interest, if nothing else, businessmen collected money, hired a lawyer to sue the local collector, and circulated a mass petition asking the governor to lower the impost to $5; all but one merchant signed the document. In July and August, after the second wave of expulsions caused retail losses as high as $10,000 a day in three southern counties, merchants who had helped expel the "evil characters" during the bandit scare became aware that *all* Mexicans were fleeing, not merely the undesirables. (Pitt 1966, p. 65)

The *hispano* was recognized by American merchants as a better customer than his more frugal Anglo counterpart (Peterson 1965, p. 64). The *Alta California*, in an editorial on March 7, 1851, joined in the defense of the *hispano*:

> Tens of thousands of miners came to California. . . . From Mexico and Peru and Chile they flocked here, better miners than our own people. . . . They usually expended nearly all of their gold as they lived onward. Even those who occasionally left for their homes, generally purchased a good stock of various articles before leaving....Our own countrymen came here only to make a pile and carry it out of the country. They seldom purchased anything to take away, and expended just as little as possible in the country while they remained here.

By 1854 many of the Sonoran miners had returned to Mexico and Mexican immigration into California was insignificant (Wright 1940, p. 326). Thousands of Mexicans also fled to the cattle counties of southern California, but they found little refuge there. In fact, the assault on them intensified during the 1850s. Lynchings and hangings were common not only in the mines but in the fields and in the cities to the south. Crime was so rampant in Los Angeles that relations between Anglos and Mexicans could be termed a race war. When the legal and judicial system did not bring the desired result, Anglos frequently took the law into their own hands. "Vigilante justice had a distinctiveness in Los Angeles, however, in that every important lynch-law episode and most minor ones involved the Spanish-speaking" (Pitt 1966, p. 154). Yet, the Californios themselves were internally divided, with the *gente de razón* often helping the vigilantes to rid the community of the "lower and undesirable element." There were two basic types of lynchers:

At El Monte lived one key group, an enclave of Texans who had served in the Texas Rangers during the Mexican War, and who, in any event, considered themselves experts at "dealing with" Mexicans. Going by the name of rangers and not vigilantes, they generally tendered their services to the vigilante committees or to the sheriffs, but sometimes took separate action. Another group, the vigilante committeemen, generally included "respectables"—old-time ranchers, merchants, lawyers, and government officials. Since they owned land titles or had a smattering of legal knowledge, the town looked to them for leadership. (Ibid., p. 155)

Although the *ricos* typically sided with the vigilantes, no Mexican was immune from persecution. The Lugos, sons of the owner of Rancho San Bernardino, for example, were charged with the murder of two men. "Although the defendants were ultimately acquitted and the case was dismissed in late 1852, the incident set off explosive ethnic tensions, led to the attempted lynching of the Lugos by an Anglo-American gang, and resulted in the wiping out of the lynch gang by Cahuilla Indians who worked for the Lugos" (Cortes 1976, p. 1).[12]

Even though Santa Barbara remained a Mexican stronghold until the 1870s, as in other parts of southern California, violence erupted. Racial violence was so pervasive during the 1850s that by 1856 the town was said to be experiencing "a racial crime wave" (Camarillo 1979, p. 19). Maynard Geiger comments on how the gold rush and the American occupation brought about significant changes in Santa Barbara:

> Lawlessness too invaded the once peaceful town. City and county felt the ravages of the gangs of Solomon Pico and Jack Powers. Robbery became a common affair. Heavy drinking became a vulgar vice. Together with gambling it was indulged in both by the affluent and the common citizen. Out of fifty business licenses in Santa Barbara in the early fifties, thirty-two were for liquor establishments. Prostitution, drunkenness, robbery and murder became the "legitimate fruits of the gambling saloon." (Geiger 1965, pp. 169-70)

Racial antagonisms were aggravated by the preponderance of Mexicans, who outnumbered Anglos by more than four to one, and by the fact that they controlled the legal and judicial system. These antagonisms were documented by eyewitness accounts. Brevet Major James Henry Carleton, who arrived in the area in 1859, felt that Mexicans were ignorant of

American customs and did not understand or appreciate the American judicial system. He saw the Mexican as lacking the capacity for self-government (Rogers 1954, p. 114). Carleton noted, moreover, that the Americans were not predisposed to grant Californians the same civil rights that they demanded for themselves (ibid., p. 115). He lamented the racial divisions, remarking that "both classes seem to have lost sight of the fact that they are American citizens in common—having equal rights and bearing equal responsibilities" (ibid.).

William A. Streeter, who came to California in 1843, described the native Californians at that time as "a simple, honest, and somewhat industrious people" (Ellison 1939, p. 272). Unfortunately, the discovery of gold brought an abundance of "rough characters" to Santa Barbara who took advantage of the openness and simplicity of the "native Californios" (ibid.). The Californians were ignorant of business and were easily defrauded of their property not only by ordinary American citizens but by the Land Commission and dishonest lawyers. Also contributing to their downfall was their love of gambling, inability to manage money, and failure to assimilate American culture and values:

> The Californian of today is an American citizen in name only. He still maintains his characteristics and his language. His sympathies are as entirely with the Mexicans as they were thirty years ago. He does not assimilate with the Americans. His feeling towards the Americans is never less than antipathy, and is more generally hatred, latent though it may be. The Californians join reluctantly in the celebration of our independence, while they are enthusiastic in the celebration of that of Mexico. (Ibid., p. 274)

The antipathy of native Californians toward Americans escalated when the body of an elderly man named Francisco Badillo was discovered at La Carpenteria, twelve miles south of Santa Barbara, on August 24, 1859. Badillo and his teenage son were found hanged about five hundred yards from their home (Rogers 1954, p. 117). John Nidever, his three sons, and several others were accused of the murder. Shortly thereafter one of the sons, George Nidever, was shot, stabbed, and beaten—allegedly by four members of a party of twenty native Californians who had traveled from Santa Barbara to investigate the Badillo murder. On September 12 a grand jury composed of eight Americans and eight native Californians met in the cases of the People vs. the Nidevers, Coates, and McKeon and the People vs. Leyba, Gutiérrez, Lugo, and Zurita, charged with assault with intent to kill George Nidever (ibid., p. 118). The grand jury was predictably split, with eight voting for indictment and eight against in both cases (ibid.). The defendants were then discharged.

Antagonisms continued and on September 25 the majority of American citizens in the town assembled at a house near the Landing. They met with Don Pablo de la Guerra, a leading citizen of Santa Barbara and senator-elect from the district, informing him that they held him responsible. Those in attendance had resolved that Pedro Domínguez-Gutiérrez, Eugenio Lugo, and Felipe Badillo would be ordered to leave the county within four days, and if they failed to comply, they would be ejected by force. De la Guerra told the crowd that "to preserve the peace he himself would advise and even persuade them to go" (ibid., p. 120). A group of armed Americans assembled at the Landing once again on October 2, but they dispersed after being convinced that the four men had left the area.

The racial crime wave was indirectly incited by the *Santa Barbara Gazette*, which vigorously protested the lack of enforcement by the Mexican city marshall of the antivagrancy law, also known as the Greaser Law, and other anti-Mexican legislation (Camarillo 1979, p. 19). By 1856 the editors of the *Gazette* and a number of Americans were openly calling for the formation of vigilante groups (ibid.). When these efforts failed, they unsuccessfully sought the aid of powerful ranchero families. The response of the *Gazette* was to launch a direct attack on powerful California families by charging them with harboring criminals (ibid.). The newspaper further charged Supervisor Antonio María de la Guerra with misconduct and negligence before a grand jury.

Recently elected mayor, Antonio María de la Guerra responded to the vigilante threat by confiscating the rifles of the Santa Barbara Mounted Riflemen (ibid., pp. 18-20). This paramilitary organization was made up of former members of the U.S. military and was the only vigilante group that constituted a genuine threat (ibid.). Perhaps the most critical factor in impeding the vigilante movement in Santa Barbara was that the *ricos* joined forces with poor Mexicans in responding to the Anglo threat.

By 1859 a racial war was in full swing. The conflict was so intense subsequent to the Badillo incident that the United States army was sent in to maintain order.

GOVERNMENT VIGILANTISM: THE TEXAS RANGERS

No analysis of the issue of vigilantism and Chicanos would be complete without some mention of the Texas Rangers (see Walter Prescott Webb Collection; Webb 1965 and 1975; Samora, Bernal, and Peña 1979). The Texas Rangers are a unique police agency in that they combine elements of vigilantism with those of legally sanctioned state or governmental violence. It is for this reason that they are perhaps best termed "police vigilantes" or "government vigilantes." Samora, Bernal, and Peña argue that although the Texas Rangers operate as a police force, they were not really created as a police agency (1979, p. 15). A police force is part of a community and operates within the parameters of that community:

> Its main function is to maintain internal order in the community. A policeman's duties may vary from pursuing and capturing criminals to giving first aid to accident victims and caring for lost children. He is supposed to be both a public servant and a functioning member of his community. In the final analysis, a police force is accountable to the people through the local electoral process. The Texas Ranger has never been accountable to the citizenry. (Ibid.)

A full appreciation of the creation and evolution of the Texas Rangers cannot be gained without first understanding the vigilante tradition of the American West, for the Rangers developed out of private ranger companies. Established as an independent state militia in order to quell Indian uprisings and to protect the Texas frontier against so-called Mexican *bandidos*, they were organized in the midst of the Texas revolt in 1835, but were preceded by a number of volunteer ranger companies, which appeared as early as 1823 (Webb 1965, pp. 22-23). Yet, according to Nackman (1975, p. 249), before the Civil War the Rangers had not acquired official status as an organization. An act entitled "An act to provide for the protection of the frontier of Texas" and approved on December 21, 1861, authorized John J. Dix to raise a company of Rangers (Adjutant General of Texas, 1862). If possible, each man was to furnish his own horse and arms.

On October 17, 1835, Daniel Parker introduced a resolution before the Permanent Council of the Revolution authorizing the creation of a group of Texas Rangers; twenty-five were to guard the frontier between the Brazos and Trinity rivers, ten were to be established on the east side of the Trinity, and another twenty-five were to be stationed between the Brazos and

Colorado. An ordinance establishing a corps of Texas Rangers was passed on November 24, 1835, setting up three companies of fifty-six men. Each company was to be headed by a captain and a first and a second lieutenant.[13] From the beginning, the Rangers were a unique and irregular force:

> The Rangers were to be always ready with a good horse, saddle, bridle, and blanket, and a hundred rounds of powder and ball. The officers were to receive the same pay as officers in the dragoons of the United States service, and in addition the pay of privates in the ranging corps . . . . The Rangers were an irregular body; they were mounted; they furnished their own horses and arms; they had no surgeon, no flag, none of the paraphernalia of the regular service. They were distinct from the regular army and also from the militia. (Webb 1965, p. 24)

The history of the Rangers over the next decade is confusing and difficult to piece together. Their service was not continuous but sporadic as "ranging men" were authorized by legislation as the need arose (Samora, Bernal, and Peña 1979, p. 23). Such laws referred to them variously as "rangers," "spies," "mounted riflemen," and "mounted volunteers" (ibid.). It was not until February 1, 1845, that the Texas Rangers were formally established as a state militia of five detachments under the command of Captain John C. Hays.

The Texas Rangers were thus born out of vigilantism. Ironically, the origin of the Rangers can be traced to the colony of American settlers established by Stephen F. Austin in 1821. While Austin was absent on a trip to Mexico City, the settlers appealed to the Spanish governor to provide protection from Indian attacks. The governor ordered fourteen men and a sergeant to be stationed near the mouth of the Colorado River (Barker 1949, p. 91). Although poorly equipped and unpaid, they provided protection and Austin urged General Garza to pay them and continue their service (ibid.). There is no evidence that these men were referred to as Rangers or whether they were Mexicans or Americans. Shortly after arriving in the settlements in 1823, Austin hired ten rangers who would be under the command of Lieutenant Moses Morrison (ibid., p. 92).

Although established as volunteer companies to protect the frontier against Indian incursions, in time the Rangers came to focus their energies on subordination of the Mexican population. Despite their many abuses and countless atrocities perpetrated against Chicanos, the Rangers have been romanticized and idealized.

Walter Prescott Webb, well known Texas historian, characterized the Rangers as "quiet, deliberate, gentle" men (Webb 1965, p. xv). When the Rangers took part in the siege of Mexico City during the Mexican War and committed numerous atrocities, their actions were either applauded or dismissed as "troublesome" behavior, or "rigorous methods." On the basis of their participation in the Mexican-American War, Webb concluded that "it was considered by everyone as the most singular and distinctive fighting organization known to the United States Army" (Webb 1975, p. 2). But for the Chicano, the Rangers were bitterly hated and resented. Numerous *corridos* (ballads) captured the prevailing attitude toward *los rinches* (Paredes 1958, p. 146). One example:

> The rangers are very brave,
> That cannot be denied;
> They have to stalk us like deer
> In order to kill us.

The mythology surrounding the Rangers has grown and developed to such an extent that in evaluating writings on the Rangers it is difficult to separate fact from fiction. Samora, Bernal, and Peña point out that Texas history is often based on the stories and memories of "old timers" (1979, p. 3). Judge Orland L. Sims, for example, glorified the Rangers as righteous supporters of law, justice, and American values:

> Of these lawmen, none have more of my respect and admiration than the Texas Rangers. They have none of the swaggering, swashbuckling attitudes attributed to them by many. They are quiet, courteous, efficient, and they are sure not afraid. Long may they wave. (Sims 1967, p. 25)

The Rangers were larger than life—brave, honest, resourceful, quiet, and strong. The esteem in which they were held is perhaps best captured in the old saying, "One riot, one Ranger" (Lasswell, 1958, p. 315). The front matter of the first edition of Webb's *The Texas Rangers* contained the following poem:

TEXAS RANGERS
Mountains that tower up solid and tall
Bulwark a country as with a stonewall.

> Oceans respect them and Tamerlanes pause,
> Stopped by the mountains' infrangible laws.
>
> Coast-dwellers chafe, "No mountains in Texas?"
> Thinking with Hood and with Shasta to vex us.
>
> Ask the Apache the why of his going,
> Ask the Comanche, he's not without knowing:
>
> Question the Mexican thief and marauder
> Why his respect for the great Texas border;
>
> Question them all, these beaten-back strangers,
> White-lipped they'll tremble and whisper, "The Rangers!"
>
> Mountains? You keep them to safeguard your rights.
> These are our peaks, our impregnable heights!
>
> Albert Edmund Trombly

In the Foreword to the second edition, Lyndon B. Johnson eulogized Dr. Webb and the Texas Rangers. Significantly, Johnson drew a parallel between traditional values of the frontier and the West, as epitomized by the Rangers, and basic American values:

> Our affluence, our abundance, our strength and power have not dulled the values experience taught us through the challenge of opening the Frontier.
>
> The Frontier—and the West—are synonymous in our minds with adventure, courage, bravery, independence, and self-reliance. Yet still another essential is not to be overlooked. Adventuresome and individualistic as they were, America's western pioneers never left far behind the rule of law. They risked much and sacrificed much to win opportunity. But they turned unfailingly to respect for the law to assure that those gains would not be meaningless.
>
> Dr. Webb memorialized one of the most storied, yet most truly effective, law-enforcement organizations in this book, *The Texas Rangers* . . . . The individual episodes he recounts are a rich part of our thrilling national heritage. But the significance of the Texas Rangers is greater than the sum of these individual stories.
>
> The never-ending quest for an orderly, secure, but open and free society always demands dedicated men. The Rangers—and Dr. Webb, himself—were just such men. Their influence was worked not by recklessness or foolhardiness, but by the steadiness of their purpose and performance—and by the sureness, among both the law-abiding and the law-breaking, that thought of self would never deter

the Ranger from fulfilling the commitment of his vows as an agent of law, order, and justice. (1965, p. x)

Richard M. Nixon was no less laudatory in his remarks in 1973 during the one-hundred fiftieth anniversary of the Rangers and the dedication of the Ranger Hall of Fame in Waco, Texas:

> For one and a half centuries the Texas Rangers have vividly portrayed the dauntless spirit of the great American Southwest, and relentlessly served the best interests of both their state and nation.
>
> I welcome this opportunity to express on behalf of all Americans the deepest admiration for the proud tradition of public service that has earned you such a splendid reputation ever since our frontier days. (cited in Samora, Bernal, and Peña, 1979, p. 5)

With the possible exception of Walter Prescott Webb, no one has contributed more to the building of the Texas Ranger mythology than the Rangers themselves.[14] According to Samora, Bernal, and Peña:

> None has been more prolific or successful in packaging and selling the image than the Rangers themselves. They have been their own most dedicated press agents: from the early frontier days through a century of stacks of autobiographies, climaxing in 1973 with the Texas Ranger Sesquicentennial Commemorative Celebration and the establishment of a Ranger Hall of Fame. (Ibid., p. 7)

It can be argued that the Texas Rangers embody values that are pervasive in American society and are, in fact, a microcosm of Anglo-Texan male society. In an article highly sympathetic to the American vigilante tradition and to the Texas Rangers, Mark E. Nackman argues that the heroes of Texas in the 1835-1860 period were its citizen-soldiers (1975, p. 231). In the struggle against Indians and Mexicans, Texas relied primarily on ordinary citizens to defend the frontier. Most, moreover, did not need any urging, and took the initiative themselves (ibid., p. 232). Prospective immigrants were cautioned against the impending perils and those who did not wish to fight were told to "stay away." "If you fear the Mexican or Indian," admonished one guide, "you are not constitutionally, morally nor physically qualified to become citizens of such a dangerous country, either in peace or in war" (ibid., p. 233).

Motivation to become a citizen-soldier extended well beyond any imminent danger and was linked to Anglo-Texan conceptions of masculinity.[15] According to Nackman, "The Texan's concept of virility was intimately bound to a man's physical prowess and martial skill. The individual who bore no battle scars was suspect" (ibid., p. 234).

As the frontier was tamed and the Rangers gained official recognition as a state agency, their initial function was altered in response to changing conditions. When first established the Rangers served the interests of "manifest destiny" and overt racism (Samora, Bernal, and Peña 1979, p. 11). They were a vehicle, in other words, for taming the frontier and displacing Indians and Mexicans from the land. They continued to act on behalf of dominant economic interests in the second half of the twentieth century but now their victims were not Mexican "bandits" but civil rights workers and strikers (Kostyu 1970, pp. 100-132; U.S. Commission on Civil Rights 1970, pp. 16-17). But the Texas Rangers "continued to live up to the description given of them by nineteenth-century observers as a police body determined to keep the Mexicans down" (De León 1983, p. 104).

There was a symbiotic relationship between the ethos of the Robber Barons and that of the Rangers. Ranger Captain Leander H. McNelly, for example, was sent to South Texas in 1875 to arrest cattle thieves and return law and order to the area. Richard King supplied beef for the Rangers and provided them with bonuses in exchange for their protection.

Captain McNelly was described by Webb as a "flame of courage" (cited in McMurtry 1968, p. 40). Another Texas historian, T. R. Fehrenbach added:

> McNelly was a great captain. He was the epitome of the Texan in action, and he set a record of courage, cunning, and audacity that was never to be surpassed. McNelly himself was young, just thirty-one. He had been a partisan soldier for the Confederacy as a teenager in the Civil War, later served in Davis's State Police. Nothing was more revealing of his ability, honesty, and his reputation than the fact that he went from the State Police to the Rangers with equivalent rank. In Davis's service he had been blunt, outspoken, incorruptible, and had been seriously wounded in battle with outlaws. (Fehrenbach 1968, pp. 575-76)

McNelly gained special notoriety in the Las Cuevas affair. In order to arrest suspected cattle rustlers, McNelly periodically crossed the Rio Grande. He had developed an intricate network of informers, including Mexican bandits who served as spies (Lea 1957, vol. 1, p. 281). According to Richard King's biographer, Tom Lea, the money used to pay the spies was provided by King and other members of the Stock Raisers Association (ibid., p. 282). King was also said to have furnished his own network of trustworthy informers along the border.

McNelly had information that shipment of eighteen thousand head of cattle was to arrive at the headquarters of General Juan Flores at Las Cuevas and that there would be as many as three hundred Mexicans protecting the cattle. He planned a surprise attack at dawn, to barricade himself and the thirty Rangers inside a house and wait for reinforcements from the U. S. troops that had been summoned (Samora, Bernal, and Peña 1979, p. 49). McNelly told his men, "We will learn them a Texas lesson that they have forgotten since the Mexican War" (Fehrenbach 1968, p. 581). Their orders were to "kill as you see except old men, women, and children. These are my orders and I want them obeyed to the letter" (ibid.).

Everything went as expected, except that rather than Las Cuevas, the Rangers mistakenly attacked an unimportant rancho, killing everyone in sight.[16] When the U. S. troops arrived, Captain Randlett hesitated in crossing the border to aid the Rangers because he felt that "without doubt McNelly's cry for help exaggerated his distress, and was made for the purpose of bringing the federal troops into Mexico (Webb 1965, p. 267). McNelly persisted, nonetheless, and despite being greatly outnumbered he refused to leave Mexico without first recovering some of the stolen cattle. It was this audacity that gained McNelly such acclaim in Texas folklore. Unless the cattle and thieves were delivered, he would attack. Fearing that the army troops would cross the border and aid the Rangers, the Mexicans agreed to his terms. Wishing to retain an element of dignity, the Mexican officials insisted on inspecting the cattle before they were returned. This infuriated McNelly:

> A Mexican official, backed by twenty-five heavily armed men, informed McNelly that the cattle could not be shipped across without inspection. McNelly, through Tom Sullivan, told the officer that the cattle had been stolen from Texas without inspection by him, and they could damn well be returned without it. The official was insulted, but McNelly was finished with Byzantine politics, parleys, and devious duplicity. He ordered his ten men to form a line and ready their rifles. What happened next was told by one of the ten: "The Captain then told Tom to tell the son of a bitch that if he didn't deliver the cattle across the river in less than five minutes we would kill all of them, and he would have done it, too, for he had his red feather

raised. If ever you saw cattle put across the river in a hurry those Mexicans did it."

So ended another confrontation of Teutonic directness and Latin subtlety, leaving a sour taste on each side. (Fehrenbach 1968, p. 584)

McNelly left Mexico and on the following day returned thirty-five head of cattle to the Santa Gertrudis Ranch, where they were welcomed back by Richard King (Lea 1957, vol. 1, p. 290). A great admirer of McNelly and the Rangers, King commented:

> That was a daring trip . . . there is not another man in the world who could invade a foreign country with that number of men and get back alive. Captain McNelly is the first man that ever got stolen cattle out of Mexico. Out of thousands of head I have had stolen these are the only ones I ever got back, and I think more of them than of any five hundred head I have. (Ibid., p. 291)

Ranger abuses continued into the twentieth century and were especially severe between 1911 and 1918. During this period of intense conflict, when a reign of terror was being waged against the Mexican population, "the most blatant abuses of police power were the Texas Rangers" (Anders 1982, p. 225). In the aftermath of a raid against a branch of the King Ranch at Las Norrias in Cameron County, the Rangers "began a systematic manhunt and killed, according to a verified test, 102 Mexicans" (Pierce 1917, p. 114). Thus, the pretext that they were quelling Mexican revolutionary raids enabled the Rangers to kill Mexicans almost at will (De León 1983, p. 104). Yet, in his biennial report for 1915 and 1916, the adjutant general of Texas concluded that "the work of the Ranger force from the inception of the border troubles . . . was of the highest order and worthy of the best traditions of the Ranger force" (Adjutant General of Texas 1915-1916, p. 11).

THE CHICANO SOCIAL BANDITS

It has often been said that history is written from the perspective of the victor, not the vanquished. Many of the so-called outlaws and cattle rustlers pursued by the Rangers were in fact innocent Mexican ranchers in pursuit of their own stolen stock. The Mexican Border Commission concluded that "the traffic in Texas of horses stolen from Mexico became a

The Lugo family at Bell Gardens, California, ca. 1888. Courtesy of Los Angeles County Museum of Natural History, Western History Collection.

Tiburcio Vásquez. From a photograph taken
while Vásquez was in jail awating trial in San
José. Courtesy of Bancroft Library, University
of California, Berkeley.

A rare old photograph of frontier days, showing Captain John R.
Hughs (on chair) with his company of Texas Rangers and a
Mexican bandit. Courtesy of Webb Collection, Archives Division,
Texas State Library, Austin.

matter of commonplace merchandise" (Comisión pesquisidora de la frontera del norte 1875, p. 12). After Webb published an article, "The Bandits of Las Cuevas," In *True West* magazine, he received a letter from Enrique Mendiola, grandson of the owner of the ranch mistakenly attacked by the Rangers. Mendiola protested:

> Most historians have classified these men as cattle thieves, bandits, *etc.* This might be true of some of the crowd, but most of them, including Gen. Juan Flores, were trying to recover their own cattle that had been taken away from them, when they were driven out of their little ranches in South Texas. They were driven out by such men as Mifflin Kenedy, Richard King, and the Armstrongs and others. (Walter Prescott Webb Papers, General Correspondence, 1962-63)

Webb responded in a letter dated January 29, 1963, by noting that his account of the incident was written from Texas and U.S. Army sources and that "to get a balanced account, one would need the records from the south side of the river"—and that he wished that the Mexicans or someone they trusted "could have gone among them and got their stories on the raids and counter raids" (ibid.).

The term "social bandit" is useful for describing and understanding the experiences of many of these men. Social historian Eric J. Hobsbawm regards social banditry as a very primitive form of social protest. Although focusing on eighteenth- and nineteenth-century Europe, especially southern Italy, Hobsbawm's study of peasant social movements is applicable to the Chicano:

> *Social banditry*, a universal and virtually unchanging phenomenon, is little more than endemic peasant protest against oppression and poverty: a cry for vengeance on the rich and the oppressors, a vague dream, of some curb upon them. (Hobsbawm 1959, p. 5)

Social bandits are regarded as criminals by the state and the prevailing power structure, but their peers consider them "as heros, as champions, avengers, fighters for justice, perhaps even leaders of liberation, and in any case men to be admired, helped, and supported" (Hobsbawm 1969, p. 13).

In applying Hobsbawm's perspective to Chicanos, Castillo and Camarillo (1973, p. 2) identify two points that are essential for understanding Chicano bandits. First, they were typically victims of injustice and abuse. They were seen as bandits by the dominant society precisely because they rebelled against abuse. Secondly, the social bandits were admired, respected, and supported by the masses of their own people. Only the Mexican elite tended to view them negatively. The social bandits were aided materially and spiritually by the Mexican population and their exploits were permanently recorded in *corridos*.

Social banditry, according to Hobsbawm "becomes epidemic rather than endemic when a peasant society which knows of no better means of self-defence is in a condition of abnormal tension and disruption" (1959, p. 5). The American occupation of northern Mexico and the imposition of a new economic, political, and judicial system proved chaotic for the *mexicano*. It not only created the social bandits but the context within which their activities took place (Castillo and Camarillo 1973, p. 3).

The importance of the economic displacement of the Chicano cannot be overstressed. The American takeover, after all, brought the rapid decline of a feudal society and the ascendancy of capitalism. Social banditry is ultimately a rural, not an urban, phenomenon, and it can be seen as a response to the decline of a feudal society and the imposition of capitalism:

> The peasant societies in which it occurs know rich and poor, powerful and weak, rulers and ruled, but remain profoundly and tenaciously traditional, and pre-capitalist in structure. (Hobsbawm 1959, p. 23)

Because of its primitive or elementary character, it should not be confused with more organized or sophisticated forms of social protest. Social banditry is ultimately a simple and individual response to injustice; not a revolutionary form of protest but a modest rebellion. "It protests not against the fact that peasants are poor and oppressed, but against the fact that they are sometimes excessively poor and oppressed" (ibid., p. 24). It generally seeks to return to a traditional world where persons are treated fairly, not a new or a perfect world (ibid., p. 5). The social bandit is, thus, poor or rebels on behalf of the poor. According to Hobsbawm, "In any peasant society there are 'landlord bandits' as well as 'peasant bandits,' not to mention the State's bandits, though only the peasant bandits receive the tribute of ballads and anecdotes" (ibid., p. 13).

Having provided a general overview of social banditry, I now turn to brief sketches of several Chicano bandits. The intent is not to present a detailed and exhaustive discussion of these individuals but to illustrate the wide range and variety of the phenomenon. Not all of those to be discussed—Joaquín Murieta, Tiburcio Vásquez, Elfego Baca, and Gregorio Cortez—were true bandits. Baca, for example, was a peace officer, lawyer, and political figure; Cortez, an innocent victim. Despite their diversity, they shared certain features in common. All were subject to the double standard of justice and were, in fact, victims of injustice, rebelled against the dominant order, took the law into their own hands, and were admired and respected by the Mexican population.

Tiburcio Vásquez

Two of the most famous California bandits, Tiburcio Vásquez and Joaquín Murieta, turned to a life of crime only after witnessing numerous abuses against their fellow Mexicans. Of special concern was protection for Mexican women. Conflict over women was a primary factor leading Vásquez to a life of crime:

> My career grew out of the circumstances by which I was surrounded. As I grew up to manhood, I was in the habit of attending balls and parties given by the native Californians, into which the Americans, then beginning to become numerous, would force themselves and shove the native born men aside, monopolizing the dance and the women. This was about 1852. A spirit of hatred and revenge took possession of me. I had numerous fights in defense of what I believed to be my rights and those of my countrymen. (Truman 1874, p. 14)

Although Vásquez is best known for his exploits as a horse thief and robber who terrorized Anglos for a quarter of a century and gained the respect and admiration of his people, he was also known as a ladies' man, and women were a determining force in his life. According to Hoyle (1927, p. 4), "In all those counties where he operated, he had the moral support and physical aid of his countrymen, and especially his countrywomen." Vásquez was good-looking and daring; one of his early exploits was an ill-fated attempt to run away with Anita, the daughter of a rancher in Monte Diablo County. The escape was foiled by the girl's father, but she was shot, and Vásquez escaped in the ensuing gunfight (May 1947, p. 125). A woman who played a critical part in his capture and prosecution, Rosario Leiva, spurned lover of Vásquez and wife of his former first lieutenant, and her husband served as key prosecution witnesses during Tiburcio's trial in San Jose. Yet, his attraction to the opposite sex remained. While in jail in San Jose, many women continued to send him flowers and he raised funds by selling cards with his picture and a brief biography on them.

Tiburcio Vásquez was born on August 11, 1835, on a ranch in Monterey County, California. He was educated in English until the age of sixteen and his papers reveal a sound command of the English language. In the spring of 1851, he attended a fandango, allegedly with "Three-Fingered Jack" García, former companion of Joaquín Murieta and José Guerra. Some Americans were said to have been rude toward the Mexican men and women in attendance. A fight broke out in which García, Vásquez, and Guerra took part, and a constable named Hardimount was killed. A vigilante organization hanged Guerra; Vásquez sought refuge in the hills. Tiburcio allegedly developed an intense hatred for Anglos as a result of this incident and said, "The white men heaped wrong on me in Monterey County" (Truman 1874, p. 42).

Vásquez spent the winter and spring of 1856 stealing horses and rustling cattle. He distributed some of his gains among the poor. He had many friends and supporters, and often depended on their aid. On the other hand, Ernest R. May argued:

> Tiburcio Vásquez was a young *caballero* of expensive tastes. The women and the card tables of Monterey and Los Angeles and the mining towns were expensive luxuries. To finance his recreations, Tiburcio had to steal and sell many head of cattle.... It is doubtful that he found many men with a talent and an inclination for rustling who possessed as well the Robin Hood proclivities ascribed to Vásquez. (May 1947, p. 124)

In the spring of 1857, he and a friend were arrested for horse stealing in Los Angeles County and he was sentenced to San Quentin. Although he escaped in 1859, the next eleven years were spent in and out of prison. Vásquez's actual career as a notorious bandit was relatively short-lived, however. In January 1873 he organized a gang that was to terrorize the state for more than one year. But it was the Tres Pinos affair that gained him the most notoriety. On August, 26, 1873 Vásquez's gang robbed Snyder's Store at Tres Pinos. In the process, three persons were killed. Prior to this incident, Vásquez's exploits had received little attention. Newspapers suddenly called for increased vigilante activity and the day after the Tres Pinos incident, the governor offered a $1,000 reward for Vásquez's capture. As Vásquez continued his exploits, every community had a vigilante committee formed and waiting for him.

On May 14, 1874, the famous bandit was shot six times and captured as he sought to escape through a kitchen window. He was kept under guard in San Jose and brought to trial on January 5, 1875. Whereas the prosecution lasted four days, the defense was very brief. On March 19, 1875, the famous bandit was hanged.

Although Hobsbawm maintains that social bandits are not revolutionaries and have little or no ideology, there is evidence to indicate that Vásquez had an ideology that was, at least potentially, revolutionary. He had many followers, especially among the poor, and the *ricos* feared that he would lead a revolution against the Americans. The *Los Angeles Express* said that Vásquez claimed that "Given $60,000 I would be able to recruit enough arms and men to revolutionize Southern California" (cited in Acuña 1981, p. 113).

George K. Beers provided an explanation as to why Vásquez took up a life of crime. This account suggests that Vásquez's actions may have had some ideological underpinnings and that he was propelled into a life of crime by

> the bitter animosity then existing, and which still exists, between the white settlers and the native or Mexican portion of the population. The native Californians, especially the lower classes, never took kindly to the stars and stripes. Their youth were taught from the very cradle to look upon American government as that of a foreign nation.
>
> This feeling was greatly intensified by the rough, brutal conduct of the worst class of American settlers, who never missed an opportunity to openly exhibit their contempt for the native Californian or Mexican population—designating them as "d—d Greasers," and treating them like dogs. Add to this the fact that these helpless people were cheated out of their lands and possessions by every subterfuge—in many instances their property being actually wrested from them by force, and their women debauched whenever practicable—and we can understand very clearly some of the causes which have given to Joaquin, Vasquez, and others of their stripe, the power to call around them at any time all the followers they required, and which secured to them aid and comfort from the Mexican settlers everywhere. (Beers 1875, p. 8)

JOAQUÍN MURIETA

Joaquín Murieta is, undoubtedly, the most famous of all social bandits, yet perhaps the most misunderstood. Although much has been written about the Robin Hood of the West, in evaluating these accounts it is often difficult to separate fact from fiction. Joaquín's fame is surprising not only because very little is known about his life but because his career was brief, spanning a two-year period.

The first account was that of John Rollin Ridge (Yellow Bird), *The Life and Adventures of Joaquín Murieta*, published in 1854. The most popular account was published by the *California Police Gazette* in 1859, a plagiarized version of Ridge's book. The serialized *Police Gazette* story was compiled into a paperback book and enjoyed wide circulation (Nadeau 1973, p. 14).

Ridge, half-Cherokee and a journalist, came to California in 1850, sympathizing with the exploited Mexicans. His small book was a detailed and vivid account of Joaquín's life, written firsthand as if the author were an eyewitness to many major events. It depicted Joaquín as being larger than life, an epic hero acting to override injustices against Mexicans in California (Nadeau 1974, p. 13). For many years the Ridge biography was accepted as accurate and authoritative, despite his own admission that only "in the main, it will be found to be strictly true."

According to Ridge, Joaquín was born in Sonora "of respectable parents and educated in the schools of Mexico" (Ridge 1955, p. 8). Disgusted with his countrymen and positively disposed toward the Americans, Joaquín set off to seek adventure in the Golden State. We first hear of him in the spring of 1850, placer mining on the Stanislaus River. Though only eighteen, the energetic young Mexican was said to have been respected and loved by those who came in contact with him and quickly developed a successful mining claim. "He had built him a comfortable mining residence in which he had domiciled his heart's treasure—a beautiful Sonorian girl, who had followed the young adventurer in all his wanderings with that devotedness of passion which belongs to the dark-eyed damsels of Mexico" (ibid., p. 9). His contented life was interrupted, however, by a band of lawless, desperate men who "visited Joaquín's house and peremptorily bade him leave his claim, as they would allow no Mexicans to work in that region . . . . They struck him violently over the face, and, being physically superior, compelled him to swallow his wrath. Not content with this, they tied him hand and foot and ravished his mistress before his eyes" (ibid., p. 10). The embittered Joaquín and his heartbroken mistress retreated to the northern portions of the mines, hoping to find peace and happiness on a small farm. But once again he was driven from his house and land by a group of unprincipled Americans. Though angered, Joaquín did not seek revenge, turning instead to dealing monte. It was not until his half-brother was hanged by an angry mob at Murphy's Diggings that Joaquín's character changed drastically and he began a life of crime. He then "declared to a friend that he would live henceforth for revenge and that his path should be marked with blood" (ibid., pp. 12-13).

Other versions differ from Ridge's account. According to Richard Mitchell (1927, p. 39), Joaquín's companion was not raped and killed by angry miners, although they did force him from his claim. She was shot, but by Joaquín himself, who was angered after she allegedly left him for a settler named Baker. Her wound was not fatal, however, and she is said to have lived to recount the shooting. Nadeau (1974, p. 24) denies the existence of a companion who was raped or killed, and maintains that the only woman linked to Joaquín by official records was Ana Benitez. References to "Rosita," "Carmela," and other women are, according to Nadeau, fictional.

The mythology surrounding Murieta cannot be understood apart from the conflict that prevailed between Anglos and Mexicans in the mines. According to Leonard Pitt, "Unquestionably, the archetypal Mexican badman was the phantom-like 'Joaquín,' who terrorized Calaveras County and neighboring parts in the winter of 1852-53 and eventually became California's greatest legend" (Pitt 1966, p. 77). Initially, Joaquín is said to have specialized in victimizing the Chinese but he soon came to be feared by Americans as well. In January 1852, after five Anglo horsemen unsuccessfully chased Murieta, they turned their anger on all Mexicans:

> Miners gathered at nearby Devil Springs and vowed "to exterminate the Mexican race from the country." Thereupon, some Yankees seized one Mexican each at Yaqui's Camp and at Cherokee Ranch for extraneous reasons and strung them up immediately. Hundreds of miners thrust guns and knives into their belts, roamed angrily over the 5-mile region from San Andreas to Calaveras Forks, and methodically drove out the entire Mexican population—as prospectors had done in previous seasons—and confiscated all property. (Ibid.)

Although fear of the noted bandit increased, his identity remained a mystery. It is commonly said that he was a Mexican from Sonora, but

Pablo Neruda claimed that he was a Chileno and wrote a drama about him in 1967. A play that ran in San Francisco in 1858 made him into a Spaniard (Nadeau 1974, p. 14). In all, at least five Joaquíns were identified. One of them, Joaquín Carrillo, lived in southern California and is said to have killed General Bean in Los Angeles, the brother of Judge Roy Bean.

In response to public outcry over the exploits of the California bandit, on February 21, 1853, Governor John Bigler offered a reward of $1,000 for his capture. The reward identified him as Joaquín Carrillo, about five feet, ten inches tall, with black hair, and a "good address." As Joaquín's exploits continued into March, the press called for a large enough sum to take him dead or alive. Philemon T. Herbert, a hot-headed Texan and Mariposa County's representative in the state assembly, introduced a bill that would establish a $5,000 reward. The bill was vehemently opposed by Assemblyman J. M. Covarrubias and Senator Pablo de la Guerra who opposed a reward for a man only identified as "Joaquín" (Pitt 1966, p. 79). Covarrubias contended that the Act was illegal:

> To set a price upon the head of any individual who has not been examined and convicted by due process of law, is to proceed upon an assumption of his guilt. . . . The offer of such reward would be likely to stimulate cupidity to magnify fancied resemblance, and dozens of heads similar in some measure to that of Joaquín might be presented for identification.
>
> The magnitude of the reward might tempt unscrupulous and unprincipled men to palm off, by purchased evidence, the head of another for that of Joaquín and thus defraud the State Treasury. (Nadeau 1974, pp. 62-64)

The bill was tabled and killed, but in April a petition, signed by residents of Mariposa County, was sent to Governor Bigler. It asked the governor "to call out a company of Rangers of at least twenty men . . . . whose duty it shall be to rid our County and state of most desperate characters by whom any community has ever been scourged" (ibid., p. 64). The petition recommended Harry Love "as a person eminently qualified to command such force" (ibid., p. 65).

Harry Love stood six feet, two inches and was considered "half man and half alligator." Nadeau described him:

> A swashbuckling Texan, Harry was a veteran of Indian warfare and border conflicts along the Brazos and the Rio Grande, where he

learned the local rule that a good Mexican was a dead Mexican. In the War with Mexico he had been an express rider for General Zachary Taylor. After the war he returned to Texas and pioneered an express route from the Gulf coast to El Paso. Then the call of gold beckoned him to California, where he settled in Mariposa County and became a professional bounty hunter. (Ibid.)

Historian Herbert Howe Bancroft added:

Harry Love was a law-abiding desperado. . . . Savages he had butchered until the business afforded him no further pleasure. He thought now he would like to kill Joaquin Murietta. Harry greatly enjoyed slaying human beings, but he did not like so well to be hanged for it; so he asked the legislature. . . . if he might go out and kill Joaquin. (Ibid.)

Love was notorious for having prisoners attempt to escape, which allowed him to shoot them.

The man who seemed "eminently qualified" to lead the Rangers had been a scout in the Mexican War and carrier of dispatches for Zachary Taylor. According to Love's great-granddaughter, he was in the Texas Rangers under Captain Jack Hayes and they probably came to California together in 1849 (Latta 1980, p. 305).[17]

On May 10, 1853, Assemblyman Herbert introduced a bill establishing the California Rangers for the purpose of capturing the five Joaquíns. The Rangers set off on a rampage, hunting down and killing suspected Mexican horse thieves, almost at will. On July 24, 1853, they rode into a camp consisting of six or eight Mexicans. One of the Rangers, Bill Byrnes, claims to have known Murieta personally and to have identified him. The Rangers killed him and another man believed to have been his first lieutenant, Three-Fingered Jack García. Joaquín's pickled head became a museum piece in San Francisco until it was destroyed in the earthquake of 1906. Although Love collected the $5,000, there is little reason to believe that the man killed by the Rangers was Joaquín Murieta. The Los Angeles Star questioned the authenticity of the head displayed by Love and reported that the notorious bandit was known to be in the south on the night of his death (1853, p. 1).

In the end, whether the man killed by Love and the Rangers was the real Joaquín is perhaps irrelevant, for the myth itself reflects the reality of racial conflict that prevailed. As Leonard Pitt noted, "the truth may be doubtful but the myth is real" (Pitt 1966, p. 81). The significance of

Joaquín is that he symbolized the resistance of Chicanos to oppression and was feared by the Anglo and admired by Chicanos:

> Joaquín in his heyday seemed possessed of an uncanny ability to strike everywhere at once; to operate under many names and guises; and to agitate, organize, and unite all the Spanish-speaking in their anti-gringo crusade. Men believed in his ubiquitousness because the hostility between Anglo-Saxons and Latin Americans now took many forms and erupted on several fronts. Vast stretches of California became a no-man's-land, as foreboding as Apache country in New Mexico Territory. "When I see a Mexican approaching," reported an experienced California traveler in 1854, "I cock my rifle and cover him with it. At the same time calling to him to raise his hand away from his lasso which hangs at his saddle-bow. In this way I keep my rifle on him until he has passed and gone beyond lasso distance." (Ibid., p. 82)

GREGORIO CORTEZ

Although Anglos had gained economic and political control, the image of the unpacified Chicano bandit struck fear in the heart of the Americans. Even a simple tenant farmer like Gregorio Cortez was widely feared and pursued as the leader of a large gang of Mexicans. While innocent of any real crime, he was branded a murderer, thief, and brigand chief. To Chicanos, on the other hand, his exploits were legendary and survive to the present day. Chicanos admired his horsemanship, his courage, and, most of all, his ability to outsmart the many posses that pursued him.

In *"With His Pistol in His Hand": A Border Ballad and its Hero* (1958), Dr. Américo Paredes skillfully researched the story of Gregorio Cortez. Cortez was born on the Mexican side of the border on June 22, 1875. He had settled down with his family to farm in 1900. Sheriff W. T. Morris, former member of the Texas Rangers, and his interpreter, Boone Choate, went to the Cortez house looking for a Mexican horse thief.

Paredes shows how an interpreter's ignorance of the complexity and subtlety of the Spanish language turned an innocent man into a fugitive from justice. Because Gregorio had recently traded a mare, when the sheriff asked him if he had bought a "horse," Gregorio answered "no." Spanish distinguishes between a horse *(caballo)* and a mare *(yegua)*. Gregorio's statement, "you can't arrest me for nothing," was probably translated as "no white man can arrest me" (ibid., p. 62). The sheriff became suspicious, drew his revolver, and shot Gregorio's brother, Romaldo. Gregorio, in turn, shot and killed Morris in self-defense. This incident, and the subsequent shooting of Sheriff Glover at the Battle of Belmont, set off one of the most famous manhunts in the history of Texas. The chase took ten days during which Cortez walked over one hundred twenty miles and rode more than four hundred. He was chased by hundreds of men in parties of up to three hundred.

Cortez was able to avoid capture by his familiarity with the local terrain, his skilled horsemanship, and the support of other Chicanos who provided him with food, shelter, and sometimes a fresh mount.

Ironically, he was arrested on June 22, 1901, after an informer named Jesús González told the authorities of his whereabouts, hoping to obtain the $1,000 reward. Although Cortez offered no resistance, the newspapers sensationalized the capture and claimed that all that was needed for the seizure of the dangerous bandit was one Texas Ranger, Captain J. H. Rogers. In the end González got only about $200, but he paid a heavy price and was ostracized by his people. The *Laredo Times* ran the following account, which was reprinted in many other papers in the state:

> The Times knows from an authentic source that Jesús González, the cowboy who assisted in the capture of Gregorio Cortez, has been entirely ostracized from his circle of Mexican friends at the coal mines on account of having rendered such assistance, effecting the capture of one of his countrymen. He has been declared as a traitor and is repeatedly and continuously insulted by certain individuals every time he meets them. Threats have been made that they were going to kill him. (Paredes 1958, p. 82)

ELFEGO BACA

The last social bandit to be discussed was also not a bandit, but a staunch defender of the law. In fact, it is ironic that some consider him a bandit because every major incident in which he took part was a response to lawlessness and an attempt to enforce the law and maintain order. The prevalence of lawlessness on the frontier, even among those charged with enforcing the law, sometimes made it necessary for him to take the law into his hands.

Elfego Baca was born in 1865 in the town of Socorro, along the upper Rio Grande.[18] Interestingly, he was reputedly born on a softball field where just a few minutes earlier his mother had played (Schaefer 1965, p. 288). Soon after Elfego was born, his family moved to Topeka, Kansas, for a safer environment and more desirable schools. Elfego grew up among Anglos and was not intimidated by them. Unlike Cortina and Cortez, he was much more fluent in English than Spanish.

When Elfego was fifteen, his father, Francisco, took the job of marshal in the small town of Belen, upriver from Socorro. After his father had killed two rowdy cowboys from Los Lunas who were shooting up the town, he was captured by some residents of Los Lunas, tried, and sentenced to a lengthy jail term. Elfego was seventeen years old, intelligent, and resourceful. He cleverly engineered his father's escape by climbing to the second floor of the courthouse, sawing a hole, and freeing his father and two other prisoners. They hid in the tall grass across the street all the next day and watched as posses rode off in search of them.

The incident that established Elfego's reputation as a fearless gunfighter was the Battle of Frisco. Socorro County was enormous, extending west to the Arizona border and a haven for drunken cowboys who loved to "raise hell" and shoot up the town. One of the worst towns was Francisco, now known as Reserve:

> The basic conflicts of the time and territory, Americanos versus Mejicanos, Texans versus New Mexicans, cattlemen versus farmers, cowboys versus townsmen, all contributing to bitter political rivalries too, came to a focus at the little town more than one hundred and thirty miles distant from the nearest other town of any consequence. (Ibid., p. 291)

Elfego was working in a store in Socorro when a deputy sheriff, Pedro Sarracino, came in for supplies and told him of the lawlessness that prevailed in Frisco. A native named El Burro had been stretched out on a counter and "right then and there poor Burro was altered in the presence of every one" (ibid., p. 292). When a man named Martínez objected, he was shot.

Baca offered his help and returned to Frisco with Sarracino. One evening, a man named McCarty of the famous Slaughter Outfit, was drunk and shot up the town. Fearing retaliation, the *alcalde*, or justice of the peace, refused to arrest him. The daring Elfego astonished the Americans by arresting McCarty in front of his friends. Several of the men from the

Slaughter Outfit, including the foreman, Mr. Perham, rode into town and demanded the release of McCarty. Baca told them he would count to three before he commenced firing. Elfego began firing and the cowboys scattered. He shot one cowboy in the leg and wounded the foreman's horse. Unfortunately, the horse reared over backward and killed Perham. The word spread quickly that the Mexicans had started a rebellion and planned to kill all Texans.

Some of the cooler heads in the crowd prevailed and got an American justice of the peace. Elfego surrendered the prisoner and McCarty was fined five dollars. Elfego sensed trouble and took refuge in a small *jacal* that gave him a clear view in all directions. The case should have been closed, but:

> A group of the hotter-heads, led by a Jim Herne, were determined to lynch the upstart "greaser." They advanced on the jacal. Rifle in hand, Herne battered on the door, shouting that he would drag the "dirty little Mexican" out of there. (Ibid., p. 295)

Herne was dropped and mortally wounded. Over the course of the next thirty-six hours, Elfego carried out a miraculous defense of the *jacal*. He held off over eighty Texans who poured hundreds and hundreds of bullets into the shack. Although almost every object inside was riddled with bullets, he remained unharmed. They even tried to set fire to the *jacal* and dynamited a portion of the building. The next morning they saw smoke coming from the chimney as Elfego was calmly cooking breakfast. He agreed to come out but would not give up his guns. He had Deputy Sheriff Ross sit in front of him on the buckboard and the escort of six cowboys also rode ahead where he could watch them. He was tried before a federal court in Albuquerque and acquitted twice.

The Frisco affair motivated Elfego to become a peace officer and a criminal lawyer. He said, "I wanted the outlaws to hear my steps a block away from me" (ibid., p. 299). He eventually became a deputy sheriff and a United States marshal. In 1890 he began to read law and passed the New Mexico bar in 1894. "He was as effective a champion of his people there as ever he was in tight spots with his guns. Innumerable were the poor 'Mexicans' who, when in trouble with Anglo law, hurried to find Elfego" (ibid., p. 302). Although he was known for his eloquence and unconventional courtroom practices, he always retained a profound respect for the law. He died of natural causes at he age of eighty.

ORGANIZED REBELLIONS

Americans have tended to label Mexican resistance to Anglo control as depredations and the work of bandits or thieves, and historians have tended to ignore or minimize the importance of such resistance. But many of these rebellions were, in fact, organized revolts or incipient revolutionary movements. Not all participants were peasants or primitive rebels lacking a political ideology, as Hobsbawm suggested. There is, thus, a need to go beyond traditional theoretical formulations such as Hobsbawm's and Castillo and Camarillo's, and recognize that many who rebelled were early Chicano guerrilla fighters (see Vigil 1974) and emergent revolutionary leaders.

Robert Rosenbaum (1981, p. 14) has identified four basic tactics employed by *mexicanos* in response to the American takeover: withdrawal, accommodation, assimilation, and resistance. The majority opted for withdrawal by separating themselves from Americans and attempting, as much as possible, to ignore the intruders. "Accommodation—interaction accompanied by jousting for position and advantage—was used by the elite and upwardly mobile, particularly in New Mexico." A few of the elite, like Miguel A. Otero who served as territorial governor of New Mexico, and others who married into Anglo families, successfully assimilated. The masses tried to ignore the Americans, but *mexicano-americano* conflict and friction were common and often resulted in violent confrontations (ibid., p. 15). Although the United States enjoyed numerical and military superiority and was never in danger of losing the acquired territory, during the nineteenth century and much of the twentieth "*mexicanos* employed violence as one means of retaining some measure of self-determination in the face of an increasingly oppressive new regime" (ibid., p. 16). The conflict was ultimately a cultural clash, but the two specific catalysts that most often provoked violent resistance were land and law (ibid.). *Mexicanos* were subjected to a legal system that was not only foreign and impersonal but "capricious and unjust" (ibid., p. 16). Competition over land was intense and there were fundamental differences in the systems of land tenure and attitudes toward the use of land (see chapter 2).

Diego Vigil similarly sees the emergence of early Chicano guerrilla fighters in the nineteenth century as a response to radical alterations in the distribution and allocation of land, organization of human labor, and distribution of wealth (Vigil 1974, p. 17). The deposed Mexican upper classes sometimes sought accommodation with the Americans and were slower to rebel, but Anglo oppression had the effect of minimizing interclass differences among Mexicans and engendering ethclass consciousness. Inasmuch as most *mexicanos* were compressed into a single class and not effectively assimilated into American society, ethclass consciousness combined "a sense of peoplehood (ethnic group) and social class position" (ibid., p. 19). What is, perhaps, most ironic about this development is that prior to the American conquest, *mexicanos*, especially those in the northern provinces, did not have a strongly developed sense of nationalism (Rosenbaum 1981, pp. 8-9).

JUAN "CHENO" CORTINA

Juan "Cheno" Cortina can be used to illustrate the concept of ethclass consciousness. Although the literature on Cortina tends to be biased and to treat him as a rogue or bandit (see De León 1983, p. 120; Rosenbaum 1981, p. 43), Cortina differs from the social bandits in several important respects. First, he was not a poor farmer or peasant but a member of an affluent Mexican family and a wealthy landlord. Secondly, he was not an ordinary bandit who held up banks and stagecoaches but a revolutionary leader. In fact, the event that gained him notoriety was the occupation of the city of Brownsville and proclaiming it the Republic of the Rio Grande on September 28, 1859, little more than a decade after the signing of the Treaty of Guadalupe Hidalgo.

The "Red Robber of the Rio Grande" was born Juan Nepomuceno Cortina on May 16, 1824, in Camargo, a village on the Rio Bravo. His great-grandfather had been captain of Camargo and was one of the original settlers in the Nuevo Santander region (Goldfinch 1949, p. 8). His family was well-off and had acquired large ranches. Cortina's mother, Doña Estéfana, was the granddaughter of José Salvador de la Garza, and one of his heirs (Woodman 1950, p. 9). When she became a widow for the second time after the death of Cortina's father in the early 1840s, she moved to her 44,000-acre Rancho del Carmen, which was part of the *Espíritu Santo* grant.

Like Vásquez and Murieta, the conflict between Cheno Cortina and the Americans, or the Cortina War as it is popularly called, can be traced directly to the racial conflict that prevailed and, specifically, to the land grab. "He had a profound dislike for Americans, occasioned initially, it was said, by their exactment of about 2,000 acres of his mother's land during an investigation of Mexican land ownership" (ibid.).

The incident which set off the Cortina War was a relatively minor one by the standards prevailing along the border at this time. Cortina went into Brownsville on a regular basis to drink coffee with friends. On July 13, 1859, he was a witness as Marshal Robert Shears attempted a brutal arrest of a disorderly Mexican who had previously worked as a servant for Cortina. Words were exchanged and Cortina shot the marshal and rode out of town with the servant on the back of his horse (Rosenbaum 1981, p. 42).

Within two months, Cortina was to lead a group of one hundred men on a raid of Brownsville, release all the prisoners from jail, shoot three Americans, and raise the Mexican flag while shouting "death to the gringos!" Two days after the raid (September 30), he returned to Rancho del Carmen and issued a proclamation explaining his actions and noting that, in defending themselves, Mexicans had invoked "the sacred right of self-preservation" (U.S. House of Representatives 1860a, pp. 70-72). He noted that "innocent persons shall not suffer" and that "we hope the government would prosecute and bring to trial our oppressors," who "number but six to eight" (ibid., p. 72). A second proclamation on November 23, 1859, was more ominous:

> Mexicans! When the State of Texas began to receive the new organization which its sovereignty required as an integrant part of the Union, flocks of vampires, in the guise of men, came and scattered themselves in the settlements, without any capital except the corrupt heart and the most perverse intentions. Some, brimful of laws, pledged to us their protection against the attacks of the rest; . . . while others, to the abusing of our unlimited confidence, when we entrusted them with our titles, which secured the future of our families, refused to return them under false and frivolous pretexts. . . . Many of you have been robbed of your property, incarcerated, chased, murdered, and hunted like wild beasts, because your labor was fruitful, and because your industry excited the vile avarice which led them. . . .
>
> Mexicans! My part is taken; the voice of revelation whispers to me that to me is entrusted the work of breaking the chains of your slavery. (Ibid., pp.80-82)

Cortina claimed that his intent in capturing Brownsville was to punish those whose punishment had long been delayed and to gain the release of an old Cortinista named Tomás Cabrera. Cheno did not behave like a bandit, however. According to Goldfinch, "Although Cortina had taken the law into his hands, he did not rob and steal when he had the city at his mercy as he certainly would have done had he been a bandit" (1949, p. 54). Instead, he took all the arms and ammunition in Alexander Werliski's store and paid him for them. Cortina killed some cattle belonging to James G. Brown and sent him a bill for them, and "apologized, by note, to the postmaster of Brownsville for stopping and opening the mails" (ibid., p. 57). Moreover, he left untouched money that was found in the mail bags.

The residents of Brownsville refused to release Cabrera. After being reinforced by Mexican troops from Matamoros, the "Brownsville Tigers" tried unsuccessfully to capture the bandit. The day after Tobin's Rangers arrived (November 10, 1859), Cabrera was hanged by a lawless mob, supposedly Tobin's men (Fehrenbach 1968, p. 514).

Cortina did not launch another offensive until after the death of Cabrera. On November 22 he defeated Tobin's Rangers and forced them to retreat to Brownsville. Cortina's army was now organized and in open rebellion against Anglo control and domination.

Cheno Cortina was eventually defeated by a combined force of Texas Rangers led by Rip Ford and U.S. Army troops under the command of S. P. Heintzelman (U.S. House of Representatives 1860b), but not before sending the citizens of Brownsville into a state of genuine panic. Even the larger-than-life Texas Rangers were awed by Cortina. The journal of a Texas Ranger, Gilbert D. Kingsbury, who was in Brownsville during the raid and subsequent takeover, is revealing. He described the attack on September 28, which was carried out with a force of some eighty or one hundred men, as a complete surprise:

> The town was unarmed and nothing like it was imagined possible. . . . We stand guard or patrol every night. For 6 weeks I have not touched a bed and nearly every man in town can say the same— This with three hours day service makes 15 hours on post every 24. Our sleep is out doors or the baracades [sic]—All the town save what is baracaded [sic] is abandoned and the families are all within our defenses. (Gilbert D. Kingsbury Papers, 1859)

All the mail routes were closed, the carriers taken prisoner, and the mail destroyed. "One carrier on a powerful horse made the attempt to escape but was cut-off and his horse is now rode [sic] by one of the Mexican officers in command under Cortina" (ibid.). Cortina was feared not only for his military prowess but for his apparent disdain for the gringo. "He has the sympathy of the whole race & makes it a war of Races. He proclaims the knife & no quarter to Americans—No one doubts but he will have 1000 armed men in a week" (ibid.). With each military success, Cortina gained additional support and new troops. He proved to be a superb military strategist and, in all, a formidable opponent:

> All the Rangers who are here agree in the immense strength of the man—and the object he has in view is all a mystery to every one of them and us. He is going no doubt to give a strong battle and his position enables him to fight four to one. They all agree that no such thing was imagined here until lately. The strength he has gained and the certainty that he is assisted from Matamoros makes it a matter of more than border interest. They say we are drifting into a war which will enable us to reclaim our slaves and settle the unstable condition of Mexico. (Ibid.)

Although it was alleged that Cortina was assisted by Mexico, troops were sent from Matamoros to support the Americans, but the Mexicans were not trusted, and their aid refused. When the Mexican troops departed Kingsbury remarked, "we felt relieved of danger and dishonor" (ibid.)

Cortina's own statements contradict the commonly held view that he sought to return Texas to Mexico. In the first proclamation he asserted, "not having renounced our rights as North American citizens, we disapprove and energetically protest against the act of having caused a force of the national guards from Mexico to cross unto this side to ingraft themselves in a question so foreign to their country" (U.S. House of Representatives 1860a, p. 72). In the second proclamation he stated that the Mexicans of Texas trusted that, once elevated to power, General Houston "will begin with care to give us legal protection within the limits of his powers" (ibid., p. 82).

Cortina set up headquarters in Mexico in January 1860 and continued to make sporadic raids across the border. Fearing that he planned to capture the King-Kenedy Steamboat *Ranchero* from the Mexican side of the border, Rip Ford crossed the Rio Grande in search of the revolutionary. Although unsuccessful, the Rangers raised havoc among the Mexican people. "The whole Mexican countryside was in alarm; women and children ran screaming from their huts as the *Rinches* rode past" (Fehrenbach 1968, p. 519).

In subsequent years, Cortina fought on the side of Benito Juárez and was imprisoned by the Mexican dictator Porfirio Díaz. In 1890 he returned to the border and was given a hero's welcome (Acuña 1981, p. 57). Cortina was especially loved and admired by the poor, who glorified his exploits in *corridos*. Even his nemesis Rip Ford acknowledged that after the war Cortina was "the idol of the Mexican masses" (Ford 1963, p. 308).

> Sometimes Cortina would make a speech in the market place and the poor would listen intently to what he had to say. He would not harm the innocent but would fight for the emancipation of the hungry *peons* . . . . They must love the land, for land was all they had. Yet their "*personal enemies*—the land-hungry imperialists to the north— were out to take the land from them. But if the Mexicans followed Cortina, the *gringos* would not have it without "*fattening it with their own gore*" (Ibid., p. 309)

Catarino Garza

Cheno's rebellion is, perhaps, the most extreme example of *mexicano* resistance to American control, but it was only one of a whole series of incidents that occurred along the border. Political unrest within Mexico itself, moreover, served as a catalyst for political activity by Mexicans north of the border. Catarino Garza, for example, a native of the Brownsville-Matamoros area, was a well-educated, liberal, ranchero and journalist who established newspapers in Eagle Pass, Corpus Christi, and Palito Blanco, and used them as a vehicle for attacking Mexican dictator Porfirio Díaz (De León 1983, p. 60). Garza led what was, perhaps, the first rebellion against *el dictadór* (Paredes 1958, p. 136), some twenty years before the Mexican Revolution and the eventual overthrow of Díaz.

In September 1888 Garza was a principal figure in the so-called Rio Grande city riot. In May of the same year, W. W. Sheley, sheriff of Starr County, arrested a man named Abraham Recéndez and charged him with robbery. While in custody, Recéndez was killed by Sheley's partner, U.S. Inspector of Customs Victor Sebree, for supposedly trying to escape (De León 1983, p. 93). The incident angered local Mexican residents, and Sebree was accused by Garza of shooting Mexican prisoners who were opposed to Díaz (Acuña 1981, p. 43). Sheley was said to have been implicated in the lynching of several Mexicans. Sebree was denounced by Garza in the newspaper *El Comercio Mexicano* for the murder of Recéndez. On September 21 Garza confronted Sebree and was shot and wounded by him:

> Sympathizers of Garza threatened to lynch Sebree and followed him out of town as he fled for refuge in nearby Fort Ringgold, where the post commander ordered the two-hundred-man mob to disperse. Mass hysteria followed. . . . Messages from Starr County reported rampant anarchy on the border and called for troops, as lives of white citizens in that region were said to be in imminent peril. (De León 1983, p. 94)

Garza recovered from the shooting and in the summer of 1891, he and his followers crossed into Mexico from Zapata County on a mission to overthrow Díaz. He enjoyed some initial success, but was eventually forced to return to Texas (Paredes 1958, p. 136). Garza continued to foment against Díaz and to plan other attacks from South Texas. Significantly, United States authorities and the Texas Rangers worked to suppress this revolutionary movement, but they had difficulty for many *tejanos* supported Garza and helped him to evade the law (De León 1983, p. 61). When he returned from Mexico, for example, Captain Hall of the Texas Rangers and a posse tried unsuccessfully to capture him and his followers (Paredes 1958, p. 136). Like Cortina, Catarino Garza was eulogized in *corridos* (folk ballads). In fact, Garza is unique in being recognized as a prominent figure in *corridos* on both sides of the border (ibid., p. 146).

It is ironic that organized movements against Mexico, rather than eliciting sympathy in the United States, simply served to reinforce the image of the Mexican as disloyal and subversive. According to De León, during the Spanish-American War there was fear not only that Spain would attack Texas but that "Mexican nationals would aid in an attack on the United States with the tacit consent of the Mexican government" (De León 1983, p. 61) and that Chicanos would support this endeavor. Ironically, those who fought for Texas independence from Mexico were characterized as "freedom fighters" and "citizen soldiers," but Garza's followers were dismissed as ignorant, lawless, low-life Mexicans *(Galveston Daily News* 1893, p. 7). Some thirty years earlier, General Heintzelman had similarly described Cortina's followers as *pelados* (low-life Mexicans), who "are an idle, thriftless, thieving, vicious people, living principally on jerked beef and corn, a frijole as a luxury" (U.S. House of Representatives 1860b, p. 14).

Conflict between Mexicans and Anglo-Texans continued throughout the rest of the nineteenth century, and appears to have peaked during the Mexican Revolution (1911-1918), especially the two-year span between 1915 and 1917. As was noted in chapter 1, above, despite a pervasive fear of "marauding" Mexican bandits and a general Mexican uprising, it was the Mexican who was typically the victim of violence and lawlessness. In retrospect, organized armed uprisings such as the Cortina War, the Garza War, and *El Plan de San Diego* appear especially significant, for they were clearly the exception rather than the rule.

Before discussing *El Plan*, it is important to note that this was not an isolated incident, but rather one that occurred in a context of open warfare along the border. Rodolfo Rocha notes, for example, that on May 30, 1915, a large contingent of heavily armed Mexicans appeared at *Rancho de los Indios*, in June the Cameron County sheriff was allegedly killed by Mexicans who crossed the river, eight incidents took place in July, and at least twenty-five in August (Rocha 1981, pp. 262-64). The conflict grew more intense and twenty-three incidents were recorded in the month of September (ibid., p. 269). However, the anticipated general Mexican uprising on September 16 failed to materialize. There can be little doubt that revolutionary activity in Mexico served as an impetus for some of these incidents. "For a brief moment in 1915, the despair of being 'Mex·ican' in the United States changed to hope as Mexican-American 'social bandits,' influenced by the ideology of the revolution, sought to redress the suffering experienced by generations of Mexican Americans" (ibid., p. 256).

EL PLAN DE SAN DIEGO

El Plan de San Diego confirmed the Anglo fear of a Mexican insurrection and helps to place the raids that occurred throughout 1915, and the Anglo response, in a meaningful context. In February a Mexican national, Basilo Ramos, arrested by Starr County Sheriff Deodoro Guerra, was found to have in his possession a copy of an irredentist plan known as *El Plan de San Diego* because it was signed in San Diego, Texas. *El Plan* called for a general uprising on February 20, 1915, and declared independence from "Yankee tyranny" (U.S. Senate 1919). This uprising was to be effected by a liberating army composed not only of Mexicans but blacks, Japanese, and Indians. The Indians were to have their land returned to them and several southeastern states were designated for blacks.

A new independent republic was to be created from five southwestern states (i.e., Texas, New Mexico, Arizona, Colorado, and California). Every white male over the age of 16 was to be shot, as were all traitors who cooperated with the enemy.

Although the plan was never brought to fruition, it was an important document in that it articulated the numerous grievances of the *tejano* population in South Texas. Unfortunately, historians and other scholars have tended to minimize the importance of *El Plan*, or to dismiss it as a wild, unrealistic scheme. Evan Anders, for examle, terms it "farfetched" and "preposterous" (1982, pp. 221-22). Others saw the plan as resulting from foreign influence and as a simple extension of the Mexican revolution to American soil. Walter Prescott Webb, for example, noted that "Mexican Revolutions tended to overrun the border and to produce in Southern Texas and New Mexico conditions similar to those that existed in Mexico itself" (Webb 1965, p. 478). The raids were frequently blamed on Carranza and his followers, for they occurred in Texas territory in areas across the border from territory under the control of one of his generals, E. P. Nafarrate, a *norteño* from the state of Sonora well known for his reputation as an "American hater" (Rocha 1981, p. 293). Others saw the plan as having been instigated by Germany, although there is no hard evidence to substantiate this view (ibid., p. 291). Although Rocha is less critical of *El Plan*, he concludes that it "failed to accomplish its purpose, probably because it had no real organization" (ibid.).

David Montejano offers a very different perspective, arguing that the Mexican Revolution and the war in Europe may have served as catalysts for this rebellion, but it was local conditions that directly fomented discontent among Mexicans in South Texas (Montejano 1982, p. 73). Ultimately, the Mexican rebellion can be seen as a response to changing economic conditions and the supplanting of traditional Mexican ranchero society with modern American farming:

> The border troubles essentially represented the armed conflict between an old ranch society and an aggressively expanding farm society. In this context, the Texas Mexican insurrectionists and the Texas Rangers constituted the opposed military forces. (Ibid., p. 74)

If one takes *El Plan de San Diego* literally, one is forced to conclude, as Rocha did, that it somehow "failed." However, if *El Plan* is viewed instead as a statement of grievances and a general call to action, it was very successful. In this sense, *El Plan* is very much like Cortina's proclamations and appears to have served a similar function. Perhaps the most important aspect of these statements is that they articulated the fears, concerns, and grievances of rank-and-file Mexican residents, and were, ultimately, an expression of Mexican resistance to Anglo domination. Although not all raiders may have understood the ideological significance of *El Plan*, most understood the oppressive nature of American capitalism and racism. According to Rocha, although the basic cause of the revolt was the deprivation of civil liberties and rights for Chicanos in the border region, the desire to regain lost lands and resistance to Anglo modernization and domination also played a prominent part in motivating the raiders (1981, pp. 279-80).

LAS GORRAS BLANCAS

Americano-mexicano conflict appears to have been most intense in Texas, but it was commonplace throughout the Southwest. Even New Mexico, which has been erroneously characterized as a territory where Mexicans were readily assimilated into Anglo society and where opposition to the American conquest was less prevalent (see McWilliams 1968, pp. 116-17), was the scene of bitter and violent confrontations. *Las Gorras Blancas*, or White Caps, are important, for the emergence of this group demonstrates that there was also organized resistance to the American takeover and the displacement of traditional society in New Mexico.

Las Gorras Blancas was a group of masked, night-riding *mexicanos* who responded to modernization and Anglo technology by engaging in numerous raids that entailed fence-cutting, rail-splitting, and intimidation (see Rosenbaum 1981; Schlesinger 1971) in the town of Las Vegas in San Miguel County, in the northern part of the New Mexico territory. Most of their attacks were directed at large landholders who had appropriated communal lands.

The Las Vegas grant was a 500,000-acre parcel of rich agricultural and timber land awarded by the Mexican government to Luís María Cabeza de Baca in 1821 (Schlesinger 1971, p. 93). Baca, however, failed to establish a permanent settlement and on March 23, 1835, the Mexican government granted a petition from thirty-one families who had been living on the land for ten years, under the condition that pasture and watering places would be free to all and that "grants are to be made according to the means and abilities of each one of the petitioners, in order that they may not leave any land which may be given them without cultivation" (ibid., p. 94). In addition to the thirty-one original inhabitants, the grant was made to future settlers who were destitute of land to cultivate. Subsequent to the Treaty of Guadalupe Hidalgo, the grant to the town of Las Vegas was confirmed by Congress on June 21, 1860.

At this time, Las Vegas was a pristine, traditional community, which had been a stop on the Santa Fe Trail, and was populated almost exclusively by Mexicans. After the Civil War, the influx of American settlers signaled the development of commercial and banking interests. The arrival of the Atchison, Topeka, and Santa Fe Railroad in 1879 brought a definite shift in the cultural and economic balance of Las Vegas (Rosenbaum 1981, p. 101). Conflict heightened during the 1870s when several Anglos purchased interests in the Las Vegas grant from the heirs of the original settlers or their legal representatives and proceeded to fence off large sections of the grant (Schlesinger, p. 95). The practice of fencing off land was common among American cattlemen who sought to separate their cattle from the flocks of Mexican sheep. Many Mexican farmers, however, found themselves cut off from sources of water and firewood, and from their communal grazing lands (ibid.).

The conflict culminated in the famous suit of Milhiser vs. Padilla, a civil suit that came to court on August 20, 1887, but was dragged out for more than two years and precipitated much of the violence involving *Las Gorras Blancas* (Rosenbaum 1981, p. 101). The plaintiffs, Philip Milhiser and his associates, claimed that in purchasing the land from the descendants of the original grantees, they had acquired absolute ownership not only in this land but a proportional interest in common lands in the grant. The defendants, on the other hand, argued that the grant had not been awarded to individuals but to the community as a whole and that any change in patterns of ownership "required the consent of the community as a whole" (ibid., p. 102). Chief Justice Elisha V. Long eventually ruled in favor of the defendants, but presented no solution for future disputes.

The decision, moreover, did not stop the land grab. During the course of the trial, Anglos continued to acquire land and to erect fences. Outraged Mexicans responded:

About midnight, November 1, 1889, 66 horsemen galloped into the town of Las Vegas. Armed with rifles and pistols, draped in long black coats and slickers, their faces hidden behind white masks, these men moved unhesitatingly and with grim determination. The thunderous clap of their horses' hooves against hard earth confirmed the worst fears of Anglo landowners and those Spanish-Americans who had come to terms with the American presence. (Schlesinger 1971, p. 97)

Significantly, the attack occurred as several persons were under indictment for fence-cutting and other damage to land and livestock. Between 1889 and 1891 numerous depredations were ostensibly committed by the White Caps, who were said to have been led by the Herrera brothers, Juan José, Pablo, and Nicanor (ibid., p. 98). On the last day of district court, twenty-six indictments were handed down against forty-seven persons, ranging in age from twenty to sixty-five, but the cases could not be tried until April 1890 when the court reconvened. In April the charges were dismissed against the forty-seven because the prosecution failed to produce any witnesses. "Loud cheers from the crowded courtroom greeted the dismissal on May 20, 1890, followed by an enthusiastic meeting in the plaza marked by speeches, whiskey, and celebratory gunshots" (Rosenbaum 1981, p. 109).

Unfortunately the official view of the White Caps espoused by persons such as Attorney General Miguel Salazar was that they were "ignorant people, easily deceived and swayed by such wicked and evil designing persons, as this leader and his lieutenants are" (Schlesinger 1971, p. 104), rather than persons responding to the dislocation of a traditional way of life. Territorial Governor Prince attempted to wage an assault against *Las Gorras Blancas*, but his efforts were thwarted not only by the fact the organization was secret, which made it difficult to issue warrants against members, but by the composition of juries "drawn from the same kinds of people who made up the White Caps" (Rosenbaum 1981, p. 110) and made convictions difficult to obtain. In the end, the White Caps appeared to enjoy the support of most Mexican residents of the county, even the "best" citizens (ibid.).

4

The Border and the Law

INTRODUCTION

The Treaty of Guadalupe Hidalgo was significant not only because it safeguarded the property and cultural rights of displaced Mexican citizens but because it recognized the Chicano as a unique national minority. The treaty, it will be recalled, provided a sort of unconditional amnesty in that it gave Mexican residents one year to either return to Mexico or to declare their intent to become American citizens. Those who did not state otherwise were assumed to be United States citizens. At the same time, the treaty distinguished between Mexicans in the newly occupied territory (Chicanos) and those residing in Mexico (*mexicanos*). The new international border was a 1,945-mile strip that stretched from San Ysidro, California, to the Gulf of Mexico.

The proximity of the border and the history of conflict between the United States and Mexico created a double oppression for Chicanos, subjected to abuse and harassment not only by local police agencies and state militia such as the Texas Rangers but also by the Border Patrol.

This chapter is concerned with the issue of the border and its impact on the experiences of Chicanos relative to the legal and judicial system. A basic thesis advanced is that the proximity of the border has placed Chicanos in a disadvantageous position within the legal and judicial system. Persons who cross the border illegally, for example, are often victims of crime or of abuses by police or the Border Patrol, but they very seldom seek redress before American tribunals. Police agencies, on the other hand, often do not bother to ascertain the place of birth or citizenship of persons of Mexican descent. Many native-born Chicanos have been subjected to unnecessary questioning and detention, and some have been deported—illegally.

Despite the presence of the border and the legacy of conflict, Mexican culture and language have transcended international boundaries. The proximity of the border and the concentration of persons of Mexican descent on both sides of it have in fact facilitated the evolution of a genuine Mexican border culture. Many *mexicanos* have friends or relatives living *en el otro lado* and American officials are frustrated by the ease with which Mexicans go back and forth across the international line. The border is, in a sense, a historical and political demarcation, and for many who cross it "illegally" the boundary has always been arbitrary and capricious.

Chicanos strongly resist the notion that they are somehow transplanted or imported "immigrants." Not only has the Chicano been in America for a long time but as Luis Valdez (1972, p. xxxiii) has astutely observed, they did not come to the United States, rather, the United States came to them:

> Now the gringo is trying to impose the immigrant complex on the Chicano, pretending that we "Mexican-Americans" are the most recent arrivals. It will not work. His melting pot concept is a sham.... The Anglo cannot conceive of the Chicano, the Mexican Mestizo, in all his ancient human fullness. He recognizes him as a Mexican, but only to the extent that he is "American"; and he accepts Mexican culture only to the extent that it has been Americanized, sanitized, sterilized, and made safe for democracy. (Ibid., pp. xxxii-xxxiii)

Inasmuch as issues surrounding immigration, legal and otherwise, and undocumented workers are broad and complex, this chapter will focus only on the impact of the border on the administration of justice on the United States side of the border. Questions such as the extent to which undocumented workers are or are not a drain on the economy, prevailing public attitudes toward undocumented workers, and alternative solutions for "stemming the tide" of undocumented workers, are important, but they extend well beyond the perview of this work. The chapter focuses instead on the development of immigration laws and policies, and their impact on persons of Mexican descent. The emergence of the Border Patrol as an agency of social control is also considered. An additional overriding concern is with abuses and injustices perpetrated against undocumented workers both by law enforcement and the public at large.

PATTERNS OF MIGRATION: AN OVERVIEW

Patterns of migration from Mexico to the United States have been inextricably linked to expansion and contraction of American capitalism. Not surprisingly, between 1850 and 1880 there was virtually no movement across the border (Samora 1975, p. 65). The war had left a legacy of conflict between "gringos and greasers," and raids across the border were common occurrences.

By the last quarter of the nineteenth century, however, economic expansion had created a demand for cheap labor. From the 1880s to about 1908 migration increased slowly but steadily. The railroads played a significant part in facilitating this migration. Porfirio Díaz, Mexican dictator from 1876 to 1910, encouraged foreign capital investment in Mexico. By 1910 almost fifteen thousand miles of railroad had been completed and one could easily travel from the interior of Mexico to the border (Galarza 1964, p. 27). Ironically, at the same time that the railroads served as a vehicle for transporting Mexican workers, Mexicans provided much of the labor for development of American railroads. In 1909, nine western railroads had a common labor force that was 17.1 percent Mexican; twenty years later the figure was 59.5 percent (Hoffman 1974, p. 7).

But the great wave of Mexican migration was yet to come. Between 1910 and 1930 it has been estimated that perhaps as much as one-eighth of the Mexican population came to the United States (Acuña 1981, p. 123). A number of factors contributed to the mass movement. Industrialization and urbanization in the United States created a great demand for unskilled labor in steel mills, mines, meat packing houses, brick yards, and canneries. Even more intense was the need for labor in the expanding agricultural industry. Opportunities for crop picking opened up throughout the Southwest and as far north as Michigan, Minnesota, and North Dakota.

The need for Mexican labor increased during World War I. There were not enough U.S. workers to meet the demands of the war effort, and the Immigration Act of 1917 set limits on immigration from Europe, established a literacy test, and a head tax for immigrants. As a result of intense pressure from industrialists and growers, these restrictions were waived in the case of Mexican workers. Between 1917 and 1920 more than seventy-three thousand temporary Mexican workers (Samora 1975, p. 66), and over a hundred thousand permanent Mexican immigrants entered the United States (ibid., p. 681; see also Neal 1941, p. 100).

Political and economic forces within Mexico also gave impetus to the northern migration. During the 34-year dictatorship of Porfirio Díaz the economic position of the Mexican peasant, *peón*, had witnessed a dramatic decline. Díaz was successful not only in consolidating his own power but the power of rich landowners, whereas the masses remained brutally exploited. The wealth of the rich came at the expense of the poor. Most *peones* were landless and forced to work for subsistence wages (Silva Herzog 1960, p. 40).

In 1910 almost half of Mexico was controlled by three thousand families and the real wages of a peasant were about one-quarter of what they had been in 1800 (Parkes 1969, p. 306). The economic and political instability of Mexico, moreover, was clearly linked to American domination and intervention. At the time of the Mexican Revolution, American interests controlled more than three-fourths of the mines and over half of the oil fields, for example. They also held substantial interests in many other industries.

The need for cheap labor was intensified by the Chinese Exclusion Act of 1882, the Gentlemen's Agreement of 1907, which effectively barred Japanese immigration, and restrictions on immigration from southern Europe (Samora 1975, p. 233). Mexican labor was also preferred by American capitalists because of the Mexican's willingness to work long hours at low wages, and because of Mexico's proximity (Cardoso 1974, p. 42).

In the early part of the twentieth century, Mexican immigration was thus not perceived as a major problem. Prior to 1908 no statistics were kept on the number of Mexicans who entered the United States, although it has been estimated that about sixty thousand were entering each year and that one-fourth to one-third of them remained (Reisler 1976, p. 13). The U.S. Congress Senate Immigration Commission (usually referred to as the Dillingham Commission) expressed what proved to be the prevailing attitude at that time toward Mexican immigration:

> The Mexican immigrants are providing a fairly acceptable supply of labor in a limited territory in which it is difficult to secure others, and their competitive ability is limited because of their more or less temporary residence and their personal qualities, so that their incoming does not involve the same detriment to labor conditions as is involved in the immigration of other races who also work at comparatively low wages. While the Mexicans are not easily assimilated, this is not of very great importance as long as most of them return

to their native land after a short time. (U.S. Congress Senate
Immigration Commission, *Abstracts*, 1911, 1, p. 691)

Because much of the employment, especially in agriculture, was seasonal
and subject to change, supply and demand for labor could be easily controlled. It was commonly assumed that the Mexicans, being so close to
their homeland, did not wish to establish permanent residence in the United
States. Mexicans were viewed as ideal workers; they would come, work
for long hours at low wages, make few demands, and return to Mexico
when the work was finished.

These beliefs were reinforced by negative racial stereotypes (see
Reisler 1973, pp. 210-45). Many saw the Mexican as a subhuman species;
a domesticated animal that would do work that a white person would not.
Dr. George P. Clemens, head of the Los Angeles County Agricultural
Department for more than twenty years (1917 to 1939) and a congressional
lobbyist favoring unrestricted Mexican immigration, expressed the view
that the lowly tasks of agriculture were those "to which the oriental and
Mexican due to their crouching and bending habits are fully adapted, while
the white is physically unable to adapt himself to them" (Hoffman 1974,
p. 10).

An interesting paradox emerged during the 1920s. At the same time
that capitalist interests favored an open border and unlimited Mexican
immigration, negativity toward Mexicans intensified. Nativism was exacerbated by World War I and the antiforeign sentiment that prevailed.
Negative attitudes toward Mexicans extended beyond blind racism and
were grounded in economic competition. Mexicans were frequently used
as a reserve pool of labor and as strikebreakers, and they, rather than
owners or employers, were held responsible for keeping wages down.

Mexican workers, however, were largely unorganized, dependent,
and extremely vulnerable to economic fluctuations. A depression in 1921
displaced many Mexican laborers suddenly superfluous and stranded
throughout the United States without work or money (ibid., p. 130). The
economy recovered in 1923 and there was once again a demand for Mexican labor. Conflict continued, however, and led to an important debate
in Congress over controls on Mexican immigration. Small farmers, unions,
and racists argued for restriction of immigration from Mexico. Dr. Thomas
Nixon Carver, professor of economics at Harvard University, gave the

following testimony before the United States Senate Committee on Immigration:

> The bringing of cheap Mexican labor brings the same situation in agriculture in California as slavery did in the South . . . .
>
> Slavery in the South . . . drove a wedge that raised those who were able to buy slaves to do their work, but lowered those who had to sell their labor to compete with that of the slaves. It made aristocrats above the wedge and poor white trash below. The same thing is likely to happen in California . . . and the introduction of Mexican peon Labor will bring a problem far worse than that caused by the introduction of Chinese and Japanese. (U.S. Congress Senate Committee on Immigration 1928, p. 9)

Industrialists and large growers, on the other hand, looked favorably on unrestricted immigration (see Lipshultz 1962, pp. 6-10). The Immigration Act of 1921 limited immigration from eastern and southern Europe. There was great pressure to include Mexicans in the provisions of the bill, but agribusiness was successful once again in lobbying Congress to exclude them (Acuña 1981, p. 131). The 1924 Immigration Act excluded most Asians and further limited immigration from southern and eastern Europe (President's Commission on Immigration and Naturalization 1953, p. 88). Despite heated debate in both houses and strong opposition by restrictionists, Mexicans were excluded from the quota. Although restrictionists did not succeed in their attempt to set a quota on immigration from Mexico, they did succeed in passing a bill that created an agency charged with the exclusive responsibility of enforcing existing immigration laws, the Border Patrol. The creation of this agency in 1924 proved to be a landmark, for it signaled the beginning of a new era of strict enforcement of immigration laws along the Mexican border.

Although attempts to pass restrictive legislation failed, by the end of the 1920s Mexican immigration was being deterred by stronger enforcement of existing laws. By August 1928, very few visas were being granted to Mexicans (ibid, p. 32). The three most common reasons for denying visas were: (1) illiteracy; (2) rigid interpretation of the Liable to Become a Public Charge (LPC) provision of the 1917 Immigration Act; and (3) enforcement of the provision that forbade "contract labor." A visa could be denied if an applicant had a work contract or the equivalent. But if applicants did not have such a commitment, a visa could be denied them on the grounds that they might become a public charge.

By 1929 the State Department had negotiated an agreement whereby Mexican officials would voluntarily limit the number of visas issued. A law making unlawful entry into the United States a felony was passed by Congress in the same year. Thus, during the decade Mexican migrants were rapidly transformed from migratory workers who crossed an arbitrary line of demarcation with relative impunity, to criminal or illegal aliens in territory that was previously theirs. Interestingly, the establishment of the Border Patrol and enforcement of immigration laws also created a new entrepreneur—the *coyote*, or person who specialized in transporting undocumented workers for profit.

Jorge Bustamante argues that contradictions within American capitalism help to perpetuate the ambiguous status of undocumented workers. The contradictions include:

> (1) A condemnation of the Mexican worker by defining him as a criminal and, at the same time maintaining a demand for his labor. This is reflected in a steadily increasing flux of Mexican workers each year. (2) Penalizing a worker from Mexico for being in the United States without a visa, but not penalizing a farmer for hiring the former. (3) Maintaining an agency for the enforcement of immigration law, and at the same time exerting budget limitations and/or political pressures to prevent a successful enforcement of the law. (1981, p. 46)

Mexican immigrant workers to the United States have been at the mercy of fluctuations within the American economy. The demand for Mexican labor has intensified with capitalistic expansion, but during times of economic contraction the demand has decreased. Juan Gómez-Quiñones has classified Mexican immigration into five basic periods: 1848-1910, 1910-1929, 1930-1940, 1941-1965, and 1965 to the present. "These periods are related to labor needs, quantity of immigration, and United States immigration laws" (Gómez-Quiñones 1981, p. 22). During periods of economic depression, harassment of Mexican workers appears to have been especially intense. Persecution was especially severe in the periods, 1920-1921, 1932-1933, 1953-1954, and 1974-1980 (ibid.).

Mexican immigration continued at a high level between 1920 and 1929, but in the early 1930s the numbers declined dramatically, as can be seen in Table 1.

TABLE 1

Number of Documented Mexican Immigrants to the U.S.A. per Year, 1920-1931

1920	51,042	1926	42,638
1921	29,603	1927	66,766
1922	18,246	1928	57,765
1923	62,709	1929	38,980
1924	87,648	1930	11,915
1925	32,378	1931	2,627

Source: Samora 1975, p. 68

The Great Depression brought nativist feelings to a feverous pitch. Not surprisingly, the Mexican worker was the first to be fired or laid off, and many reluctantly turned to public relief. Pressure mounted to limit immigration and to deport illegal entrants.

The push for exclusion was grounded on three basic rationales (Kiser and Silverman 1979, p. 48). The first blamed unemployment on Mexican workers. A letter dated March 4, 1930, to the commissioner-general of immigration asked:

> Can we not send back the thousands of Mexicans and give the American working men a chance to make an honest living? It would stop a great deal of want. . . . Many families are hungry because they cannot get work. (Ibid.)

The second rationale was more overtly racist and expressed alarm at the invasion of Mexicans, which would inevitably lead to a decline in the moral fiber of American society. The final rationale warned of possible rebellion by American workers if the influx of Mexican workers was not halted (ibid., p. 49).

LA MIGRA: THE BORDER PATROL

In 1924 restrictionist pressure led the United States Congress to appropriate $1 million for the creation of the Border Patrol. The force was initially handicapped by not having uniforms, by an absence of qualified personnel, and by a very high rate of turnover (Hoffman 1974, p. 31). By

1930, it had almost doubled its personnel and appropriations, and had become a much more efficient operation. Although the extent to which the Border Patrol actually deterred illegal entrants is questionable, in the seven years after its creation it could boast of having captured more than one hundred thousand illegal aliens and more than twenty-six hundred smugglers of aliens (ibid.).

Like the fate of undocumented workers, the Border Patrol has been influenced tremendously by fluctuations in the economy. Interestingly, the agency was ostensibly created not so much for the purpose of apprehending Mexicans but rather to arrest Europeans and Asians who were entering illegally through Mexico (García 1980, p. 107). In 1904, Sam Webb, a customs officer in Nogales, Arizona, recommended having a rider to search for smugglers of aliens. The smugglers were Americans and the aliens were Chinese (Myers 1971, p. 18). President Theodore Roosevelt liked Webb's idea and named Jeff Milton Chinese Inspector (ibid., p. 17).

Initially housed within the Department of Labor, throughout the 1920s Border Patrol activities were concentrated on controlling the smuggling of contraband items (ibid.). Most of its officers were ignorant of immigration law and saw themselves more as law enforcement officers than immigration officers.

During the 1930s, as a massive program of deportation and so-called voluntary repatriation was carried out by local governmental and law enforcement agencies, the flow of illegal entrants decreased dramatically. Questions were raised at this time concerning the very need for a border patrol. Secretary of Labor Francis Perkins considered placing the agency under the Treasury Department, but it remained within the Department of Labor (ibid.). Although the force was reduced in 1933, it was increased in 1935 and Border Patrol agents started to be trained as immigration officers (ibid.).

Although the Border Patrol was not established until 1924, it had been preceded by several other patrol units. The Army Air Service Armed Patrol was in existence along the United States-Mexico border from 1919 to 1921. The unit was established on June 19, 1919, as personnel from the 20th Aero Squadron stationed at Ellington Field, Texas, were assigned to Fort Bliss at El Paso, Texas. According to Stacy C. Hinkle, an original member, this was the inception of the Border Air Patrol, organized to protect the entire border against raids of Pancho Villa and Mexican bandits (Hinkle 1970, p. 6). Villa had made several incursions into the United

States, the largest of which was an attack on Columbus, New Mexico, on March 9, 1916, which resulted in the death of seven United States cavalrymen and eight civilians, as well as the wounding of five cavalrymen and two civilians. Villa, on the other hand, had one hundred ninety men killed or wounded (ibid., p. 4). Raids of Mexican bandits across the border were common occurrences between 1915 and 1918. On June 14-15, 1919, Villa attacked the border city of Ciudad Juárez for the third time and U.S. troops at Fort Bliss crossed the Rio Grande to aid Mexican federal troops. Villa's army was defeated and dispersed; over two hundred of his men were killed.

The Border Air Patrol included twenty-nine flying officers, seventy-one enlisted men, and a medical unit with one officer and four enlisted men. The first task of the flying officers was to ascertain where Villa and his men had gone following their defeat at Juárez on June 15 (ibid., p. 11). They were to search for bands of men and report their whereabouts to the nearest cavalry outpost. Although they were officially instructed not to fly across the border, it was not uncommon for them to enter Mexican territory (ibid.). Lieutenant Hinkle noted:

> These patrols were effective in stopping the raids from across the border. The raiders, with their stolen horses and cattle, were sure we could always see them from the air. . . .
>
> The ranchers in the Big Bend and Upper Big Bend country where so much of the raiding, stealing and murdering had gone on for so many years, were most grateful that our patrols ended such raids. They referred to us as the "River Pilots." (Ibid., p. 12)

On August 10, 1919, Lieutenants Peterson and Davis disappeared, apparently captured by a Mexican "bandit" named Jesús Renteria.[19] He demanded $15,000 ransom but received only half this sum. After the release of the two pilots, three hundred 8th Cavalry troopers crossed into Mexico. Lieutenant Cooper, using a Lewis machine gun, killed Renteria from the air (ibid., p. 251). Four other outlaws were captured and killed by their civilian scouts, five others were captured and taken prisoner to Ruidoso, Texas, and eight others were captured by the Mexican cavalry, court-martialed, and shot to death (ibid.).

The Border Air Patrol was the immediate precursor of the Border Patrol, but it too had had predecessors. As early as 1904, a small band of men known as "mounted inspectors" (later called "mounted watchmen" or "mounted guards") were given the nearly impossible assignment of guarding the 2,000-mile border, a task described as "akin to sweeping back a flood with a broom" (Rak 1938, p. 2).[20] This token force of mounted guards, appointed by the commissioner-general of immigration, proved woefully inadequate in patrolling the border (U.S. Department of Justice 1978). Despite the existence of the mounted inspectors, Mexican residents generally went freely back and forth across the border.

Because of the absence of adequate patrolling, local residents often resorted to vigilante tactics in attempting to control the flow of illegal entrants. In Fort Hancock, Texas, for example, American farmers had complained of depredations allegedly committed by Mexicans who crossed the river at night. The local sheriff was to have sought the aid of a retired Texas Ranger who would be given a "free hand" in dealing with the Mexicans (Rak 1938, p. 2). The old Ranger and a local cowboy who served as his lieutenant were outnumbered but determined to outwit the enemy, nonetheless. To this end, the Ranger reportedly acquired a long length of very heavy log chain with a series of smaller, lighter chains. As half-drunken Mexicans stepped from the local saloon, "One by one the prisoners' necks were clasped by a padlocked chain until the whole length of log chain was alive with angry, bewildered and frightened men" (ibid., p. 3). The message was sent to local communities in Mexico that the men would be kept in chains until all properties stolen from Americans were returned. Within twenty-four hours, the hostages were released and the jubilant American farmers went to the river to pick up their property (ibid., p. 4), once again confirming the old adage, "one riot, one Ranger."

The parallels between the Border Patrol, especially in its early years, and the Texas Rangers are inescapable. Both were created to protect American capitalists and their property from the so-called depredations carried out by Mexicans. The Border Patrol was in a sense the national—or more accurately, international—equivalent of the Texas Rangers. Not surprisingly, the Border Patrol recruited heavily among Texas Rangers. Jeff Milton, for example, resigned from the Rangers in 1883 to become a U.S. Immigration Border Guard, which preceded the Immigration Riders (Perkins 1978, p. xii). Milton served in Ranger Captain Charles L. Nevill's famous Frontier Batallion Company. Miles Scannel, assistant chief of the U.S. Border Patrol in 1924 at the Marfa subdistrict, was an ex-Texas Ranger and Cavalry Scout. He was killed by Mexican bandits in 1929 (ibid., p. 97). Clifford Alan Perkins, who served in the Border Patrol from 1910 to 1954, indicated that he went over the patrol rosters in San

Antonio and selected twenty inspectors who were ex-Rangers and who had not been seen in Duvall County for several years, for the purpose of effecting a raid on Laredo and arresting every illegal alien and Mexican prostitute in sight (ibid., p. 113).

An additional parallel is that, like the Texas Rangers, most of the information about the Border Patrol has been written either by ex-Border Patrolmen or sympathizers of the force (for example, Hinkle 1970; Rak 1938; Perkins 1978; and Myers 1971). Such works seek not so much to understand, as to romanticize and idolize the Border Patrol. In the Preface to *Illegal Mexican Aliens in the United States,* for example, Johnson and Ogle (1978) openly express their support and admiration of the Border Patrol vis-à-vis Mexican aliens:

> Journalistic accounts frequently stress the plight of Mexico's alienated poor. They devote less attention to the human rights of Americans whose lives are affected, often adversely, by illegal immigration. And very little attention has been given to the emotional and physical toll which the enforcement of immigration law has had on INS and Border Patrol officers.

The Texas border was, thus, heavily patrolled at this time. United States army units were concerned with a possible invasion by Mexican troops, whereas the Texas Rangers sought to apprehend violators of state statutes and bandits operating on both sides of the border. The Arizona Territorial Rangers were similarly organized (Myers 1971, p. 15). The Border Patrol, on the other hand, was specifically charged with the enforcement of federal laws. This neat division of labor was not always observed, however (Perkins 1978, p. 102).

In the early years, it was difficult to control patrolmen who emulated the tactics of the Rangers. The chief patrol inspector in San Antonio, Clifford Alan Perkins, in 1926 lamented:

> Many early Patrolmen were acquainted with the Texas Rangers and their activities and started to emulate them despite the fact that the Patrol was dealing with the general public, not criminals. . . . It took considerable indoctrinating to convince some of the inspectors they were not chasing outlaws, and we never did get it out of the heads of all of them, for we had to discharge several for being too rough. A good percentage had not been well trained, so that once in a while conditions arose that became serious before either the sector or district offices were aware of what was going on. (Ibid.)

Violence was common along the border. Perkins recalls that between 1924 and 1926, twenty-four smugglers and two officers were killed in gunfights along the river (ibid., p. 97). "Some of the first Patrolmen were a little too quick with a gun, or given to drinking too much, too often, and had to be let out, but in the main, we managed to pull the recruits into line, and several made outstanding officers" (ibid., p. 95).

Among such outstanding officers was one Pete Torres from New Mexico, who was said to have spoken English with an "accent" and fluent border Spanish. According to Perkins:

> He was an extremely valuable man on the river, for he thought like a Mexican and looked like one. He could meander through the Mexican sections without arousing suspicion, especially at night, and he had no nerves at all. He may have been a little quick on the trigger, but his actions in every shooting match during which smugglers were killed always proved justified by the circumstances. The men had to be good shots, for if they were not, they did not last long. (Ibid., p. 96)

During the 1930s and 1940s, the Border Patrol continued to be plagued by internal problems such as inadequate funding, poor organization, ineffective leadership, and low morale.[21] In 1940 the Immigration and Naturalization Service (INS) was shifted from the Department of Labor to the Justice Department, but this did little to alleviate these problems. Enforcement of immigration laws appeared haphazard and the Border Patrol was criticized both by those who called for stronger enforcement of immigration laws and proponents of an open border. As Juan García observed:

> In retrospect, it appears that the Border Patrol was caught up in a vicious circle. Its critics, both in and out of Congress, accused the Border Patrol of gross inefficiency and pointed to the growing number of "illegal" entrants to support their arguments. Yet part of the reason for its failure to stem the influx lay with its outdated equipment and its lack of personnel. However, until it could prove that it could do the job, Congress was not prepared to increase its appropriations enough to purchase the equipment and hire the extra personnel necessary to control the border. (García 1980, p. 110)

Rather than enforcing the law in a systematic and unbiased manner, the Border Patrol typically functioned as an instrument of the dominant economic interests. When there was a high demand for cheap Mexican labor, the agency decreased its apprehension activities:

> From time to time Border Patrol officials and line officers testified publicly that they had been ordered to hold back until after the harvest season was over. In testimony before the President's Commission on Migratory Labor, three officials from the INS in Arizona testified that a powerful group of agribusiness interests had compelled the suspension of law-enforcement activities against undocumented workers. Carson Morrow, Arizona Chief Border Patrol Inspector at Tucson, stated that he had received orders from the District Director at El Paso, Texas, to stop the deportation of undocumented workers. According to Morrow these orders had been issued during each harvest season. O.W. Manney, Phoenix Chief of the Immigration Service, told the commission that the legal and illegal contracting of Mexican workers because of domestic labor shortages had been abused to the extent that there always seemed to be "a year around emergency." (Ibid., p. 111)

In the fall of 1925, the Immigration Bureau staged a series of raids in the Imperial Valley. These raids severely restricted the supply of Mexican workers and raised wages for agricultural workers in the region (Reisler 1976, p. 61). Incensed growers protested vociferously to the Department of Labor and established the Associated Labor Bureau to represent them (ibid.). I. F. Wixon, Labor Department representative, worked out a "gentlemen's agreement" aimed at protecting the growers' labor supply. Each undocumented worker in the Imperial Valley was to register with the Associated Labor Bureau:

> Upon registering, a worker would be given an identification card, which would protect him from deportation. In return he agreed to pay $18.00 to cover the cost of the head tax and visa fee in weekly $3.00 installments. Once $18.00 had accrued, the Mexican worker would be taken to a nearby border immigration station, and his entry into the United States would be officially legalized. The Immigration Bureau's chief supervisor informed growers that this arrangement should "permit all Mexicans now in the country to remain here." (Ibid.)

In subsequent years the Border Patrol increased in size and grew increasingly more efficient and sophisticated. In 1984, 1,246,981 aliens were apprehended (U.S. Department of Justice 1984, p. 188). Today, some twenty separate sectors are under the direction of chief patrol agents, who serve under the supervision of a regional commissioner and his staff (U.S. Department of Justice 1982, p. 12).

Despite its increased size and sophistication and the push for professionalism within the force, the INS and the Border Patrol remain closely tied to agricultural interests. For most Mexicans in the United States, moreover, the Border Patrol (*la Migra*), like the Texas Rangers, remains a symbol of American domination and exploitation. This attitude has been documented in song, as in the *corrido* of "El Deportado" ("the deportee"):

Los gueros son muy maloras,	The blonds are very bad fellows,
los gueros son muy maloras,	The blonds are very bad fellows,
se valen de la ocasión,	They take advantage,
y a todos los mexicanos,	And to all the Mexicans,
y a todos los mexicanos,	And to all the Mexicans,
nos tratan sin compasión.	They treat us without pity.
Hoy traen la gran polvadera	Today they bring about a great disturbance
y sin consideración,	And without consideration,
mujeres, niños y ancianos,	Women, children and old people,
mujeres, niños y ancianos,	Women, children and old people,
nos llevan a la frontera	They take us to the border,
nos echan de esta nación.	They eject us from this country.
Adiós paisanos queridos,	Good-bye, dear countrymen,
adiós paisanos queridos,	Good-bye, dear countrymen,
ya nos van a deportar;	They are going to deport us:
pero no somos bandidos,	But we are not bandits,
pero no somos bandidos,	But we are not bandits,
venimos a camellar.	We came to toil.
	(Foster 1939, p. 182).

Abuses and mistreatment of undocumented workers have been common, especially during periods of economic recession, when the demand for Mexican workers declines. The Depression in the 1930s, for example, introduced a "reign of terror" among Mexicans living in the United States as a massive program of deportation and repatriation was effected by the INS in cooperation with local welfare and other governmental agencies. Nellie Foster commented on the prevailing atmosphere:

> The government policy of deporting undesirable aliens and those "likely to become a public charge" which has been in effect in recent years and which is still being followed, brought terror to the hearts of Mexicans in the United States, and especially in Southern Califor-

nia. In Los Angeles and other parts of the southern section of the state, where the Mexican population is said to be the next greatest to that of Mexico City, the deportations began with raids on the unemployed or those found on the streets and in other public places who were unable to present evidence of citizenship or of legal entry. Since few people carry with them their valuable documents, and also since strict enforcement of the immigration laws did not begin until recently [1939], it was but natural that many Mexicans were unable to comply with the demands of the immigration officers. The terror, bewilderment, and anguish caused by the methods of officials in deporting laborers, and later in the deportation of families under the complaint that they were public charges, is vividly described in a report by Mrs. Daisy Lee Worcester concerning deportation in San Diego. (Ibid., pp. 47-48)

In retrospect it is clear that the establishment of the Border Patrol in 1924 dramatically altered the status of undocumented workers in the United States. Previously, Mexican workers crossed the border openly and were free to select the most desirable occupation available. Inasmuch as only a judge could order a deportation, aliens felt relatively safe as long as they did not run afoul of the law (Bustamante 1972, p. 269-71). Significantly, information on the number of aliens apprehended by the INS was first recorded in 1925 (U.S. Department of Justice 1984, p. 188). With the establishment of the Border Patrol, Mexican workers were placed at a disadvantage not only relative to the legal and judicial system but relative to their employer. Employers were given tremendous leverage. Because it was illegal to be an undocumented worker but not illegal to hire one, employers held the threat of detention and deportation over the head of their workers. It was not uncommon for them to turn illegal aliens over to the INS without paying them (Bustamente 1972, p. 271). Jorge Bustamante has summarized the plight of undocumented workers:

After the establishment of the Border Patrol a new factor came into being, namely the factor of being apprehended and thus returned to Mexico. Thus, the threat of being turned in presented a new dimension to the disadvantage of the Mexican worker. Since anyone can turn in an "illegal," such a threat began to narrow down the social contacts which the Mexican worker might establish, with the exception that he must always have some relationship to the employer. The implicit or explicit threat of being turned in even by the employer, brings a new element into the situation with regard to wages and working conditions. In a real sense the Mexican worker is at the mercy of the employer, the alternatives of accepting or not accepting a job are not necessarily open to the Mexican worker because an employer can in fact insist that the wages and working conditions be accepted by the worker or face the possibility of being turned in to the Border Patrol. (Ibid.)

OPERATION DEPORTATION: "WETBACKS GO HOME"

Fluctuations in the American economy have had a direct and consistent effect on Mexican immigration. Mexican immigration increased steadily between the turn of the century and the mid 1920s. In 1924, for example, 87,648 Mexican workers entered the United States legally, but by 1931 the number had declined to a mere 2,627 (see Table 1 above). During the Depression, Mexican workers became a convenient scapegoat and were seen not only as causing unemployment and depressing wages among American workers, but as a drain on welfare rolls. Thousands of Mexicans were excluded through Operation Deportation, a program of deportation and repatriation initiated in 1930 by the INS in cooperation with local authorities:

> Although no statistics were kept for this operation, the general procedure was to require all those suspected of being alien, to prove that they were born in the United States. The person who could not satisfy this requirement was expelled from the country under the administrative procedure of "voluntary departure." (Bustamante 1981, p. 43)

While repatriation was ostensibly a "voluntary" program, the line between deportation and repatriation was very thin, and at times nonexistent. Coercion and intimidation were, thus, integral to the program. Many Mexican workers were termed indigent and a public charge by local welfare officials and coerced into returning to Mexico. If they did not return voluntarily, they were told, it would seriously jeopardize any opporunity of returning to the United States at some future date when economic conditions improved.

William N. Doak took office as secretary of labor on December 9, 1930, with the promise that work would be provided for unemployed Americans by deportation of employed illegal aliens (Hoffman 1974, p.

39). In carrying out raids by the Labor Department's Bureau of Immigration, the new labor secretary succeeded in sensationalizing what had previously been a routine bureaucratic procedure (ibid.). "Doak's immigration agents carried out the order to intensify their hunt for deportable aliens with dedicated zeal. They raided private homes and public places in a search that extended from New York City to Los Angeles" (ibid.).

That unemployment was blamed on Mexican workers was an ironic twist, for unemployment had been a serious problem in the Mexican community long before the Great Depression. The 1921-1922 depression had set a precedent: Mexicans were blamed for unemployment and thousands were forced to return to Mexico (Kiser and Kiser 1979, p. 33). In fact, thousands of Mexican workers had been stranded throughout the United States without a job or enough money to go back to Mexico. Yet in 1928 representatives of the Mexican community in the United States looked to Herbert Hoover with the hope and anticipation that the new administration might solve the problem of chronic unemployment among Mexican workers (Reisler 1976, p. 227). A Mexican newspaper in Chicago stated:

> There is a multitude of men whose sole occupation is to walk the streets from day to day waiting for the uncertain time when someone might give them a nickel with which to buy a cup of coffee.
>
> If Hoover has the power to eliminate this suffering, his accession to the Presidency will be a blessing for our countrymen who have come here to barter their labor for an honest living. (Ibid.)

The glut of labor was such that in California in 1933 it was estimated that there were 2.36 workers for every agricultural job (Reisler 1973, p. 376). Many Mexican workers lost their jobs to unemployed white workers, and a number of states and municipalities enacted legislation requiring that all persons employed in public works projects be citizens (Reisler 1976, p. 228). Not only were many Mexican workers unemployed but those who worked saw their wages reach incredibly low levels. A 1935 study of 775 migrant families in California reported an average yearly income of $289 (ibid., pp. 228-29). In addition, Mexican nationals and some American citizens of Mexican descent were denied assistance because of a "citizen only" policy (Balderrama 1978, p. 1).

The attack on immigrant labor was supposedly aimed at all foreigners, but in reality it was the Mexican who bore the brunt of this assault. The mass exodus was especially intensive in southern California. Special trains were set up in Los Angeles to transport over eighty-thousand Mexicans, their families, and essential belongings across the border. A significant number of them were children who were citizens of the United States. So successful was the program that it is estimated that approximately five-hundred-thousand persons were repatriated or deported (Kiser and Kiser 1979, p. 33). The mass Mexican migration between 1910 and 1925 was, thus, effectively reversed and the number of Mexicans living in the United States declined dramatically.

The efficacy of Operation Deportation was predicated on the massive violation of civil guarantees. Legal deportation was difficult and cumbersome, in that it required a formal hearing and proof that the person entered illegally (Reisler 1973, p. 380). In addition, as Commissioner-General Harry Hull noted, the Immigration Bureau was prevented from effecting mass deportations of Mexicans on relief:

> They had "fallen into distress through inability to obtain employment" arising from depression conditions. The law mandated expulsion of only those individuals who had become public charges within five years of their arrival from causes "not affirmatively shown to have arisen subsequent to entry." (Ibid., p. 381)

Although only a limited number were formally deported, informal channels proved extremely effective in pressuring Mexicans to return. Many were induced into voluntary repatriation by the granting of temporary relief by welfare agencies or the offer of free transportation to Mexico (ibid., p. 383); others were coerced by the threat of possible deportation. In addition, pressure from local public officials and the press for the government to intensify its deportation program was said to have literally "scared" thousands of Mexicans out of the southern California region (ibid., p. 381).

Operation Deportation led not only to the exclusion of many United States citizens but to the separation of families. A leading newspaper in Mexico, *El Excélsior*, protested this practice:

> Another exceedingly serious aspect of the mass deportation of Mexicans is the lack of consideration shown for marriage contracts. Upon being deported to Mexico, Mexicans are separated from their wives, if the latter are Americans.
>
> Notwithstanding the protests and even entreaties of the unfortunate Mexican husbands, or wives, if the husband is an American, the authorities in question show no consideration and separate husbands and wives under the pretext, it itself, an insult, that Mexicans live in a manner irreconcilable with Yankee customs. Neither

labor nor marriage contracts are respected, Mexicans being separated from their wives as if they were animals. (Kiser and Kiser 1979, p. 37)

The situation grew so serious that the Mexican government encouraged its citizens to repatriate and welcomed them back home. The *repatriados* were allowed to bring back their material goods without having to pay duty, including machinery, large appliances, and animals (Hoffman 1974, p. 136). The government also waived fees normally charged by Mexican consuls and provided free transportation from the border to the interior of Mexico (ibid.). As an additional inducement, Mexico set up colonization projects. The intent was to utilize the skills acquired in the United States by setting up colonies of *repatriados* in remote parts of Mexico and providing land at a low cost (ibid., pp. 138-42). Despite the lofty goals of the colonization project, the colonies were short-lived. In retrospect it is clear that "most repatriates had returned not with the intention of participating in colonization projects or land purchases, but because Mexico seemed preferable to the United States in a period of depression" (ibid., p. 135).

Mexican consuls encouraged repatriation and offered to help *repatriados*. Enrique Balderrama notes that the Mexican population in the United States maintained strong ties with the *madre patria* (homeland) and turned to local consulates for help. The *consulados*, in turn, responded with a massive campaign in their defense (Balderrama 1978, p. 1). The problem was especially acute in colder climates, in the East and Midwest. In Detroit, Mexican Consul Ignacio L. Batiza advised Mexicans to return to their homeland:

> As winter approaches, life in this region becomes more and more difficult for persons without work. All of the circumstances which produce the crisis still prevail without hope of amelioration in the near future; for which reason this Consulate reiterates its call to our Mexican residents that for their own interest they accept this opportunity which is offered by the Government of Mexico for their repatriation and return to their country. The Mexican Government, within its power, is disposed to aid these repatriates that they may later make themselves important factors in our national economic structure. (Kiser and Kiser 1979, pp. 44-45)

By 1937 repatriation had declined to the point where it was no longer considered a mass movement and public interest in the topic decreased. Yet Mexican President Lázaro Cárdenas continued to pursue the idea of a rigorous repatriation program (Hoffman 1974, p. 151). Cárdenas advocated agricultural reform, expropriation of foreign investments in Mexico, and repatriation of Mexican nationals (ibid., pp. 152-53). In the spring of 1939 the Mexican government announced the establishment of a colony near Matamoros, Tamaulipas. The colony was named "18 de Marzo," the date of the expropriation decree issued the previous year (ibid., p. 154). On April 5 Minister of Foreign Affairs Ramón Beteta set out on a whirlwind tour across the barrios of the United States from Texas to California. He informed Mexican nationals and Chicanos of the new colony and of available land for colonization and cultivation in the states of Sinaloa and Baja California (ibid., p. 155). Beteta was so effusive that the offer to settle in Mexico was even extended to Anglo-Americans (ibid.). The foreign minister's efforts were widely acclaimed by journalists in Mexico City, but the success of Mexican repatriation efforts was grossly exaggerated (ibid., p. 156).

THE BRACERO PROGRAM:　"WELCOME BACK, *AMIGOS*"

Despite the push to expel Mexicans during the Great Depression, throughout the 1930s powerful interests strongly opposed Operation Deportation. The most prominent opponents were large growers and ranchers who coveted cheap Mexican labor (Kiser and Silverman 1979, p. 63). They argued that a reduction in Mexican labor would have very negative consequences (ibid., p. 51). These powerful interest groups prevailed in the 1940s. Economic recovery and World War II created a labor shortage and increased the demand for cheap, temporary labor once again. The mass exodus of Mexican workers out of the U.S. was reversed.

Operation Deportation gave way to the Bracero Program and the "Good Neighbor Policy of Uncle Sam," which welcomed back its *amigos* to the south with open arms. The Bracero Program of 1942, however, was not the first contract labor program in the United States.[22] The first such program was implemented during World War I, as temporary Mexican labor was informally exempted from the Immigration Act of 1917. An order issued by the secretary of labor permitted temporary Mexican workers to enter the United States without having to abide by the head tax, contract labor, or literacy provisions of the Act (Kiser and Kiser 1979, p. 10).

Although both programs resulted from intense pressure from agriculture to permit temporary Mexican workers, they differed in important respects. First, the 1917 accord grew out of de facto policies, whereas the agreement reached on August 2, 1942, was formally enacted. Secondly, the first program was established unilaterally; the second was a binational accord. Thirdly, the Bracero Program set up general guidelines and included safeguards for the protection of Mexican labor. There were four general principles underlying the program:

1. It is understood that Mexicans contracting to work in the United States shall not be engaged in any military service.
2. Mexicans entering the United States as a result of this understanding shall not suffer discriminatory acts of any kind in accordance with the Executive Order No. 8802 issued at the White House June 25, 1941.
3. Mexicans entering the United States under this understanding shall enjoy the guarantees of transportation, living expenses and repatriation established in Article 29 of the Mexican Labor Law.
4. Mexicans entering the United States under this understanding shall not be employed to displace other workers, or for the purpose of reducing rates of pay previously established. (Statutes at Large 1942, p. 1766)

Contracts would be made between the employer and worker and would be written in Spanish. Other benefits included in contracts were provisions for adequate housing, a minimum number of work days, and payment of minimum wages or the prevailing wage in cases where it was higher.

The Mexican government entered the agreement in good faith and was genuinely concerned with the welfare of its workers. Unfortunately, the basic provisions of the agreement were often not honored. The "prevailing wage" was typically established arbitrarily by the employer and was almost always lower than the wage for domestic workers (Craig 1971, p. 68). In California the Standard Work Contract established a minimum wage of $2 per day, but growers could easily avoid paying the wage. If a bracero was charged $1.75 for board and 9¢ for insurance, for example, he would be left with a net pay of 16¢ per day (Anderson 1961, p. 133). In addition to payroll deductions, growers avoided payment of the minimum wage by use of the piece-rate system, which they defended as the backbone of the wage structure in agriculture (ibid., p. 135). The system was defended because it was said to encourage greater efficiency among workers and stabilized labor costs for growers. In fact, labor contractors often served as middlemen who contracted directly with the employer and subcontracted the work to farm laborers (ibid.). Although the system had many advantages for growers, it resulted in a form of peonage or debt servitude:

> We had a very bad contract. I would only make 10 to 12 dollars a week. Only one day out of the six weeks did I work by the hour. Then I got 90 cents an hour. The rest of the time we picked berries by contract. We got 40 cents for each crate. It took us almost an hour to pick a crate because the crop was very poor and the good berries were scarce. One of the crews of 30 to 40 men went on strike, their pay was so low. All the big chiefs of the association came out to talk to them. They said that the wages we were receiving were the same as the locals. (Ibid., p. 137)

Organized labor, on the other hand, has traditionally opposed the piece rate as it has been implemented in agriculture. The rate of pay was set arbitrarily by agriculture and manipulated so as to maximize profits. Often the rate was designed to prevent even the best workers from earning the prevailing wage. A seasoned sugar beet worker in San Joaquin County, California, commented in 1959 on the unilateral imposition of the piece rate:

> Last week, when the beet thinning started, my crew started out at 90 cents an hour. We were all experienced workers, and we were earning our 90 cents. But I guess the growers didn't want to pay that much. One morning, after we had been picked up by the truck and had gotten out to the field, they told us we were being changed to a piece rate. We would get a certain amount for thinning a half-mile row. So we tried it out. We found that the most we could make under the piece rate was 65 cents an hour. It was the same field we had been in before. It was the same crew. We were all experienced. We were doing our best. But we couldn't possibly make anywhere near 90 cents an hour.... I don't know who decided to change to piece rates; I know we never found out about it until we got out to the field that morning, and they told us to take it or leave it. (Ibid., p. 135)

Although many of the basic provisions of the Bracero Program were not observed, the Mexican government attempted to use the program as a lever for reducing discrimination against Mexican workers (Kirstein 1973, p. 70). Discrimination was so blatant in Texas that Mexican secretary of labor, Roberto Medellín, proclaimed that no contract labor would be sent until positive action was taken to end abuses against Mexicans. Not only

Mexican nationals, but Chicanos in uniform and visiting Mexican dignitaries had been subjected to discriminatory treatment (Scruggs 1979, p. 88). Governor Coke Stevenson urged the legislature to pass the "Caucasian Peace" resolution, approved by him on May 6, 1943, affirming "the right of all Caucasians within the state to equal treatment in public places of business and amusement, and denounced those who denied such privileges with 'violating the good neighbor policy of our state'" (ibid.).

The war helped to dramatize the contradictions experienced by Mexicans in the United States. At the same time that Chicanos supported the war effort, as many were drafted or volunteered to fight overseas and Mexico had recently declared war on the Axis powers, discrimination against Mexicans had grown more extreme. Aware of the impact that adverse publicity would have on its Good Neighbor Policy, the Office of the Coordinator of Inter-American Affairs (OCIAA) drafted an educational program to study the problems experienced by the Spanish-speaking in the Southwestern states (ibid.). The State Department also pressured for elimination of the ban. Governor Stevenson embarked on a "good will" tour of Mexico and promised to work to end discrimination against Mexicans. Despite these efforts, the blacklist of Texas was not lifted until after 1947 (ibid., p. 95).

Although the Bracero Program, officially termed the Emergency Labor Program, went into effect in 1942, congressional approval for it did not come until 1943 with passage of Public Law 45. Public Law 45 expired on December 31, 1947, ending the Bracero Program of World War II (Craig 1971, p. 53). Temporary Mexican labor continued to be recruited, however, by passage of a series of postwar accords. Although similar to the wartime agreement, they also differed in several respects. The responsibility for recruiting labor was shifted from the government to individual growers (ibid.). Before growers were permitted to recruit, they had to obtain certification from the Department of Labor indicating that there was a shortage of labor; previously certification had come from the Department of Agriculture (ibid., pp. 53-54). The cost of transporting a worker was to be absorbed by the employer, rather than the government:

> Work contracts between bracero and employer also differed substantially from their wartime predecessors. In this respect, the following 1948 contract stipulations are notable. First, a minimum hourly wage for braceros was not specified, as it had been under the wartime accord. Second, there was no minimum piece-rate guarantee, which

had existed previously. Third, no formal compliance mechanism was established, although the United States Employment Service was granted undefined power in this area. Fourth, an employer bond was required prior to contract in order to guarantee the bracero's cost-free return to Mexico. No such bond had been required previously. Fifth, the former unemployment payment of three dollars per day was not included. Instead, a stipulation on prospective earnings was utilized. Finally, employers utilizing wetbacks were declared ineligible for bracero contracting. (Ibid., p. 54)

In 1951 Congress amended the Agricultural Act of 1949, by inserting title V, which was to regulate the admission of braceros. The amendment, known as Public Law 78, empowered the secretary of labor:

> To recruit Mexican farm workers, bring them to reception centers near the border, assist them in negotiating contracts, and guarantee that the contracts would be carried out by the employers. Wetbacks who had been in the United States five years or longer might also be placed under contract. Again, however, there were to be a number of restrictions and safeguards. The workers could not be imported until the Secretary of Labor had certified that there was a need for them. The government was to be reimbursed for transportation costs and legal losses, and, in accordance with the executive agreement of 1951 and its later extensions, employers must pay the prevailing wage, guarantee work for 75 percent of the contract period, provide compensation for occupational injuries and diseases, and furnish adequate housing, sanitary, and transportation facilities. (Ibid., p. 100)

The new law was strongly criticized by organized labor, Chicano activists, and others who sought to provide a minimum wage and greater safeguards for temporary workers. Despite these criticisms the measure remained in effect for fourteen years. In 1964 public pressure brought the program to an end, some twenty-three years after the first braceros had entered the United States. Yet the bracero proved to be a valuable asset to American capitalism. Between 1942 and 1950 alone, more than 430,000 contract laborers were provided by principal recruiting centers in Hermosillo, Chihuahua, and Aguascalientes (Galarza 1964, p. 52). From the figures below it is clear that the year in which most braceros entered was not during the war but 1949:

1942	4,203
1943	53,098
1944	62,170
1945	49,494
1946	32,043
1947	19,632
1948	35,345
1949	107,000
1950	67,500

(Ibid., p. 53)

The Bracero Program was ostensibly designed as a measure that would provide temporary labor and stem the flow of illegal entrants, but the presence of braceros did not appear to deter illegal immigration. From 1951 to 1964, more that four million braceros entered the United States, as compared to only 430,000 between 1942 and 1950 (Allsup 1982, 113). In the 1950s, approximately three million braceros and 273,000 permanent residents entered the United States. During the same decade, more than three million undocumented workers were captured by the Immigration Bureau (Samora 1975, 71).

OPERATION WETBACK: MASS DEPORTATION DURING THE 1950S

The 1950s are often perceived as an era free of political turmoil and strife, but for Mexicans living in the United States it proved to be a very difficult period. The Korean War created a demand for temporary Mexican labor once again. With the end of the war in 1952 and the recession of 1953-1955, however, antiforeign sentiment increased dramatically and pressure mounted to exclude Mexican workers. It was a time of intense and brutal political repression. During the McCarthy era, political dissent was not tolerated. Anticommunist and antiforeign sentiment were, thus, closely intertwined. Not surprisingly, the Mexican was a visible symbol of the foreign element in American society. Many Chicano political activists were blacklisted for being subversive or un-American; others were denaturalized and deported (Acuña 1981, p. 158).

Attorney General Herbert Brownell played a critical role in the process. Shortly after his confirmation in 1953, Brownell indicated that he favored other alternatives to increased appropriations for the Border Patrol.

Four months later, however, as public concern over the "wetback" problem mounted, the attorney general took a tour of the border and spoke with Border Patrol officials and more than one hundred persons who were affected in some way by illegal immigrants (García 1980, pp. 157-58). Representatives of the Border Patrol actually took him to a section of the border where he could personally witness large numbers of illegals coming on foot. When Brownell returned to Washington, he reversed his position and called for increased appropriations for the Border Patrol.

During the tour of the border region, Brownell met Lieutenant General Joseph M. Swing, who commanded the Sixth Army and was termed a "professional, long-time Mexican hater" by the Los Angeles Committee for Protection of the Foreign Born (Morgan 1954, p. 3). In 1953, shortly after Swing's retirement from the army, Brownell selected him to be commissioner of the INS. Swing had been at West Point with President Eisenhower and had participated in the punitive expedition against Pancho Villa in 1916. When Eisenhower responded to the public outcry in 1954 by asking Brownell to devise a way to get rid of the wetbacks, Swing was put in charge of Operation Wetback. Swing was proud of the deportation program, which he described as "pursued with military efficiency and the result was that over a million wetbacks were expelled from the country in 1954" (Bustamante 1981, p. 43).

It is important to note that the military approach to solving the problem of undocumented workers had been pursued by Brownell long before the implementation of Operation Wetback. In a plan reminiscent of the Army Air Service Armed Patrol of the United States-Mexico Border, the attorney general had recommended that army troops, with the support of light planes, concentrate on patrolling a 250-mile sector of the Arizona-California border (García 1980, p. 169). The plan was not well received by army officials, however. News of the proposed plan and charges of inhumane treatment of illegals by the Border Patrol generated great concern in Mexico and a strong outcry over the use of the army to patrol the border. The outcry led Franklin C. Gowan, counselor for the American embassy in Mexico to remark:

> The slant of these comments, which are being overheard in typical local cafes, restaurants, and other like places patronized by Mexicans, is that we are an imperialistic, war-mongering and ruthless people and that the poor and wretched wetbacks who want to return to the

lands which the United States forcibly took from Mexico, will be met by a hail of American bullets. (Ibid., p. 170)

A fuller appreciation of the impact of Operation Wetback is gained when one looks at patterns of apprehension and deportation of undocumented workers in historical perspective. In 1920 only 1,268 Mexicans were deported (Galarza 1964, p. 59). The figures below show that the number of deportations of Mexican workers increased in the decade from 1944 to 1954 when they went beyond one million:

1941	6,082
1942	5,100
1943	8,860
1944	29,176
1945	69,111
1946	101,478
1947	199,282
1948	203,945
1949	293,000
1950	480,000
1951	509,040
1952	528,815
1953	885,587
1954	1,108,900

(Galarza 1964, p. 59)

Available figures seriously question the popular assumption that temporary labor stems the tide of undocumented workers, as was previously noted. Julian Samora has observed that "it is rather sobering to consider the enormous traffic in people that these population movements suggest" (Samora 1975, p. 72). Overall, he concluded that up to the mid-1970s, more than one and a half million Mexicans were legal immigrants to the United States, over five million contract laborers entered, and more than seven million were apprehended and returned to Mexico (ibid., pp. 72-73).

With termination of the Bracero Program in 1964, the modern era of relations between Mexico and the United States began. Increased demand for cheap labor and the growing economic dependence of Mexico forced unprecedented numbers to cross the border. Restrictive legislation was passed in 1968 but it was not effective in controlling the problem. The number of undocumented workers apprehended increased from only 43,844 in 1964 (Samora 1975, p. 70) to 870,000 in 1976 (Acuña 1981, p. 170) and more than one million in 1977, the highest total since Operation Wetback in 1954 (Associated Press 1977c, A-3).

One of the most unfortunate dimensions of Operation Wetback was that the prevailing xenophobia served as a smokescreen to hide the wholesale abridgment of civil liberties, not only for undocumented workers but for all persons of Mexican descent living in the United States. Senator Pat McCarran of Nevada, for example, sponsored a bill designed to limit immigration and to rid society of subversives. "To forestall the impending breakdown in American culture, Senator McCarran had been busy since 1947 with hearings and drafting of legislation; his aim: the codification of all the scattered immigration and naturalization acts in the federal statute books" (Lieberman 1968, p. 106). Title I of the McCarran Internal Security Act of 1950 set up a Subversive Activities Control Board, which was to identify and investigate subversive activities. Title II gave authority for establishment of concentration camps where suspected subversives would be kept without a trial or hearing, in the event of a national emergency (Acuña 1981, p. 159). In addition to giving the INS broad powers to interrogate aliens, the Immigration and Nationality Act of 1952 (McCarran-Walter) provided for:

> (1) The codification of previous immigration acts, relating to national origins; (2) the abolishment of racial bars to entry and citizenship; (3) the establishment of a complicated procedure for admitting Asians; (4) the inclusion of a long list of grounds on which aliens could be deported or exluded; (5) the inclusion of conditions whereby naturalized citizens could be denaturalized. (Ibid.)

The 1952 act passed despite President Truman's veto and was severely criticized by the more liberal segments of society. The president's Commission on Immigration and Naturalization, for example, noted that the Immigration and Nationality Act of 1952 "does not adequately solve immigration and naturalization problems, and that the codification it contains fails to embody principles worthy of this country" (President's Commission 1953, p. xi). Specifically, the commission argued that the United States is characterized by cultural diversity and that, if the nation was to grow and prosper, it needs immigrants. The McCarran-Walter Act was based on a negative immigration policy that looked upon aliens with suspicion and negativity (ibid., p. xiv). The law was vague and set up a category of second-class citizens by rescinding retroactively the statute of limitations (ibid., p. 198). Thus, persons could be deported if it was discovered during naturalization proceedings that they had committed a minor offense twenty or forty years after entering the United States. The commission concluded:

> We cannot be true to the democratic faith of our own Declaration of Independence in the equality of all men, and at the same time pass immigration laws which discriminate among people because of national origin, race, color, or creed. We cannot continue to bask in the glory of an ancient and honorable tradition of providing haven to the oppressed, and belie that tradition by ignoble and ungenerous immigration laws. We cannot develop an effective foreign policy if our immigration laws negate our role of world leadership. We cannot defend civil rights in principle, and deny them in our immigration laws and practice. We cannot boast of our magnificent system of law, and enact immigration legislation which violates decent principles of legal protection. (Ibid., pp. xiv-xv)

Unfortunately, views such as this did not prevail. Repressive legislation like the McCarran Internal Security Act of 1950 and the McCarran-Walter Act of 1952 set the stage not only for the blacklisting and deportation of Chicano activists but also for union busting:

> These two laws led to gross violations of human rights. The law intimidated many activists who feared being placed in a concentration camp, being labelled a subversive, or being deported. The Los Angeles Committee for the Protection of the Foreign Born, an affiliate of the American Committee for the Protection of the Foreign Born, was placed on the subversive list by the Subversive Activities Control Board because it challenged the two acts. The committee, as well as many of its members, was cleared after extensive litigation. (Acuña 1981, p. 160)

These acts also "thwarted the development of effective organization both in the barrios and among working-class Chicanos by deporting some of its most effective leaders and intimidating others with the threat of deportation" (ibid.).

UNDOCUMENTED WORKERS AND CRIME

Although undocumented workers have been welcomed by the United States government and agribusiness during periods of economic expansion, during economic downturns much negativity has been directed at the wet-back. Some of the more common charges are:

1. There are many millions of undocumented Mexican aliens.
2. Undocumented workers take jobs away from citizens, particularly minorities. They are in direct competition with poor whites and members of minority groups for jobs.
3. They are a burden on public, social, educational, and medical services—that is, on the United States wage earner and taxpayer.
4. They are responsible for increasing rates of crime; they are a threat to peaceful society and public morality.
5. Undocumented workers undermine existing wage rates and unionization efforts.
6. Undocumented workers and their families are a "threat" to the ecological balance of the United States.
7. Undocumented workers threaten the political and military security of the United States (Gómez-Quiñones 1981, p. 30)

These attitudes have been held and propagated not only by members of the dominant society but by Mexican-Americans as well. In fact, the mobilization of bias has been so intense that Mexican-Americans often internalize and espouse negative attitudes against wetbacks. Because of the prevalence of racism, it is not uncommon for assimilated and upwardly mobile Mexican-Americans to proclaim themselves "100 percent Americans" and dissociate themselves from "Mexicans." The American G.I. Forum of Texas, an organization of Mexican-American War veterans, asked rhetorically in 1954, "What Price Wetbacks?":

> Truly, the American people are entitled to ask: "What price wet-backs?"
>
> What is the price in terms of depressed wages for citizens of the United States who have a right to a wage on which they can live according to American standards of living?
>
> The 25-cent hourly wage of the wetback cannot support American citizens.
>
> What is the price in disease and death?
>
> Disease and death rates in the areas of heaviest wetback concentration are an indication of the stupendous price we pay in that regard.
>
> What is the price in criminal activities?

Crime is a natural result of the presence of thousands of people who already are living beyond the law.

What is the price in danger to our national security?

An open border is a constant invitation to subversives and spies.

What is the price in lost business?

Dollars not paid in wages don't go into trade channels; dollars sent to Mexico don't ring cash registers in the United States.

What is the price in human misery?

(American G.I. Forum of Texas 1954, p. 59)

The report carried out in conjunction with the Texas State Federation of Labor asserted that illegal workers displace American workers and that the answer to the "Wetback Problem" was tougher immigration laws and stronger enforcement.[23] It concluded, "Only then can the American people relax, secure in the knowledge that the threat of the wetback invasion has been halted" (ibid.).

A full discussion of the relative merit of these allegations is beyond the scope of this chapter; suffice it to say that there is overwhelming evidence indicating that undocumented workers contribute far more to the economy and society than they take out (see Villalpando 1977; North and Houstoun 1976; Bustamante 1977 and 1981; Gómez-Quiñones 1981). The focus here is simply on the impact of undocumented workers on crime.

The issue of immigration and crime is not new. It has often been asserted that immigrants, including those from Mexico, are criminally prone, despite the absence of hard data to support this contention. As early as 1882, a congressional act was passed stipulating that upon arrival in the United States, "all foreign convicts except those convicted of political offenses" were to be sent back to their nation of origin (U.S. National Commission on Law Observance and Enforcement 1931, p. 45). Concern with crime and the foreign-born was exacerbated by the commonly held belief that a number of European nations were systematically exporting undesirable elements, including convicts and criminals, to the United States.

In 1911 the Immigration Commission (also know as the Dillingham Commission) issued a massive 42-volume report on the effects of immigration. Volume 36, which the Wickersham Commission was to later term the "Grand Inquest" (U.S. Congress Senate Immigration Commission 1931, p. 52), was devoted entirely to the subject of immigration and crime. The "Abstracts of Reports" of the Immigration Commission concluded:

While control of the immigration movement so far as physical and mental defectives are concerned has reached a high degree of efficiency, no adequate means have been adopted for preventing the immigration of criminals, prostitutes, and other morally undesirable aliens. The control of the latter classes is a much more difficult matter. In spite of the stringent law, criminals or moral defectives of any class, provided they pass the medical inspection, can usually embark at European ports and enter the United States without much danger of detection. A considerable number of criminals or aliens with criminal records are debarred annually at United States ports, but this results from the vigilance of immigrant inspectors or from chance information rather than from our system of regulation. (U.S. Congress Senate Immigration Commission 1911, vol. 1, p. 27)

At the same time, the commission came to the startling conclusion that criminality among the foreign-born did not appear to increase "the volume of crime in proportion to the total population" (ibid.). In fact, a comparison of foreign- and native-born prisoners showed that the proportion of foreign prisoners actually decreased between 1890 and 1904 (ibid., vol. 36, p. 4). In addition, the native-born appeared to commit more serious crimes than did immigrants (ibid., p. 5).

At a hearing of the United States Congress Senate Committee on Immigration in 1928 on a bill to subject certain immigrants from the Western Hemisphere to quotas under immigration laws, Mr. Edward H. Dowell, vice-president of the California State Federation of Labor and a member of the San Diego City Council, testified:

There are in the California State penitentiary at San Quentin, 3,358 prisoners. Of that number, 438 are Mexicans. In other words, about one-twelfth of the population of California are Mexicans and about one-seventh of the prison population are Mexican. Data supplied with the above figures shows that at least 60 per cent of the violations of prison laws and rules in that penitentiary were credited to those few Mexicans that were in there. (U.S. Congress Senate Committee on Immigration 1928, p. 5)

Concern with crime and the foreign-born did not abate. In 1931 the U.S. National Commission on Law Observance and Enforcement issued a 14-volume report. Report no. 10, of what was generally known as the Wickersham Commission, was a volume devoted entirely to *Crime and the Foreign Born*. Significantly, the report appeared as Operation Deportation was in full swing. The commission pointed out that because of the recent increase in immigration from Mexico, there was much concern with Mexican crime and delinquency. Reports from three distinguished authorities in the field (Paul S. Taylor, Max S. Handman, and Paul Livingston Warnshuis) were included in the volume.

Because of prejudice against Mexicans and selective enforcement of the law, Taylor concluded that arrest statistics are not accurate indices of criminality (U.S. National Commission on Law Observance and Enforcement 1931, p. 409). Professor Handman found that there was no evidence to support the contention that Mexicans are more frequent law violators than non-Mexicans (ibid., pp. 409-10). Mr. Warnshuis similarly found that "While numerous arrests and frequent convictions of Mexicans tend to make it appear that they are inclined to be delinquent, it is quite likely that such things point rather to misfortune, the lack of ingenuity and resources, and in some instances to discrimination against them" (ibid., p. 411). The committee concluded:

> Thoughtful reading of these three reports dealing with the Mexican tends to lead to the formation of an opinion that the lack of fairly exact population data which would permit corrections for sex and age makes it impossible to determine whether or not Mexicans commit more crimes than do the native white, but that there is reason to doubt that the popular belief as to excessive criminal behavior among Mexicans is justified by the facts; that the character of crimes committed by Mexicans points to a definite and serious conflict between customs and habits acquired in Mexico and legal codes applied in the United States, rather than to any innate criminal tendency as a basic factor; and that the Mexicans, when accused of crime, are probably at a greater disadvantage than other foreign born white individuals, having to suffer from a racial prejudice that is very real in certain regions, in addition to the handicaps under which all immigrants labor in common. (Ibid., p. 412)

A survey of Los Angeles conducted in 1919 by the Interchurch World Movement of North America (1920, p. 12) revealed that "Contrary to public opinion the percentage of crime among Mexicans is no higher than the average of the city at large," Jay S. Stowell similarly reported that "So far as we have the facts, there is every reason to believe that as a peaceful, law-abiding member of the community the Mexican ranks well with the native-born American. Thus in the city of Los Angeles in the year 1919 the percentage of Mexican arrests to the total number of arrests for the entire city was 5.5 per cent in a population which is five per cent Mexican" (Stowell 1921, p. 48).

From the preceding discussion it is clear that the issue of undocumented workers and crime should be placed within a historical context, for criminal tendencies have been attributed to Mexican immigrants since the first great wave of immigration from Mexico began around 1908.

As in previous epochs, it is commonly asserted that the high level of crime among undocumented workers not only threatens the public safety but severely taxes the capabilities of law enforcement. Special divisions of the Los Angeles Police Department (LAPD), for example, estimated:

> Illegal aliens commit 50% of all pickpockets, 30% of all hit-and-run accidents, 25% to 30% of all shoplifts, 20% to 25% of all burglaries, 20% of all auto thefts, and 5% of all homicides. It is also estimated that illegal aliens comprise 15% to 20% of the burglary victims, 20% of the pickpocket victims, 4% of the rape and homicide victims, 4% of the robbery victims, and 8% of the extortion victims. (Villalpando 1977, p. 67)

An additional cost is incurred in housing undocumented workers during court proceedings as well as transporting them back to their native country. Undocumented workers are also alleged to increase the flow of narcotics and contribute to a general increase in crime statistics (ibid., p. 66).

An LAPD "briefing" paper in 1977 asserted that the illegal alien population had increased by more than 200 percent and that there would soon be a "hidden" population of over one million (Johnson and Ogle 1978, p. 9). The LAPD argued that the department is responsible for serving a population that is 23 percent larger than the official statistics suggest. Undocumented workers were said to cost the city about $37 million per year and to account for 36.6 percent of all felony arrests (ibid., pp. 10-11).

The police view is shared by significant segments of the population. A person who was previously a United States attorney in Arizona asserted that the illegal alien is not simply a worker but:

> Also a cheat and a fraud, willing to exploit the generosity of the American people. . . . We are all expected to contribute to his support simply because his mother country will not. He does not seem to care that he is stealing from the poor and helpless of this country.

Now he even insists on his *right* to do so by bringing suit in our courts of law. (Ibid., p. 10)

In El Paso it is estimated that undocumented workers account for 10 to 15 percent of the criminal cases, although according to official police statistics only 6 percent of those arrested are illegal aliens (Tinsley and Ahlgren 1983, p. 94). Courthouse experts also maintain that it costs more to prosecute "illegals":

> District Judge Sam Callan said bail bondsmen are less likely to post bonds for illegals. So they remain in jail at a cost of $28.50 a day. Most are indigents and the court must therefore appoint lawyers for them at an average cost of $400. (Ibid.)

In addition, the average cost for an assistant district attorney's time is $400 and for a judge it is $260 per day. The article unfortunately does not delve into the human cost of processing an illegal alien through the criminal justice system; many of those incarcerated have committed no crime and many are held simply as federal witnesses against *coyotes* or smugglers.

One of the few studies that has systematically examined the impact of undocumented workers on local law enforcement agencies was carried out in San Diego County. Although San Diego makes up only about 3.3 percent of the border area between Mexico and the United States, it accounts for roughly 43 percent of all apprehensions of undocumented workers along the southern border and 25 percent of all apprehensions (Villalpando 1977, p. i).

The San Diego study reported that 267,711 undocumented workers were apprehended in the Chula Vista section and that approximately 92,138 undocumented workers were believed to be living within the county (ibid., p. 72). In 1975, out of 546 undocumented workers booked for a variety of offenses in the San Diego county jail, 529 were of Mexican origin. Out of 971 undocumented workers booked between March 1, 1974, and March 1, 1976, 933 or 96 percent were Mexican. Undocumented workers were charged with a broad range of offenses, not just property crimes, but those for which they were most often charged were auto theft (139), driving under the influence (107), petty theft (72), burglary (71), and possession of marijuana (69). At the same time, it is important to note that they were not charged with an inordinate number of serious violent crimes. None was charged with homicide, 16 with assault with a deadly weapon, 7 with rape, 1 with attempted rape, and 13 with armed robbery (ibid., pp. 76-77).

Data from the Juvenile Probation Department showed that 188 juvenile undocumented workers were processed between January 1975 and April 1976, at a cost to the county of approximately $161,969. The most common offenses were burglary, shoplifting, assault, and transporting drugs (ibid., p. xiv).

These data indicate that crime does occur among undocumented workers as it does among legal residents, but it hardly supports the stereotypical conception of a "wetback" crime wave. They suggest instead that the rate of crime is probably no higher among undocumented workers than among the population as a whole, and that it may, in fact, be lower, especially with regard to violent offenses.

One of the most unfortunate aspects of the mobilization of bias against undocumented workers, especially in the mass media, is that by focusing on the so-called crime wave perpetrated by "wetbacks," the extent to which they themselves are victims of crime is neglected or ignored. The problem of the victimization of illegal aliens is so extensive that the Border Crime Task Force (BCTF) was implemented in an effort to apprehend border thieves who prey on helpless victims who cross the border illegally. The task force is made up of bilingual police officers passing as illegals (Villalpando 1977, p. 113). Crime is so rampant at night that the region has often been described as a "war zone." Although the BCTF has been criticized by those who do not believe that American tax dollars should be wasted on "wetbacks," it appears to have enjoyed relative success (ibid.). The crimes perpetrated against undocumented workers include robbery, assault, rape, and homicide:

> In 1975, the crimes against illegal aliens included 290 robberies, 16 attempted robberies, 21 assaults, 16 rapes, 5 attempted rapes, and 4 murders. In 1976, the crimes included 156 robberies, 3 rapes, and 3 homicides for a total of 162 cases. According to the San Ysidro police log, the majority of these crimes are committed between the daytime hour of 4:00-5:00 P.M. due to the fading sunlight. During the summer months, the average time of travel for illegal entrants is around 7:00-8:00 P.M. Robbery is the principal crime against unsuspecting illegal aliens. (Ibid., p. 114)

A number of factors make the illegal alien an easy target for criminals. Most of them are unarmed and unfamiliar with the rugged terrain, whereas the so-called border raiders are armed and very familiar with the terrain (ibid.). The perpetrators are also secure in the knowledge that their crime will not be reported. Law enforcement officials estimate that only about 10 percent of the crimes against undocumented workers are reported (ibid., p. 115). Using these estimates, almost four thousand illegal entrants would have been victimized.

In 1975 Mexican and American law enforcement agencies embarked upon a joint effort to deter crime against Mexican nationals on both sides of the border, "Operation *Pollero*." A *pollero* is a "chicken herder" and the project was aimed at those who prey upon undocumented workers. During the Labor Day weekend in 1975, some 407 persons were apprehended on the San Diego side and 50 on the Mexican side (ibid., p. 117). Of the 457 arrested, 150 were kept in custody in Baja California and 87 were subsequently charged with a variety of offenses (ibid.).

Undocumented workers have been victimized not only by *polleros* and San Diego gang members but by conservative paramilitary groups who have acted as vigilantes to protect the United States against the invading horde of foreigners.[24] The Ku Klux Klan established a "Klan Border Watch" to patrol against illegal aliens. The Klan charged that the Border Watch was necessary to protect the border because the Border Patrol had failed to do its job (Associated Press 1977a, p. A-1). Grand Dragon of the Knights of the Ku Klux Klan David Duke said that some two hundred thirty members would patrol in southern California, one hundred fifty in Texas, and between sixty and seventy-five in New Mexico (ibid.). Several barrio clubs in Texas responded by establishing their own patrol to monitor Klan activities (United Press International 1977, p. A-8).

Not only are undocumented workers victims of crime and harassment but they are typically deprived of civil and constitutional rights. Apprehended aliens are sometimes held by the INS in"deplorable" and "dismal" conditions (Associated Press 1977b, p. A-2). As many as two hundred aliens waiting to be deported, for example, have been "held inside a barbed wire-topped, chain-link enclosure containing crude toilet facilities and seating for only 80 persons" (ibid.). It was noted previously that undocumented workers are also often held and detained in prison without being accused of any crime. The response of Sheriff Mike Davis of El Paso to this practice was: "If you're asking me if this is OK morally, I don't know. If you're asking me if it's legal, yes" (Tinsley and Ahlgren 1983, p. 94). Undocumented workers can thus be kept in jail indefinitely without charges being brought against them.

Undocumented workers are also less likely to be able to post bail or to get bail bondsmen to post bond for them. They have an additional language handicap and are typically represented by inferior, court-appointed counsel. In fact, it is only recently that the California Supreme Court recognized the right of defendants to an interpreter.

STEMMING THE TIDE: AN OVERVIEW OF LEGISLATIVE PROPOSALS

The United States is popularly known as a nation of immigrants, but there has been great variation among groups both in their mode of entry and their subsequent treatment. The Irish in the 1800s, for example, "were considered as completely unassimilable to American society" (Samora 1975, p. 63) and were the objects of discrimination in wages and employment. Americans have always held an ambivalent attitude toward immigrant labor:

> The doors have always been open for unskilled labor to fill unskilled occupations at low wages. There has also been a demand and a necessity for labor for industrial expansion and development, yet negative reactions to these workers have been expressed in forms of prejudice and discrimination. (Ibid.)

There have also been significant differences in the experiences of white immigrants and those of persons of color. Although some whites came to the United States as indentured servants, most entered freely and individually. Persons of color (i.e., Native Americans, Blacks, Chicanos, Chinese), on the other hand, first entered society by force and en masse. Blacks were of course slaves, many of the Chinese had been shanghaied, and American Indians and Mexicans became involved with the United States as a result of military conquest. In addition, for obvious physical reasons, it was much easier for white immigrants to assimilate and gain acceptance.

Paradoxically, at the same time that the United States is ostensibly a nation of immigrants, there has been a long history of conflict between native and immigrant workers. Industrial expansion during the 1830s ushered in an era of mass immigration. The nativist movement originated during this period, as low wages and unemployment were blamed not on capitalist exploitation but on the abundance of cheap immigrant labor. Jobs were thought of as a scarce commodity that workers had to compete for. Poor working conditions and low wages also were blamed on the new immigrants, rather than on employers (Bustamante 1972, p. 262). Those immigrants who more readily conformed to dominant values and expectations by their ability to speak English, their knowledge of the system and how to manipulate it, and so forth, were less vulnerable to conflict with the host society (ibid., pp. 262-63).

By the second half of the nineteenth century, there was considerable concern about regulating immigration.[25] One of the first immigration laws to be passed was the immigration law of 1875, which excluded convicts and prostitutes. On August 3, 1882 the first act to regulate immigration was passed by Congress. It placed a head tax of fifty cents on each immigrant and prohibited idiots, lunatics, convicts, and persons likely to become public charges (Statutes at Large 1882, p. 214). The first law prohibiting temporary contract labor was passed in 1885 and in the 1890s,

> We tightened our immigration laws to exclude people with loathsome or dangerous contagious diseases, persons convicted of moral turpitude, paupers, and polygamists. We also were to deport all aliens who had entered illegally. The law of 1903 excluded epileptics, insane persons, professional beggars, and anarchists. The statute of 1907 excluded the feeble-minded, those with physical and mental defects, children under sixteen without parents, and we effectively barred, through the Gentlemen's Agreement, the immigration of Japanese. (Samora 1975, p. 82)

The Immigration Act of 1917 added a literacy requirement and a head tax, and excluded immigration from Asia and islands of the Pacific, but these restrictions were not applied to immigrants from Mexico. The Immigration Law of 1921 established a quota system based on the proportion living in the United States. The Immigration Act of 1924 excluded those likely to become a public charge, applied a head tax, excluded most Asians, and further limited immigration from southern and eastern Europe. Although restrictionists were unable to include a quota on Mexican immigration in the 1924 legislation, a compromise was reached when the sponsor of the bill, Albert Johnson of Washington, agreed to introduce another bill creating the Border Patrol (Acuña 1981, p. 132). Mexican immigration, it was argued, could be controlled without a quota by simply enforcing existing laws, especially the literacy requirement.

Thus, prior to the creation of the Border Patrol in 1924 and stronger enforcement of existing laws in the late 1920s, Mexican immigration to the United States had been unregulated. By the end of the summer of 1928, however, few visas were being granted to Mexicans. By 1929 an agreement was reached between the United States and Mexico, according to which Mexico would voluntarily limit the number of visas issued. It was also in 1929 that a congressional law was passed that made illegal entry into the United States a felony.

Mexicans were deported and coerced into "voluntary" repatriation in the 1930s and welcomed back once again as temporary labor in the 1940s. The Immigration and Nationality Act of 1952 sought to codify existing laws (Samora 1975, p. 64). It also attempted to exclude drug addicts and those with two or more offenses (ibid.). The 1952 act stipulated that the first 50 percent of those admitted in the quota would be highly skilled and the rest would be close relatives (ibid.). The Immigration Act of 1965, effective in 1968, did away with the quota system by country and set up broad quotas for the Eastern and Western Hemispheres (ibid.).

Passage of the Immigration Act of 1965 and abolishment of the Bracero Program in 1964 ushered in the modern period of Mexican immigration. During this period, legal Mexican immigration has been curtailed at the same time that the demand for cheap Mexican labor has increased. In addition, the Mexican economy has grown increasingly dependent on the United States and unprecedented high levels of unemployment have driven thousands of workers northward. As economic conditions worsened in the United States and unemployment rose, antipathy toward undocumented workers increased. The result was mass hysteria:

> The threat of an insurmountable wave of "illegal" migration from Mexico was fomented by politicians, the INS, and certain organized interest groups hoping to evoke anti-Mexican sentiments in the general public. Immigrants were blamed for the country's economic ills. Hysterical propaganda was directed at the undocumented worker, and public pressure by officials led to national legislative solutions. A new element against it was introduced: the argument for national security. In 1972, Congressman Peter Rodino introduced a bill to amend existing immigration legislation. Known as the Rodino Bill, H.R. 14381 sought to make employment of undocumented workers a crime and provided penalties for employers who knowingly hired illegal workers. Although the bill passed the House of Representatives, it failed to receive ratification in the Senate. Sanctions on employers continued to be stressed in following debates. (Gómez-Quiñones 1981, p. 26)

Even a cursory examination of recent legislative proposals to control the flow of undocumented workers reveals that such "new" alternatives are based on very old solutions to a perennial "problem." Proposed solutions range from those that would seal off the border through stronger enforcement, increased raids by the INS, or the building of a "tortilla curtain," to those at the other extreme, who want an open border and complete amnesty for undocumented workers. Johnson and Ogle (1978, pp. 130-40) have identified five possible alternatives: (1) Do nothing. (2) Impose severe penalties on employers of illegal aliens. (3) Set up with Mexico a program of temporary contract labor. (4) Create "fortress America" by closing off the border. (5) Create an open Border and abolish all immigration laws.

It goes without saying that the last proposal would not engender much congressional or public support. There is, however, substantial support for "fortressing America." Johnson and Ogle, for example, state that although this alternative should be adopted only as a last resort, "many United States citizen residents of the border are prepared to 'Fortress America,' indeed they have told us so. They fear that the border may get 'moved north' " (ibid., pp. 131-32). Fear of Mexicanization or *reconquista* ("reconquest") extends to academic circles. In *Immigrants—and Immigrants*, Arthur F. Corwin notes that, thanks in large part to the openness of the melting pot, Mexico-America has become institutionalized:

> Perhaps, after all, there would be little justification for "white flight" from the Mexican renaissance or for taxpayer revolts. Many Raza leaders, exhilarated at the swelling ranks of brown power, have promised to be generous with their former Anglo conquerors and patrons, and, moreover, to provide new sources of cultural enrichment and a better cuisine: just keep the border open, you'll see. Such is the nature of the subject. (Corwin 1978, p. 354)

Most proposals to control the border have been based on a combination of the second (penalties for employers), third (contract labor program), and fourth (stronger enforcement) alternatives isolated by Johnson and Ogle. From the Johnson Bill (1924) and the Bracero Program (1942) to the Carter Plan (1977) and the Rodino Bill (1978), proposals have demonstrated amazing consistency. Public Law 94-571 (i.e., the Eilberg Bill), amended the Immigration and Nationality Act. The bill went into effect on January 1, 1977. Its basic stipulations were:

1. Mexican legal immigration was cut by roughly 60 percent by setting a 20,000 quota for each nation in the Western Hemisphere.
2. The exception for skill and job requirements was eliminated.

3. Priority categories were equalized for the Western and Eastern Hemispheres but 60,000 more visas were alloted to the Eastern Hemisphere.
4. Standards of labor certification were invoked on professionals.
5. Persons who had entered the United States illegally were prohibited from legalizing their status. (Gómez-Quiñones 1981, p. 27)

The Eilberg Bill had an adverse effect on Mexican immigration not only by limiting the number of legal entrants but by decreasing opportunities for families to reunite, and by precluding legal status for undocumented workers. In 1977 President Carter presented a proposal that would have granted limited amnesty to illegal aliens. Those who had entered the United States prior to 1970 would be eligible, but only if they met certain conditions. Those who came between 1970 and 1977 would be eligible for temporary resident status, and those who came subsequent to 1977 would be repatriated immediately. The plan would also have added two thousand additional immigration officers, provided penalties for employers who hired undocumented workers and required all residents of the United States to carry a national identification card. Although presented as a proposal for amnesty, the Carter plan was basically a piece of repressive legislation and strongly opposed by the Chicano community:

> The Carter Plan was not a set of novel measures; it sought to synthesize past experience. It did provide, however, for more repression and greater control over the regulation of labor and the population as a whole. It sought to please business and public opinion. For the industrialists, the plan offered them labor without any declared benefits or rights for workers. The plan excluded these workers from receiving social services such as pensions, health benefits, unemployment insurance, and injury compensation. For the public in general, it promised more effective methods of control and deportation of undocumented immigration, i.e., the growth of this country's Mexican population would be deterred. (Ibid., p. 27)

The plan, introduced in 1978 as House Bill 9531 by Congressman Rodino and Senate Bill 2252 by Senators Kennedy, Eastland, and Bentsen, failed to pass.

In 1980 a bill that called for a temporary 180-day guest worker program, stronger penalties for violations of visa restrictions, assurances that temporary workers would not displace domestic workers, and authorization to the attorney general to set quotas on visas was introduced by Senators Schmitt, Hayakawa, and Goldwater. The bill, however, failed to pass the Senate.

The Simpson-Mazzoli Bill incorporated many elements of its predecessors and generated strong opposition from Chicano rights organizations; they saw it as a very serious infringement of civil liberties (see del Olmo 1983, p. 123; Strickland 1983, p. 103).[26] Also known as the Immigration Reform and Control Act of 1982 (S. 2222 and H.R. 5872), the primary provisions of the bill were to:

(1) Impose fines on employers and entities hiring, recruiting or referring for employment persons not authorized to work in the United States by Immigration and Naturalization Service ("INS").

(2) Require the President, within three years of enactment of the law, to develop a "secure" system to determine workers' eligibility to be employed in the United States.

(3) Restructure the categories of immigrants who may lawfully enter the United States by establishing an overall annual immigration ceiling of 425,000. This system would include a new "independent" group of immigrants having access to 75,000 visas annually, and would abolish the ability of siblings of United States citizens to immigrate on the basis of their family relationships.

(4) Streamline the process of United States agricultural employers to obtain permission to import temporary foreign labor.

(5) Regularize the status of many undocumented immigrants by granting them either lawful permanent resident status or "temporary resident status" depending on the length of their residence in the United States.

(6) Eliminate various procedural protections available to immigrants and refugees in INS administrative proceedings. (Schey 1983, pp. 53-54)

One of the provisions most strongly criticized was that of sanctions against employers who hire undocumented workers. The Mexican-American Legal Defense and Education Fund (MALDEF) and other groups argued that the provision would be used by employers as a justification for discriminating against Latinos (del Olmo 1983, p. 123). The bill would require the creation of a national employment identification system, which many Chicanos believe would constitute an additional infringement on civil liberties. The system may be designed for all residents but it would be implemented largely against Latinos and Asians.

Another area that drew strong opposition was the amnesty provision. Those persons who came to the United States before 1977 and who had resided here continuously would be given the opportunity to legalize their status, but it did nothing to clarify the legal status of those who had entered subsequent to this date or who would enter at a future time. There was fear and concern among Latinos that the bill would not only violate their civil liberties but:

> Lead to an increase in the budget and manpower for *la migra*—the Immigration and Naturalization Services and its uniformed arm, the Border Patrol. The two agencies have long been feared and detested by Latinos because of their past history of indiscriminate raids in Latino neighborhoods. (Ibid., p. 124)

Perhaps what is most ironic is that such legislation would most likely not curtail the flow of immigrants to the United States, but instead, would increase immigration among professionals and better educated persons and discourage the legal migration of the poor and uneducated (Schey 1983, p. 71). Chicano groups have long held that an employer sanctions law will not deter the hiring of undocumented immigrants, will be very costly, and will encourage discrimination against Hispanics.

On November 6, 1986, President Reagan signed into law a compromise bill that constitutes the most sweeping immigration reform bill in decades (Scripps Howard News Service 1986). The bill penalizes employers who knowingly hire undocumented workers, and offers possible amnesty to qualifying individuals who are already in the United States. Amnesty is offered to those who have lived continuously in the United States since before January 1, 1982, and to those who have worked in American agriculture for at least ninety days prior to May 1986.

A full discussion of possible solutions to the so-called problem of undocumented workers is beyond the scope of this book, but it is clear that the "new" alternatives are based on old time-worn approaches. The most fundamental criticism of these proposed solutions is that they attack the effects rather than the root causes of the problem. The problem of undocumented workers, after all, cannot be divorced from the long legacy of conflict between the two nations and the economic dependence of Mexico on the United States. The problem cannot and will not be resolved by building of a massive "tortilla curtain," additional funds for the INS, guest worker programs, or limited amnesty proposals. The bottom line is that Mexicans cross the border to the United States not only because there are not enough jobs in Mexico and because wages are higher in the United States, but because it is more profitable for American capitalists to hire cheap temporary foreign labor than to hire domestic workers. The problem will be resolved only when Mexico gains economic and political independence, and when workers on both sides of the border are paid a decent wage, regardless of their nationality or resident status.

5

La Placa: The Police

Police agencies are created to enforce the law, maintain order, and protect the citizenry from unlawful elements in society.[27] Unfortunately, many Chicanos have a perception of the police not as a symbol of law and justice, but rather of lawlessness, injustice, and abuse (see Trujillo 1983). The agencies that have undoubtedly elicited the most fear, resentment, and distrust are the Texas Rangers and the Border Patrol. Since these two have been discussed at length in previous chapters, the focus of this chapter is on the relationship of the police as a whole to the Chicano community. After presenting an overview of Chicano-police conflict, three specific cases are examined—the Sleepy Lagoon case, the United States servicemen's riots of 1943, and the Los Angeles police riots of 1970-1971. The chapter concludes with an assessment of relations between Chicanos and law enforcement agencies.

AN OVERVIEW OF CHICANO-POLICE CONFLICT

Police misconduct, excessive use of force, and related issues are of concern to all citizens, but the problem is especially acute among blacks, Native Americans, and Hispanics (National Institute of Law Enforcement and Criminal Justice 1979, p. ix). The United States Commission on Civil Rights has had a long-standing interest in police abuse. In 1961, the Commission reported that "police brutality in the United States is a serious and continuing problem" (U.S. Commission on Civil Rights 1981, p.vi). Twenty years later, in an extensive report on police practices, *Who Is Guarding the Guardians?*, the Commission concluded that "violations of the civil rights of minority people by some members of police departments is a serious national problem" (ibid., p. ii).

In response to allegations that Chicanos were subjected to abuse and harassment by law enforcement officers and to discriminatory treatment by the legal and judicial system, the Civil Rights Commission carried out an extensive investigation of the problem — *Mexican Americans and the Administration of Justice in the Southwest* (1970). Interviews were conducted with approximately four hundred fifty persons throughout the Southwest, including police officers, probation officers, judges, prosecutors, and public defenders (U.S. Civil Rights Commission 1970, pp. iv-v). Also interviewed were leaders of Chicano organizations and private citizens. Three state advisory committee meetings and a commission hearing were held. A questionnaire was sent to 793 local and state law enforcement agencies in the five states, covering recruitment policies and procedures, employment of Chicanos, policies relative to assignment and training of officers, citizen complaint procedures, and police-community relations.

Based on the information obtained and the testimony presented, the Civil Rights Commission observed that it had

> heard frequent allegations that law enforcement officers discriminated against Mexican-Americans. Such discrimination includes more frequent use of excessive force against Mexican-Americans than against Anglos, discriminatory treatment of juveniles, and harassment and discourteous treatment toward Mexican Americans in general. Complaints also were heard that police protection in Mexican-American neighborhoods was less adequate than in other areas. The Commission's investigations showed that belief in law enforcement prejudice is widespread and is indicative of a serious problem of police-community relations between the police and Mexican-Americans in the Southwest. (Ibid., p. 13)

The Subcommittee on Criminal Justice of the U.S. House Committee on the Judiciary similarly conducted hearings on police misconduct and found that blacks and Hispanics are much more likely to be victims of police shootings (Committee on the Judiciary 1984, p. 1). In the ten previous years there were four thousand fatal shootings of civilians by police and more than half of the victims were minorities (ibid.).

Complainants often feel not only that the police use excessive force, but that they would not have been treated in this manner if they were Anglos. The following case presented before the Civil Rights Commission is typical of such abuse. A South Texan man

went to the courthouse to inquire as to his father's case. He was told
that he was going to be tried at 7. So he went to find out whether
or not the man was going to be tried at 7 A.M. or 7 P.M. And this
inquiry was made of the justice of the peace.

When this inquiry was made, the sheriff walked in and said:
"What do you want, Mexican?" Of course they don't call you "Mexican" . . . they call you "Meskin." And the man said: "Well, this
is none of your concern," and they proceed to pistol-whip him. Both
the sheriff and the judge. The man had a very severe gash across
his scalp. He was beaten about the face, and he was dragged from
the court. . . . And he kept yelling that he was going to die, that he
was bleeding to death. (U.S. Civil Rights Commission 1970, p. 2)

Alfred Figueroa, a native of Blythe, California, testified before the
California State Advisory Committee that he was severely beaten by local
police. Mr. Figueroa indicated that he was having a soda in a bar when
the police entered and ordered him to come outside and talk to the officers.
Figueroa, believing that the police were mistaking him for a migrant farm-
worker, told them "they were barking up the wrong tree." According to
Figueroa:

> When he refused to leave, one of the policemen said that he was "just
> another smart Mexican," threw him on the floor, kicked him and
> handcuffed him. Figueroa claimed that he made no move to resist
> the arrest, yet the officers threw him in a car and when he could not
> get in because of the narrowness of the door, slugged him and kicked
> him inside. By this time, according to Figueroa, a great crowd had
> gathered because he was well known in town. (Ibid., p. 3)

Mr. Figueroa was jailed and charged with drunkenness, despite the fact
that he was not drinking alcohol. Figueroa was subsequently acquitted of
this charge. He brought a civil suit and obtained a judgement of $750
against one of the officers (Ginger 1967-68, p.76).

The foregoing case is, according to Figueroa, only one of many incidents of police harassment of his family. The Figueroas are lifelong residents
of the area and outspoken supporters of civil liberties. In 1968 his brother
Gilbert filed a complaint against law enforcement officials in the city of
Blythe and the County of Riverside, charging that two off-duty
plainclothesmen assaulted him "because he is a Mexican-American
and . . . one of the Figueroa brothers whose opposition to police malprac-

tice and . . . activities in urging and aiding Mexican-Americans and other minority persons to assert their rights are well known in the area" (U.S. Civil Rights Commission 1970, p. 3). The complaint also asserts that two Riverside County sheriff's officers were on duty but refused to protect him from the plainclothesmen. The Blythe chief of police, moreover, allegedly failed to permit the plaintiff to file a complaint against the officers.

The commission heard numerous other allegations that the police use excessive force against Chicanos. This occurred not only in the major cities but in many small towns throughout the Southwest. Although the function of the commission was not to adjudicate or to establish the validity of complaints, their prevalence indicated that this was a very "serious" problem (ibid., p. 6). This inference was supported by the large number of formal complaints of police brutality lodged. Between January 1, 1965, and March 31, 1969, the United States Justice Department received 256 complaints of police abuse against Hispanics in the Southwest (ibid.). Over a two-year span, the American Civil Liberties Union of Southern California filed 174 complaints of serious police brutality against Chicanos (ibid.).

The problem of police abuse is more pervasive in some areas than others. About fifteen percent of the 7,500 complaints received nationwide by the Justice Department originate in Texas (National Institute of Law Enforcement and Criminal Justice 1979, p. 54). Between 1970 and 1978, the Justice Department investigated 4,449 incidents of alleged police abuse in Texas, about half of all complaints received in the state. From these 4,449, only twenty seven incidents involving fifty officers were prosecuted, and eight incidents including twenty officers resulted in convictions by Texas juries (ibid).

Officers who engage in misconduct are sometimes not only not disciplined but they even receive commendations, awards, or promotions as a result of these incidents.

> One Houston officer shot four persons in five months, killing one. He received five commendations in the same 5 months, four of them related to shootings. This officer also had eight complaints against him, five for physical brutality. Two years after the shootings he was promoted to detective (U.S. Civil Rights Commission 1981, p. 89).

Although police abuse appears endemic, the U.S. Civil Rights Commission (1970) has isolated several areas that seem especially problematic for Chicanos. Among the most common complaints in Chicano neighborhoods were unequal treatment of juveniles, lack of courtesy and respect, inequalities in the treatment of traffic violations, excessive arrests for "investigation" and "stop and frisk" practices, harassment of narcotics addicts, and inadequate police protection.

The commission received a large number of complaints of discriminatory treatment of juveniles. Anglo juveniles were often released to their parents without being charged, whereas Chicanos who committed the same or similar offenses were jailed or placed in reform school. The former chief of police of Las Vegas, New Mexico, Arthur Esquibel, told the commission about an incident in which it was proposed that a Chicano gang and an Anglo gang be given very different types of punishment (ibid., p. 7). The gangs were both guilty of vandalism and were in competition to see which could be more destructive. Initially, it was difficult for Esquibel to convince the community that there was in fact an Anglo gang, because the common belief was that the Chicano gang was responsible for all of the destruction. When local officials called a meeting, they proposed that since most of the Chicano boys already had arrest records, charges should be brought against them. The proposed punishment for the Anglo boys, on the other hand, was that they not be allowed to play basketball for three weeks. It was only as a result of Esquibel's vigorous protest that no charges were brought against members of either group.

Another common complaint is that parents are not promptly notified subsequent to the arrest of their children. Mrs. Jesusita Vigil of Silver City, New Mexico, alleged that her son was arrested for truancy and placed in jail for two days before she learned of his arrest (ibid.). Mrs. Amelia Zamora of Portales, New Mexico, similarly indicated that she was never notified that her son had been arrested and jailed for truancy (ibid.). An ex-policeman in Portales, Carleton Crane, testified that Chicano parents are seldom informed when their children are arrested. The commission suggested that "lack of notification may be attributable in some areas to the view of law enforcement officials that Mexican-American parents do not care about their children" (ibid.). The chief of police of Center, Colorado, alleged in a field interview that Chicano parents "spend money on a six pack or a bottle of wine rather than buy cookies for their kids" (ibid.).

It is also charged that Chicanos, especially youth, are treated more severely than Anglos for traffic violations. According to the chief of police in Tucson, Arizona, recent police recruits observed that Mexican-Americans were much more apt to be ticketed for a traffic violation (ibid., p. 9). Chicanos are often stopped on the pretext of a traffic violation in order to check for drugs or needle marks, or simply as a form of harassment.

Another common practice is for the police in the barrio to arrest someone on "suspicion" or "for investigation," while an attempt is made to gather evidence against them. Random "stop and frisk" practices are also rampant. In some communities, all Chicanos are apt to be stopped, even if they have no police record:

> Henry Trujillo of Alamosa, Colorado, reported that until he complained about the practice, the state highway patrol would stop all Mexican-Americans leaving Lariat, Colorado [a predominantly Mexican-American town adjoining Alamosa], on the way to work and search many of their cars. Trujillo, an investigator for the district attorney's office, reported that he discovered the practice because his wife was stopped by a highway patrol officer. Trujillo said that when his wife asked the patrolman what he was doing, he replied: "Just checking cars." (Ibid., p. 10)

These police practices are so extensive that in many communities, Chicano youth come to expect that they will get in trouble with the police. In a study of adolescents in Los Angeles, one of the most ambitious young men interviewed, who was also president of his graduating class, reported:

> Mostly everybody gets in conflict with the police once in a while, whether it is a parking ticket, whether it is being arrested for drunk driving, for narcotics, or something else. You always seem to get caught at the other side of the thing. . . . I got into trouble once. It was right after the school dance. . . . I was going home and I think it was about four blocks from the dance that they pulled me over, a police car pulled us over and pulled guns on us. They opened my eyes and wanted to know whether I was on dope. I wanted to know what I did. They just said that there was a report of some activity, that some Mexican boys were taking dope, that there was a *cholo* party. So they opened my eyes and everything, rolled up my sleeve, whether I was taking dope. Then they said that I was O.K. and let me go. But they had no reason for stopping me. (Heller 1966, pp. 63-64)

If one applies a sociological labeling perspective to such instances, it is little wonder that Chicano youth have a relatively high rate of delinquency. As Heller observed, however, "the extent [to which] the high rate of Mexican-American delinquency is an expression of the heavy policing

[handwritten margin note: so do chicanos cause more crime, or are they targeted by police]

of the areas where large numbers of Mexican-Americans are concentrated has not as yet been ascertained" (ibid., p. 64).

The issue of police deployment practices has aroused considerable controversy within the Chicano community. Chicanos have argued that barrios are subjected to excessive patrolling and that this artificially raises crime rates. The police maintain, on the other hand, that they are deployed according to need. The late William H. Parker, former chief of the Los Angeles Police Department (1950 to 1966) asserted:

> Every department worth its salt deploys field forces on the basis of crime experience. Deployment is often heaviest in so-called minority sections of the city. The reason is statistical—it is a fact that certain racial groups, at the present time, commit a disproportionate share of the total crime. Let me make one point clear in that regard—a competent police administrator is fully aware of the multiple conditions which create this problem. There is no inherent physical or mental weakness in any racial stock which tends it toward crime. But, and this is a "but" which must be borne constantly in mind—police field deployment is not social agency activity. In deploying to suppress crime, we are not interested in why a certain group tends toward crime, we are interested in maintaining order. (Parker 1957, p. 161)

Do Chicanos commit a disproportionate share of the total crime? Armando Morales sought to answer this question by examining police deployment practices in Los Angeles. Morales (1972, p. 51) compared the LAPD Hollenbeck Division, which is predominantly Chicano (73.4%) and has a low median family income, with the Wilshire Division, which is mostly white (68.6%) and has a much higher median income. Morales found that more police are deployed in the Chicano community, despite the fact that the incidence of crime is greater in the middle-class Anglo community (ibid., p. 52).

These findings suggest that police deployment practices are influenced by subjective factors and that higher rates of arrest of Chicanos for certain offenses may reflect a self-fulfilling prophecy. Police department policies regarding drunkenness arrests, for example, vary widely from department to department. The President's Commission on Law Enforcement and the Administration of Justice reported that the number of arrests may be more a reflection of police policy than of the actual incidence of drunkenness (1967a, p. 234). Morales similarly reported that arrests for drunken driving accounted for more than half of all arrests in East Los Angeles, a predominantly Chicano community. Thus, one is led to conclude either that the incidence of alcohol abuse is much greater among Chicanos or that there is selective enforcement of the law. The rate of arrest for drunk and drunken driving was much higher in the Chicano than in the Anglo district, however, despite the fact than according to the California Department of Public Health the two areas have identical rates of alcoholism (Morales 1972, p. 55). From this data, Morales concludes that "more police are present to observe drinking infractions of the law in the East Los Angeles area, and that drunk and drunk driving arrests increase as the number of police per population and square mile increase" (ibid.).

Perhaps the most persistent overriding concern expressed by Chicanos is that the police treat them with less respect and courtesy, and with less regard for their rights. A national survey of police-community relations carried out for the President's Commission on Law Enforcement reported extensive complaints by blacks and Hispanics relative to verbal abuse, discourteous treatment, and the employment of "trigger words" (National Center on Police and Community Relations 1967, p. 30). The U.S. Commission on Civil Rights also received numerous reports of rude and disrespectful treatment of Chicanos by the police (1970, p. 8). In San Antonio, Chicano youth complained that some police officers call them "Pachucos" or that they will say "Hey, punk, come here" (ibid.). Those who argue back are arrested. The commission also found that police are much more likely to enforce curfew violations and to break up parties and dances in the barrio. Chicanos are often verbally harassed, or stopped and questioned for no apparent reason, other than the fact that they are Chicano. The following incident is typical of such abuse:

> A young Mexican-American was stopped by a Denver policeman as he was escorting a blonde Anglo girl home from a party. The girl was driving, Mr. Rosenberg stated, and the officer told her she was speeding. The policeman then asked her escort: "Mexican, what are you doing with a white woman?" and arrested him. The young man was charged with four traffic violations which were dismissed in court since he was not driving the car. According to Mr. Rosenberg, the officer called the girl's mother to tell her that her daughter was out with a "Mexican." (Ibid., p. 9)

Testimony received by the U.S. Civil Rights Commission also showed that there is a double standard in the treatment of Chicanos by police. When responding to calls in Chicano or black communities, the police are much less likely to be courteous and to refrain from using force. A report in San Diego on police-community relations commented on the prejudicial treatment experienced by barrio residents:

> If a policeman knocks on a door and receives no immediate response, even though he may hear someone inside, he would kick the door down and enter. Yet, police officers in La Jolla go to the back door when they are on official business. (Lohman and Misner 1966, p. 82)

One of the most serious consequences of this differential treatment is that it reinforces the prevailing belief in minority areas that the basic function of the police is not to protect the community but to protect the white population from blacks and Chicanos (ibid., p. 83). Chicanos are alienated from the police and do not see them as providing protection or other badly needed services. A national survey of police-community relations commissioned by the President's Commission on Law Enforcement found that blacks and Latinos also tend to "look upon the police as enemies who protect only the white power structure" (National Center on Police and Community Relations 1967, p. 30).

The alienation of Chicanos relative to law enforcement has been intensified by the absence of prompt and effective mechanisms of redress. The U.S. Civil Rights Commission observed that "in most southwestern cities the only body to which complaints of malpractice by law enforcement officers can be addressed is the local law enforcement agency itself" (1970, p. 20). The fact that complaints against the police must, in most instances, be processed by the police clearly discourages persons from filing them. In addition, complaints must be filed in English. Chicanos also often lack the necessary knowledge or economic resources to seek redress through the courts. An added impediment is that many attorneys are reluctant to bring suits against the police because they are costly, time-consuming, and have a low probability of success. According to Armando Morales, "most Mexican-American attorneys in Los Angeles are unwilling to jeopardize their good relationship with the district attorney's office by representing plaintiffs in police malpractice cases" (ibid., p. 23). Mr. Alfred Figueroa, for example, had difficulty in finding an attorney who would bring a suit against the Blythe police department. One attorney told him:

> I'm sorry, Alfred, I can't do nothing about it because I've got to live here in this town and I am going to make bad relations if I do this. (Ibid.)

Signficantly, before Mr. Figueroa's suit only one Chicano in California had ever successfully brought a civil suit against the police (ibid.). Finally, the commission documented numerous cases of direct and indirect retaliation by police officers against complainants.

Remedies against police abuse have proved even less effective on the federal level. The principal federal criminal sanction against unlawful action by law enforcement is 18 U.S.C. 242, a statute that makes it illegal for state officials to deprive persons of their constitutional rights. The statute is supposed to be enforced by the Civil Rights Division of the U.S. Justice Department. After reviewing Department of Justice records, the Civil Rights Commission found that 256 complaints from the Southwest involving Chicanos had been investigated from January 1965 to June 1969 (ibid., p. 31). Commission staff members reviewed one hundred of these files and found that only two cases were actually prosecuted. Because in most cases the victim and the police officer presented contradictory testimony, the Department of Justice generally required independent evidence before it would seek prosecution. The commission's review of the files suggested, however, that the criteria used for assessing "independent" evidence may have been too rigid:

> In several instances, members of the victim's family made statements which corroborated the victim's claim that excessive force was used but no effort was made to interview these witnesses to assess their credibility. For example, a Mexican-American family called the police because one of its members collapsed from alleged drunkenness. When the chief of police arrived, according to their statements to the FBI, he beat the victim unconscious with his gun. It was determined that the case lacked prosecutive merit on the ground that there was no independent evidence of whether the victim's injuries were inflicted by the chief of police or by the fall he had suffered before the chief's arrival. Members of the family could have testified to events before the chief's arrival and medical evidence uncovered by the FBI investigation tended to confirm that the injuries were the result of a beating. The incident occurred late at night and there were no witnesses other than members of the family. (Ibid., p. 31)

There were other cases where friends of victims witnessed arrests but because they were usually Chicano, poor, and had sometimes themselves been involved with the police, their testimony was not sought.

The tendency to ignore relevant testimony by relatives and friends of the victim illustrates the "hierarchy of credibility" concept. According to Howard Becker, there is a hierarchy of credibility so that "in any system of ranked groups, participants take it as given that members of the highest group have the right to define the way things really are" (1967, p. 241). The police, for example, are assumed to be more responsible and credible than Chicano citizens, who are considered "biased."

The review of the files by the Civil Rights Commission also revealed that illegal police action was often tolerated. In one instance, the U.S. attorney did not recommend prosecution even though "technically more than reasonable force may have been used" (1970, p. 33). Incredibly, in another case involving a Chicano who was shot and killed by a San Antonio police officer, the Department of Justice closed its investigative files on the grounds that "prosecution of a white police officer for the shooting of a Mexican would have little chance of successful prosecution in the Southern District of Texas" (ibid.).

SLEEPY LAGOON: THE CHICANO COMMUNITY ON TRIAL

During 1942 and 1943 a great deal of violence was directed at Chicano youth by the police and American servicemen. Ironically, although Chicanos were typically the victims of these unprovoked attacks, the incidents were popularly known as the "zoot-suit riots." The prevalence of such terminology is not only unfortunate but pernicious, for it implied that Chicanos had been perpetrators rather than victims of the violence.

Although the U.S. servicemen's riots took place in 1943, antipachuco sentiment was evident long before the eruption of this incident. As early as August 17, 1941, Los Angeles newspapers began to carry sensationalized stories of zoot-suit crime when the death of two boys after a party-crashing fight in the Rose Hill section was reported. According to Patricia Adler, "Both gangs were composed of Mexicans—as the papers called them without distinction as to their individual citizenships—and some of the boys were dressed in the bizarre style favored for 'jive' dancing, the 'zoot-suit' " (Adler 1974, p. 145). The prevalence of gang fighting was consistent with the stereotype of the Mexican as a criminal, a stereotype in existence since the nineteenth century:

The existence of gang fighting and zoot-suit styles in the Mexican district did not come as a revelation, but rather as a confirmation, of the Los Angeles stereotype of Mexican conduct. According to the stereotype, there was always violence in the barrios, hidden behind the picturesque "Old California" facade which fascinated the tourists. At the same time, Mexicans were thought of as ignorant and lazy. (Ibid.)

The double-edged nature of this stereotype seemed to invite the hostility of the Anglo community which could always see the "Mexican problem," but never the Mexican people (ibid.).

The blatant prejudicial and stereotypical attitudes toward Mexicans in this period were strongly manifested in the Sleepy Lagoon case in Los Angeles. The case received much publicity and resulted in the conviction of seventeen young Mexican men for conspiring to commit a murder that was never confirmed (see Sleepy Lagoon Defense Committee 1942; Endore 1944). The young men were accused and convicted of conspiring to murder one José Díaz on the night of August 2, 1942, after he left a drinking party on the Williams Ranch near a reservoir called the Sleepy Lagoon by the defendants. Members of the 38th Street Club had crashed the party and a fight ensued, but the conviction was obtained without evidence to prove that they had beaten Díaz or even that he had been beaten. Díaz had been drinking heavily and may have been run over by an automobile. The entire "gang" was arrested and twenty-two members were charged with criminal conspiracy. Each defendant, even if he was not involved in the killing, was to be charged with the murder of Díaz.

The Sleepy Lagoon defendants were in jail for three months without being permitted to get haircuts or a change of clothing because the prosecution argued that the "appearance of the defendants is distinctive" and that "their style of haircut, the thick heavy heads of hair, the duck tail comb, the pachuco pants and things of that kind" were important "evidence" (Endore 1944, p. 31). Also, despite repeated objections by the defense, the prosecution went out of its way to call attention to the ethnic origin of the young men. Judge Fricke was so confused as to the identity of the boys that each defendant was asked to stand up as he was discussed during a particular phase of the trial:

The boys were seated in a special section across the room from the jury and as their names came up, they kept popping up and then sitting down. In this particular case the effect was not only ludicrous, it was incriminating. For when you are made to stand up when you are being accused of this and that, the effect on the jury must be as if you had acknowledged your guilt.

The witness might for example be asked: "Did you see Padilla fighting?" And Padilla would be asked to stand up. And whether this particular testimony was torn to pieces or not by the lawyers, the one memorable picture that is left in the mind is that of Padilla standing up as the witness testifies against him. (Ibid.)

The defense of the young men was further impeded by the actions of Judge Fricke. He ruled, for example, that the defendants were to be prohibited from sitting with or otherwise conferring with their counsel. The judge ordered that they be taken to the prisoner's room during recess and that counsel not be allowed to talk to them. The defense lawyer, Mr. Shibley, protested strenuously and pointed out that prosecution witnesses had been allowed to sit with the district attorney throughout the trial:

"I [Shibley] am simply contrasting the treatment of the witnesses for the People and the treatment of the defendants." He then asked if at times it would be permitted for a "defendant to walk over to the counsel table and consult with me during the trial."

Judge Fricke: "I certainly won't permit it."

Mr. Shibley: "You will not permit it?"

Judge Fricke: "No."

Mr. Shibley: "Well, that is just the sort of thing I am making an objection to."

Judge Fricke: "All right then. I understand you thoroughly."

Mr. Shibley: "If your Honor please, I object on the grounds that this is a denial of the rights guaranteed all defendants, and each one of them, both by the Federal and State constitution. I think their right to consult and be represented by counsel at all stages of the proceedings demands that they have the right to come to their counsel during the proceedings and speak to them." (Ibid., p. 32)

Although it was up to the jury to determine whether a murder had been committed, in his instructions the judge told them that there was in fact a killing:

You are instructed with regard to Count 1 of the indictment, which charges murder, as to this count only, that in determining the intention of the defendants at the time of the transaction complained of, it is important to consider the means used to accomplish the killing. (Ibid., p. 33)

The defendants were also repeatedly referred to as a "gang" during the trial, even though there was no leadership, no membership, and no evidence that they engaged in illegal activities. According to Guy Endore, "These boys and girls simply lived near each other, knew each other, liked each other and hung around together" (ibid., p. 14). They referred to each other as the "bunch" or the "crowd," but were not really a criminal gang. Nonetheless, "the judge, in a statement to the jury, deliberately linked the horror of Chicago gangsterism with these boys" (ibid.).

Alice Greenfield, Executive Secretary of the Sleepy Lagoon Defense Committee, also did not view the 38th Street boys as a gang. In a personal interview with the author (December 8, 1986) she noted:

I would strongly disagree with anybody who would call them a gang. . . . Groups, you know, were referred to as "gangs," even if they sort of hung out on the same corner, and gang was a word that didn't mean anything. *Our* gang, was our group, and prior to this period, and after, you would hear people talking about our gang goes to this or our gang goes to that. They don't mean gangsters at all. They simply mean a group of people who hang out. . . . The kids who lived on 38th Street were said to belong to the 38th Street gang. . . . but it didn't mean at all, anything like what was inferred by people and was implied in the newspapers. The implication was that it was a group of criminal or hostile marauding people who always went around together. That simply wasn't true. . . . I don't think 38th Street went around defending their turf. . . . *and, you know*, and so on. And they could get in a fight with another group, or somebody could beat up on Henry [Leyvas], as is alleged in this whole thing, and probably did, and he might get some of his friends to say "Well, the next time we see them, we'll get even," but it wasn't nearly as structured.

As the trial progressed, the newspapers ran sensationalized stories of "zoot-suit gangsters" and "pachuco killers" who were running amuck, terrorizing countless innocent victims. The conviction of the Sleepy Lagoon defendants was therefore a foregone conclusion long before the trial began for, in the end, it was not the defendants, but the Mexican community that was on trial (Adler 1974, p. 148).

Captain Ed Duran Ayres, chief of the Foreign Relations Bureau of the Los Angeles Sheriff's Office, and self-proclaimed anthropologist, presented to the grand jury a report that was an indictment not only of the Sleepy Lagoon defendants but of the Mexican. Although the report acknowledged the presence of discrimination and segregation in employment, certain trades, defense plants, and in public establishments (e.g., restaurants, swimming pools, theaters, and schools), it concluded that in explaining the causes of Mexican delinquency, "the biological basis is the main basis to work from" (Sleepy Lagoon Defense Committee 1942, p. 14). Ayres argued:

> When the Spaniards conquered Mexico they found an organized society composed of many tribes of Indians ruled over by the Aztecs who were given over to human sacrifice. Historians record that as many as 30,000 Indians were sacrificed on their heathen altars in one day, their bodies being opened by stone knives and their hearts torn out while still beating. This total disregard for human life has always been universal throughout the Americas among the Indian population, which of course is well known to everyone.
>
> The Caucasian, especially the Anglo-Saxon, when engaged in fighting, particularly among youths, resort to fisticuffs and may at times kick each other, which is considered unsportive, but this Mexican element considers all that to be a sign of weakness, and all he knows and feels is a desire to use a knife . . . to kill, or at least let blood. That is why it is difficult for the Anglo-Saxon to understand the psychology of the Indian and for the Latin to understand the psychology of the Anglo-Saxon or those from Northern Europe.
>
> Representatives of the Mexican colony . . . may be loathe to admit that [this crime wave] is in any way biological—for reasons one can quite understand, pride of race, nationality, etc., but the fact remains that the same factors, discrimination, lack of recreation facilities, economics, etc., have also always applied to the Chinese and Japanese in California, yet they have always been law abiding and have never given our authorities trouble except in that of opium among the Chinese and that of gambling among both the Japanese and Chinese, but such acts of violence as now are in evidence among the Mexicans has been entirely unknown among these two Oriental peoples. . . .

Again let us repeat: the hoodlum element as a whole must be indicted as a whole. The time to rehabilitate them is both before and after the crime has been committed, as well as during his incarceration, but it appears useless to turn him loose without having served a sentence. . . . It is just as essential to incarcerate every member of a particular gang, whether there be 10 or 50, as it is to incarcerate one or two of the ringleaders. (Ibid., pp. 14-18)

The Sleepy Lagoon case is significant not only because it was a historic miscarriage of justice but because it exposed major contradictions within American society. Chicanos had enthusiastically supported the war effort. According to Ruth Tuck, "patriotism and military action had a strong appeal; enlistments in the Mexican districts swelled" (1943, p. 314). A lot was happening in the summer of 1942. Shortly after Captain Ayres testified that Mexicans were biologically disposed toward crime, the first wave of temporary Mexican contract labor (braceros) arrived in California—on September 29, 1942. Mexico had declared war against the Axis powers on May 22. The United States government characterized the bracero program as a "ticklish experiment in racial relations" and President Roosevelt declared that "Hidalgo and Juarez were men of the same stamp as Washington and Jefferson" (Sleepy Lagoon Defense Committee 1942, p. 15). "Pachuco madness" prevailed, despite the protestations of prominent Americans like Orson Welles and Carey McWilliams, who saw the "zoot-suit" and "pachuco" hysteria as dividing the war effort and established the Sleepy Lagoon Defense Committee. The committee sought not only to reverse the conviction but to counter this divisive racist philosophy:

As we take the offensive against the Axis enemies everywhere in the world, we take the offensive against their agents and stooges and dupes in California.

Against Ed Duran Ayres and his "biological basis."

Against Sheriff Eugene Biscailuz who complained, "I advocated months ago that we handle them like criminals, but it is hard to make society understand that children can be treated like that."

Against the Hearst press and its headline-made "crime waves."

Against the Sinarchists and the Falangists, and against every organized group, Mexican or American, that tries to disrupt our unity.

For this offensive we need an army, a big army and a united army. We need the united strength of the American trade unions with their more than eleven million members, fighting for the solidarity of labor at home and throughout the hemisphere.

We need the churchmen of all faiths, and their congregations to proclaim the unity of all races, creeds and colors, at home and throughout the hemisphere.

We need Americans of all strains and origins, Filipinos and Chinese, Poles and Czechs, Negroes and Jews and Puerto Ricans and Scandinavians and Irishmen to fight together against the attack on the Mexican minority as an attack against themselves. (Ibid., pp. 22-23)

Predictably, the conviction of the Sleepy Lagoon defendants was exploited by the Axis powers. On January 13, 1943, the following message in Spanish was beamed to Latin American countries:

In Los Angeles, California, the so-called City of the Angels, twelve Mexican boys were found guilty today of a single murder and five others were convicted of assault growing out of the same case. The 360,000 Mexicans of Los Angeles are reported up in arms over this Yankee persecution. The concentration camps of Los Angeles are said to be overflowing with members of this persecuted minority. This is justice for you, as practiced by the "Good Neighbor," Uncle Sam, a justice that demands seventeen victims for one crime. (Ibid., pp. 18-19)

Although the Sleepy Lagoon Committee, couched its support of the defendants within the context of the war effort, several members, including its chair Carey McWilliams, were harassed and red-baited by the press, law enforcement agencies, and the California Committee on Un-American Activities, better known as the Tenney Committee. The Tenney Committee accused McWilliams of being a communist and tried to determine whether the Sleepy Lagoon Committee itself was a "communist front."

The emergence of the Sleepy Lagoon Defense Committee was significant not only because it sought to protect the rights of the Sleepy Lagoon defendants and of Chicanos in general, but because it forged an alliance between the Mexican community and liberal whites. This was certainly not the first case of discrimination or abuse vis-à-vis Chicanos. What was unique was the vociferous protest of white liberals. What prompted the strong reaction by the liberal community in Los Angeles? The extremity of the abuse was undoubtedly a factor, but the fact that the United States was at war was no less significant. The Sleepy Lagoon Defense Committee literature was filled with patriotic references. One pamphlet requests not only that readers buy United States Savings Bonds and Stamps but implores them to also "DO YOUR PART TO WIN THE WAR ON THE HOME FRONT!":

> You can help to crush the Axis Fifth Column in our midst by helping to free the 17 boys convicted in the Sleepy Lagoon Case. Much Axis propaganda has been made over these unjust convictions. It is up to you to help show our minority groups that through our democratic institutions and the organized will of the people, such grave injustices are rectified. (Sleepy Lagoon Defense Committee 1942, back cover)

The Sleepy Lagoon Defense Committee was successful in appealing the verdict. On October 4, 1944, the District Court of Appeals reversed the conviction of all of the defendants. Unfortunately, they had already served almost two years in San Quentin Prison. The District Court also reprimanded the trial judge for his conduct and criticized the manner in which the prosecution had obtained the conviction (see People v. Zammora et al., 1944).

The process through which Chicano youth were transformed from normal adolescents to "pachuco killers" and "zoot-suit gangsters" is an excellent example of the mobilization of bias. The media, the grand jury, law enforcement agencies, and governmental committees successfully perpetuated, by the manipulation of symbols, numerous negative myths and stereotypes about Chicano youth. Gangs had persisted in Los Angeles long before the war, but Mexican gangs were not considered much of a problem:

> They were characterized as docile, or shiftless, or cowardly, according to the point of view of the organization with which they came in contact. The neighborhood of the really "hard guys" used to be Echo Park, a non-Mexican district. (Tuck 1943, p. 313)

According to a Los Angeles probation officer report, the juvenile delinquency rate in 1942 for the city as a whole was 1.6 percent and for the Mexican population it was three percent (ibid.). Tuck found, moreover, that "while the rate of delinquency for all juveniles in Los Angeles has increased since the war, the increase for the Mexican groups has been less than that for the city as a whole and less than that of any other statistically segregated group" (ibid., p. 314). The Los Angeles district attorney noted that, contrary to popular belief, Mexican boys accounted for only 26.3 percent of the boys who came before the juvenile court (Adler 1974, p. 145). Although the rate of delinquency was increasing less rapidly among Mexican boys, the public was most concerned with Mexican delinquency and believed that violence was unique to Mexican gangs (ibid., p. 144). Much of the negativity was a direct result of exaggerated media coverage:

> A comparison of local news reports in the Los Angeles press during 1942 and 1943 with the statistics compiled by the district attorney, and later confirmed by other officials, indicates that the newspapers, especially those published by William Randolph Hearst, were presenting a highly distorted picture of delinquency. Beginning a few weeks after the Japanese relocation story had left the front pages, the war news was frequently interspersed with news about roving gangs of Los Angeles teen-agers and the crimes of violence they supposedly committed. (Ibid., p. 145)

Xenophobia reached such extreme proportions that on August 10 and 11, 1942, the police carried out a massive raid in Mexican barrios. Every car containing Mexicans was stopped as it left or entered the neighborhood; occupants and vehicles were searched for weapons. The raid is described in a letter dated August 12, 1942, from Captain Joseph Reed to Chief of Police C. B. Horrall:

> C. B. Horrall,
> Chief of Police.
> Sir:
>
>   The Los Angeles Police Department in conjunction with the Sheriff, California Highway Patrol, the Monterey, Montebello, and Alhambra Police Departments, conducted a drive on Mexican gangs throughout Los Angeles County on the nights of August 10th and 11th. All persons suspected of gang activities were stopped. Approximately 600 persons were brought in. There were approximately 175 arrested for having knives, guns, chains, dirks, daggers, or *any other implement* that *might have been used in assault* cases. . . .
>
>   Respectfully,
>   Joseph F. Reed
>   Administrative Assistant
>   (McWilliams 1968, pp. 235-36)

Seventy-two Chicano youths were similarly arrested following a fight at a party in the Crenshaw district (Adler 1974, p. 149).

In the meantime the Los Angeles grand jury was providing a legitimate forum in 1942 for the police theory that crime was, at bottom, racially inspired (ibid.). The following year the grand jury recommended that all delinquent and "pre-delinquent" Mexican youth be removed to special facilities and "that juvenile court jurisdiction be denied for participants in zoot-suit gang offenses" (ibid.).

There was, however, strong opposition by more liberal forces to the "pachuco madness" and the raids on Chicano neighborhoods. Harry Braverman, a member of the grand jury who had been against indicting the Sleepy Lagoon defendants, called for a special hearing of the grand jury on October 8, 1942, to attempt to correct some of the damage caused by the Ayres report (McWilliams 1968, p. 237). Several persons, including Carey McWilliams, Manuel Aguilar of the Mexican consulate, and Walter H. Laves of the Office of the Coordinator of Inter-American Affairs, argued against the biological basis of Mexican criminality. The Report of the Special Committee on Problems of Mexican Youth of the 1942 grand jury of Los Angeles County also concluded:

> young people of Mexican ancestry have been more sinned against than sinning in the discriminations and limitations that have been placed on them and their families. The evidence is convincing that the great majority of the Spanish-speaking community is composed of excellent, law-abiding people. The records of the Probation Department of the County for the first six months of 1942 reveal that fewer youth of Mexican descent have been detained for violations of law than in the same period of 1941 (December 22, 1942, p. 45, Manuel Ruiz Collection, MS #295, Box 15, Folder 16).

The special committee offered a number of recommendations, including the elimination of discrimination in housing and public facilities, employment of more Spanish-speaking teachers and teachers who do not discriminate against Mexican youth, more adequate recreational facilities, and elimination of police brutality. Representatives of the Coordinator of Inter-American Affairs also appealed to local newspapers to cease their campaign against the Mexican population, arguing that the campaign was seriously undermining the war effort and the Good Neighbor Policy of Uncle Sam (McWilliams 1968, p. 237). Ironically, the appeal seems to have had the effect of intensifying, rather than quelling, the mobilization of bias against Mexicans:

The representatives of the Coordinator's Office urged the newspapers in particular to cease featuring the word "Mexican" in stories of crime. The press agreed, but, true to form, quickly devised a still better technique for baiting Mexicans. "Zoot-suit" and "Pachuco" began to appear in the newspapers with such regularity that, within a few months, they had completely replaced the word "Mexican." Any doubts the public may have harbored concerning the meaning and application of these terms were removed after January 13, 1943, for they were consistently applied, and only applied, to Mexicans. Every Mexican youngster arrested, no matter how trivial the offense and regardless of his ultimate guilt or innocence, was photographed with some such caption as "Pachuco Gangster" or "Zoot-suit Hoodlum." (Ibid., p. 238)

It should be noted that prior to this the wearing of zoot suits was not perceived as an exclusively Mexican phenomenon. According to Ruth Tuck:

Peg bottoms and long coats, common enough in other large cities, had been worn for quite some time in Los Angeles, not only by Mexicans but by whites, Negroes, Filipinos, and other youth of certain economic and social status. The wearing of exaggerated clothing as a means of achieving distinction and recognition denied in other fields is a well recognized phenomenon. "High rise" trousers and bell bottoms were worn by the same groups a few years ago, but no mention was made of a high rise crime wave. Until June 13, 1943, the *Los Angeles Times* had for many months run a comic strip which glorified the wearer of a zoot suit as a sort of Superman. (Tuck 1943, p. 315)

THE VERDICT IS IN: KILL THE "ZOOTERS"

Patricia Adler has accurately depicted the 1943 clash between American servicemen and Chicano youth as being but a "Brief Episode in a Long Conflict." Although the government riots lasted only from June 3 to June 10, they were the culmination of a vicious and intense campaign waged against Mexican residents of Los Angeles by the press, the police, and the public at large. In the end, the rioting sailors were certainly not the cause of the riots; they were simply an instrument for the expression of a generalized societal antipathy toward the Mexican. Carey McWilliams commented on the conditions that prevailed on the eve of the riots:

The following elements were involved: first, the much-publicized "gangs," composed of youths of Mexican descent, rarely over eighteen years of age; second, the police, overwhelmingly non-Mexican in descent, acting in reliance on the theories of Captain Ayres; third, the newspapers, caught in a dull period when there was only a major war going on, hell-bent to find a local scapegoat, "an internal enemy," on which the accumulated frustrations of a population in wartime could be vented; fourth, the people of Los Angeles, Mexican and non-Mexican, largely unaware that they were sponsoring, by their credulity and indifference, a private war; and, fifth, the men of the armed services stationed in or about the city, strangers to Los Angeles, bored, getting the attitudes of the city from its flamboyant press. They entered the plot, however, only at the climax. (McWilliams 1968, pp. 238-39)

The riots began on June 3, 1943, as several off-duty policemen staged a vigilante hunt for "zoot-suiters" who had reportedly attacked several sailors in the Mexican district. According to Solomon Jones, however, conflict between sailors and zoot-suiters had been building throughout California since the beginning of 1943 (Jones 1969, p. 20). Reports of reciprocal attacks and of Mexican gang fights became increasingly more common in the press. "Thus, explosive conditions were evidenced in Oakland, Venice, Belvedere, in the little districts of Palo Verde, Alpine, on streets, alleys, and in centers of entertainment throughout Los Angeles County" (ibid.). In April, marines and sailors launched an attack on black and Chicano areas in Oakland and "cleaned up on" some two hundred zoot-suiters.

The Lick Pier riot occurred less than one month before the incident on June 3. The move to end discrimination in public facilities had opened up a number of areas that had previously been off limits to Mexicans. Lick Pier, a public recreation area in Venice, had recently become a popular hang-out for Chicano youths but their presence only served to intensify anti-Mexican sentiment. The trouble started on Saturday night, May 8, 1943, when a group of boys from Venice High School went to the Venice Amusement Pier to "clean up" the zoot suiters (ibid.). The high-school boys came up to the sergeant who was on duty at the Aragon Ballroom:

"It's talk the zootsuiters have taken over the beachfront . . . we're going to straighten things out." Some sailors came around. "A sailor's been stabbed . . . let's get the zooters!"

> The sergeant assured them that the "Mexicans" jitterbugging inside the Aragon were okay. "The troublemakers have been kept out. . . . No sailor has been stabbed." But the sailors and high-school boys talked loud and tough. A crowd quickly gathered. Someone yelled that two boys had been beaten up on the beach, and the fight was on. As one eyewitness said, "They didn't care whether the Mexican kids wore zootsuits or not, and for that matter most of the kids dancing inside were not in drapes—they just wanted Mexicans." (Griffith 1948, p. 18)

Despite assurances from the police that the Mexicans inside the ballroom were "okay" and that no one had been stabbed, an angry crowd gathered outside. When the Mexican boys and girls attempted to leave the ballroom:

> Someone yelled that "a sailor has been knifed and killed by pachucos. . . . Let's get 'em. . . . Let's get the chili-eating bastards." Thus a riot ensued. It did not matter whether the kids affected zoot-suits or not. They were *Mexican;* they were *zoot-suiters;* they were *criminals.* (Jones 1969, p. 20)

The rioting continued until two in the morning. In the end, twelve zoot-suiters were arrested and charged with unlawful assembly. The pattern that emerged—arresting only Mexicans—was to continue during the riots on June 3-10. Because the servicemen were viewed as being beyond the law, the police felt that they had no choice but to arrest the Mexicans. Although the charges were dropped because of a lack of evidence, Judge Arthur Guerin used the opportunity to admonish the youngsters and to render a lengthy lecture on "Americanism," suggesting that those with "belligerent ideals" should go to a recruiting office. One of the accused, Alfred Barela, offered the following rebuttal in a letter dated May 21, 1943, and addressed to Judge Guerin:

> You gave us quite a severe lecture, said we were a disgrace to our people and you said that Mexican boys are a grave problem and you don't understand yourself what's wrong.
>
> You asked us whether we know but you didn't wait for any answer. . . . I wanted to tell our side of the story because for one thing I was glad to get out of this trouble since I've never been in any kind of trouble before. . . .
>
> Ever since I can remember I've been pushed around and called

names because I'm a Mexican. I was born in this country. Like you said, I have the same rights and privileges of other Americans. . . .

We're tired of being told we can't go to this show or that dance hall because we're Mexican or that we better not be seen on the beach front, or that we can't wear draped pants or have our hair cut the way we want to. Why didn't you bawl those cops out? How come he said there were twenty five hundred people in that mob and only a few Mexican kids in that mob, but all the arrests were of the Mexican kids and none of the others were arrested. . . . My people work hard, fight hard in the army and navy of the United States. They're good Americans and they should have justice. (Manuel Ruiz Collection, MS #295, Box 15, Folder 16)

The stage was set for the June 3-10 clash. Rumors of attacks on sailors abounded, especially in the Chicano communities of Alpine and Palo Verde. Taxis carrying sailors began to cruise through Chicano neighborhoods a week before the riot. "The prejudice fanned by the biased campaign of the press coupled with frequent mass arrests by police aggravated this tense situation" (Jones 1969, p. 23). On Sunday, May 31, 1943, eleven servicemen were allegedly attacked as they walked along the 1700 block of North Main Street.

The riots officially began on June 3, 1943, when the LAPD Vengeance Squad staged a vigilante hunt for zoot-suiters who had attacked the sailors. The next night, after the police Vengeance Squad had failed to find the "culprits," two hundred sailors cruised through the barrio in a fleet of taxicabs, beating zoot-suiters and ripping their clothing (Adler 1974, p. 150). The police aided and abetted these criminal acts not only by providing an escort for the rioting sailors but by arresting their victims. Military officials were also implicated, as one naval officer commented: "We knew where they were going, and the guards looked the other way. Most thought it high time that something was done" (Jones 1969, p. 24).

The violence directed at Mexicans during four consecutive nights of rioting by American servicemen was so severe that it is difficult to escape the similarity between the racism that prevailed at this time in Germany and in the United States. The *New York PM Magazine* noted that there is a deadly parallel between pictures of naked Mexican boys lying on the streets of Los Angeles in pools of blood with mobs standing around, and pictures of mobs standing over Jews in the streets of Vienna (*New York PM Magazine* 1943b, p. 4).

Incredibly, these vicious attacks on Mexican youth, most of whom were American citizens, were applauded by the press as symbolic of patriotism and heroism:

> Sailors made it a landing party, sought out the zoot-suiters in their hangouts, then proceeded with mopping up operations, which then included stripping the trousers off the enemy. (*Los Angeles Daily News* 1943, p. 3)

The newspaper treatment of the riots also served to announce the riot and to encourage public participation. The revelation that there was going to be trouble on Main Street on Monday night came at least twenty-four hours before it occurred, as crowds gathered in anticipation of the riot (McWilliams 1943, p. 819). Despite this forewarning, the police and the military did nothing to avert the attacks.

Los Angeles servicemen were joined not only by civilians but by fellow servicemen from throughout California. Seven truckloads of sailors arrived from the Las Vegas Air Base, for example (Jones 1969, p. 30). A soldier from Lockheed Air Terminal was armed by his commanding officer: "He gave me a gun and some small shot. . . . He told me to 'go out and quiet the zooters down' " (Griffith 1948, p. 24). On Monday, June 7, the attacks reached a peak as the mob set off on an indiscriminate search for zoot-suiters:

> The mob pushed its way into every important down-town motion-picture theatre, ranged up and down the aisles, and grabbed Mexicans out of their seats. Mexicans and a few Negroes were taken into the streets, beaten, kicked around, their clothing torn. . . . Zoot-suiters, so-called, were attacked in the streets, in the theatres, in the bars; street cars were stopped and searched for Mexicans; and boys as young as twelve and thirteen years of age were beaten. Perhaps not more than half were actually wearing zoot-suits. (McWilliams 1943, p. 819)

Many were stripped of their clothes and left naked and bleeding (*New York PM Magazine* 1943a, p.3). The rioting finally came to an end when military authorities declared Los Angeles off-limits for enlisted personnel.

Mexicans were thus a visible symbol of the "foreign element" that was to be extricated from American society. The swarthy, dark-skinned and dark-haired pachuco, with his long, slicked-down hair, contrasted sharply with the fair-skinned, blond, crew-cutted Anglo sailor (Scott 1971, pp. 237-38). The uniform of the pachuco, the zoot suit, may have also represented a symbolic challenge to the military uniform. According to Edward McDonagh, "it is probably true that many of the Mexican boys desired the patriotic status of the military uniform and many of the sailors wanted the freedom symbolized by the zoot-suit" (1949, p. 451).

The so-called zoot-suit riots illustrate how the mobilization of bias is an effective, and brutal, mechanism of social control. By creating a very negative stereotype of the zoot-suiter, violence could be directed at Mexican youth with impunity and without any moral obligation (Scott 1971, p. 236). In a content analysis of articles found in the *Los Angeles Times* between January 1933 and June 1943, Turner and Surace found a consistent and significant decline during the 1940-1943 period in the total number of articles mentioning the word "Mexican." As Mexicans became invisible, there was a concomitant increase in unfavorable presentations of zoot-suiters and pachucos. With the rise of the zoot-suit theme, "the symbol 'Mexican' tended to be displaced by the symbol 'zoot-suiter' as the time of the riots drew near" (Turner and Surace 1956, p. 19). This transformation provided an unambiguous, unfavorable symbol against which violence could be legitimately directed:

> The "zooter" symbol was a recasting of many of the elements formerly present and sometimes associated with Mexicans in a new and instantly recognizable guise. This new association of ideas relieved the community of ambivalence and moral obligations and gave sanction to making the Mexicans the victims of widespread hostile crowd behavior. (Ibid., p. 20)

Although numerous explanations have been offered, it is not possible to pinpoint a single factor or incident that led to the riots. The motives underlying the U.S. government riots were not only racial but sexual. "The most prominent charge from each side was that the other had molested its girls" (ibid., p. 16). A common rumor was that zoot-suiters had assaulted white females. Mexican youth, on the other hand, were even more protective of their females. American servicemen considered the Mexican district a good place to pick up loose women and "raise a little hell." The initial clash between zoot-suiters and sailors, in fact, was over pachuquitas:

> The Mexican *pachuquitas* were very appealing to American servicemen, and jealously guarded by the Mexican-American boys. They scandalized the adults of the "Anglo" and Mexican communities

> alike, with their short, tight skirts, sheer blouses, and built-up hair-
> dos. (Adler 1974, p. 152)

The beating and stripping of the zoot-suiters were, thus, attacks not only on their culture but also their manhood. The pachuco was left bleeding and naked, stripped of his masculinity or machismo. Such defeats of Mexican manhood became "symbolic conquests of at least the access to the then-undefended *pachuquitas*" (ibid.).

Mauricio Mazón presents a very different interpretation of the zoot-suit riots and is critical of Carey McWilliams, Beatrice Griffith, Luis Valdéz, and others who have viewed the riots as symptomatic of a racist conspiracy against Mexicans. The violence, Mazón argues, was not directed against all Mexicans. Braceros, for example, were exempted, for they were part of the Allied effort against the Axis, as were Mexicans who lived in Mexico (Mazón 1984, p. 69). The so-called riots defy simple classification or explanation because they were not "riots" in the usual sense of the word. There were no deaths or massive injuries, and property damage was minor (ibid., p. 1). Moreover, "neither the zoot suiter nor the 'riots' make sense" (ibid., p. 9). For Mazón, the zuit-suit riots were not simply rooted in racism. In addition to their manifest meaning, the riots had an important symbolic function: they represented a symbolic annihilation of the enemy and a mechanism for dealing with the tensions, ambiguities, frustrations, and anxieties experienced by American servicemen. In the end:

> The ritual, in the Zoot-Suit Riots, was . . . more important than the reality. The zoot-suiters, attacked by servicemen and civilians in June 1943, were symbolically annihilated, castrated, transformed, and otherwise rendered the subjects of effigal rights. Among the bizarre processes was the transformation of the real zoot-suiter into an imaginary zoot-suiter. (Ibid., pp. 2-3)

The prevailing mood is revealed in a letter written to Chicano attorney Manuel Ruiz and his wife Claudia by a man stationed at the Victorville Army Flying School in California and dated mid-June 1943. Ruiz's friend "Johnny" asks:

> What in the hell is being done about these god-damn mexican punks, I think the city officials and police are scared of them. . . .
>   They are certainly raising hell in L.A. raping women and knifing lone soldiers, one of our men came back to the outfit all cut up and it's really getting us hot. This will naturally lead to a bunch of

(Right) *PM Magazine*, June 10, 1943; p. 3.

(Below) Youth stripped, another beaten. Associated Press Photo, Los Angeles, June 7, 1943. Wide World Photos.

Zoot Suit Pffft!

PIEROTTI

WASHINGTON, Oct. 28.—What was described as "the death knell for zoot suits" was sounded yesterday by the War Production Board, which issued an order extending wartime restrictions to all types of men's and boy's clothing.

Wide trouser legs, tucks, bellows, gussets, yokes, belted backs, vents and extra trousers have been banned heretofore only in wool garments. The amended order includes rayon, cotton and other non-wood garments.

Sleepy Lagoon defendants leaving Hall of Justice after their release. October 4, 1944. Courtesy Department of Special Collections, University Research Library, UCLA.

East Los Angeles police riots, January 31, 1971. Courtesy Professor Paul Ruiz, California State University, Northridge.

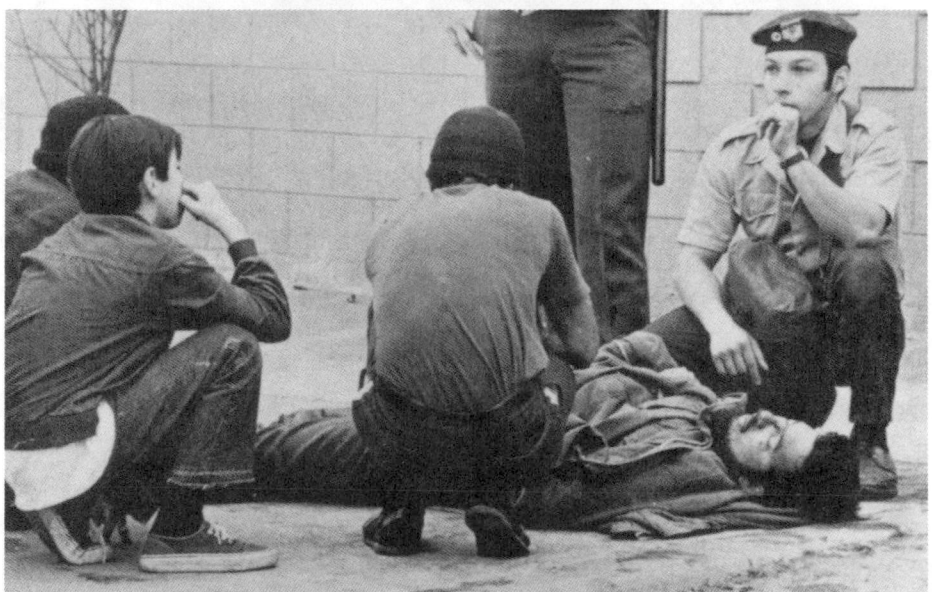

our men going into L.A. and there will be a lot of sorry Mexicans.
I know you don't like to hear of more fighting, being their coun-
cil but I for one would kill any of them. (Manuel Ruiz Collection,
MS #295, Box 1, Folder 3)

Interestingly, although "Johnny" is clearly a family friend and considers
Ruiz to be an exception to the rule, the letter makes no reference to zoot-
suiters or pachucos. Contrary to Mazón's thesis, it suggests, instead, a
generalized antipathy toward Mexicans, or at least Mexican youth.

THE LOS ANGELES POLICE RIOTS (1970-1971)

The atrocities perpetrated against persons of Mexican descent during the 1940s served not only to increase political awareness and intensify
ethnic consciousness among Chicanos but to lay bare contradictions
inherent in the American capitalistic system. Some have argued, in fact,
that the Sleepy Lagoon victory marked the beginning of the contemporary
Chicano movement. It was certainly not the first time that Chicanos had
suffered inequities, or that they had struggled to redress wrongs committed against them, but it may have been the first time that they won a significant victory before American tribunals. Carey McWilliams described the
reaction when the charges were finally dropped against the Sleepy Lagoon
defendants:

Hundreds of Mexicans crowded the corridors of the Hall of Justice
to greet the boys. "Hysterical screams and shrieks," reported the *Los
Angeles Times*, "laughter and cries of jubilation welled from the
crowd. The atmosphere was electric with excitement as the liberated
men were besieged by well-wishers who enthusiastically pumped their
hands and slapped their backs. Tears flowed unashamedly." For the
first time in the history of Los Angeles, Mexicans had won an organized victory in the courts and, on this day, bailiffs and deputy sheriffs
and court attachés were looking rather embarrassed in the presence
of Mexicans. (McWilliams 1968, p. 231)

At the same time that Chicanos were joining the armed services in
record numbers and distinguishing themselves in battle, and braceros were
providing badly needed labor to help the war effort, Mexicans in the United
States were being labeled foreigners, pachucos, and greasers. The response

to the patriotism that prevailed in the barrios was clear and unambiguous. Mexicans were part of the foreign element that had to be expelled from American society.

Sleepy Lagoon and the zoot-suit riots proved a diplomatic embarrassment for both the United States and Mexico. Mexico had recently joined the Allied forces, and the United States was seeking to develop a strong alliance with its southern neighbor. At the same time that the United States was exhorting the virtues of its Good Neighbor Policy, a domestic war was being waged against racial minorities within its own borders.

As in World War II and Korea, Chicanos were grossly overrepresented among combat troops and casualties in Vietnam. It has been estimated, in fact, that about 20 percent of all casualties in Vietnam were Chicano. As the Chicano *movimiento* grew in intensity, and as resistance to United States involvement in Southeast Asia increased, opposition to the war solidified in the barrio. Opposition culminated in the Chicano Anti-War Moratorium on August 29, 1970. The significance of the moratorium was that it dramatized the contradictions experienced by Chicanos within American society. Chicanos were urged to resist fighting an unjust war abroad and instead fight for social justice at home (Morales 1972, p. 101). Ironically, the response to the moratorium was an unprecedented level of police violence.[28] Most of the violence during the 1940s had been aimed at Chicano youth, especially those termed pachucos or zoot-suiters. But the violence in East Los Angeles in 1970 was widespread and indiscriminate, touching all segments of the Chicano community, including women and children.

Chicanos were victims of police abuse and, as in the past, anti-Chicano bias was mobilized by the media. As a result, the incidents became known as the East Los Angeles riots, not the Los Angeles police riots. Channel 7 (KABC) in Los Angeles gave the following editorial in the aftermath of the January 31, 1971, incident:

> This weekend, a wave of senseless, pointless violence in East Los Angeles left damages totalling over $200,000 in its wake.
>
> It was a largely teen-aged response to the Chicano Moratorium rally attended by an estimated 4,000 Mexican-Americans on Sunday.
>
> Police and Moratorium leaders—Rosalio Muñoz in particular—deserve credit for the fact there were no outbreaks at the Belvedere Park rally or during the three-day march preceding it. Both factions promised to exert every effort to avoid violence. Those promises were kept.

It was afterward it happened. About a thousand angry youth, perhaps inflamed by rally speeches, certainly frustrated by the ghetto conditions in which they live, turned to meaningless destruction and violence. They first attacked the Sheriff's station on 3rd Street, then stores on Whittier Boulevard.

Sheriff's officers still did not appear in force until after firemen attempting to put out blazes were met by a hail of rocks.

The Moratorium was to protest alleged police brutality in the Mexican-American community. But there can be little question about the validity of Sheriff Peter Pitchess' statement that: "They can't say we provoked them this time."

Moratorium leaders are already claiming police over-reaction. The final facts are tragic. A young man is dead, 35 others wounded, a number of community businesses destroyed—and no positive purpose has been served.

There's no question that there was over-reaction—but it was initiated by young Chicanos who ignored pleas by Rosalio Muñoz that they disperse peacefully after the rally ended.

The Mexican-American community is a vitally-important part of our Southern California society. But such immature displays by a minority of the citizens there are major obstacles in keeping it from gaining the position of respect it deserves. (Ibid., p. 119)

The KABC editorial created the impression that the violence was provoked by Chicano youth who waged a senseless attack on law enforcement officers and looted stores along Whittier Boulevard. It suggested, in other words, that Chicanos perpetrated the violence. The editorial failed to consider that this was not an isolated incident but one that had been preceded by numerous unprovoked attacks by the police. In responding to the editorial, Dr. Armando Morales noted that the violence was not "senseless" or "pointless":

The violence *had* a sense of direction and a point to make. The violence was directed at black and white cars, white business and the police. This was an effort of an active minority announcing their unwillingness to continue accepting indignity and frustration without fighting back. Their point was that they were communicating their desperation through violent acts since no other channels of communication were open to them.

The focus of Mr. McMahon's editorial was on Chicano violence and ignored other expressions of violence. Violence is a destructive force that injures persons. When social institutions begin to injure persons, it becomes *institutional violence*, as expressed through a Los Angeles political system that does not permit one Mexican-American city or county elected representative; a school system with a 50% drop-out rate; inhumane welfare and Medi-Cal cutbacks; a severe over-representation of Mexican American Vietnam casualties; innumerable acts of police brutality; and a strict law enforcement shooting policy that allows for "ricochetting bullets" that wounded thirty-five Mexican Americans. These are the necessary ingredients that result in overt violence.

The Moratorium demonstrations unintentionally led to the uplifting of a scab that revealed a deep, unhealed wound in the Mexican American community caused by years of societal neglect and current institutional violence. The broader community does not want to be reminded of this neglect as expressed by the Mayor who, critical of the Sheriff's Department "low profile" strategy, promises an even higher profile police retaliation if this symptom expresses itself again. This type of leadership will only serve to escalate the violence and it is in *this* respect that it becomes a "senseless, pointless" exercise. The violence in the streets will end when society no longer permits the day to day institutional violence. Let us, together, be against *all forms* of violence. (Morales 1972, pp. 119-20)

A full understanding of Chicano-police conflict cannot be gained by looking at an isolated incident. It is necessary to look not only at the series of incidents that took place in Los Angeles in 1970 and 1971, but also at the social and political climate in which they occurred. The 1970-1971 police riots can be seen as symptomatic of the broad and consistent pattern of police brutality that has characterized relations between the police and the Chicano community not only in Los Angeles but throughout the Southwest.

Although the moratorium of August 29, 1970, was the most widely publicized, other incidents took place on January 1, 1970, September 16, 1970, January 9, 1971, and January 31, 1971. All told, thirty-five persons were shot, one fatally, and hundreds were injured. At least thirty riots, moreover, followed on the heels of the East Los Angeles incidents in cities throughout the Southwest, but they were largely ignored by the media.[29] Rather than being viewed as evidence of a pervasive pattern of Chicano-police confrontation, they were treated as isolated incidents of lawlessness.

Morales compared conditions that preceded the Los Angeles police riots with those found in riots in one hundred fifty cities throughout the United States in the 1960s and found many more similarities than differences. In fact, in comparing the U.S. Riot Commission Report findings with East Los Angeles one could easily substitute "Chicano" for "black" and "barrio" for "ghetto" (ibid., p. 91).

A detailed analysis of three of the East Los Angeles incidents (January 1, 1970; August 29, 1970; September 16, 1970) revealed conditions very similar to those found in the earlier riots involving blacks and the police. Similarities included the following key conditions:

1. Social, economic, political, and psychological oppression of the ethnic minority group.
2. White racism toward the ethnic minority group.
3. Ethnic minorities feel they are being politically and economically exploited by the white power structure.
4. Ethnic minorities lack influence and channels of communication.
5. Ethnic minorites are frustrated by a feeling of powerlessness.
6. There is alienation and hostility toward the institutions of law and government and the white society which controls them.
7. Major outbursts were precipitated by routine arrests of ethnic minorities by white police.
8. Police have come to symbolize white power, white racism and white repression to ethnic minorities.
9. There is a widespread perception among ethnic minorities of the existence of police brutality and corruption, and of a double standard of justice and protection—one for ethnic minorities and one for whites (ibid., pp. 98-99).

The August 29, 1970, Chicano Moratorium March was undoubtedly the most significant of these events. Between fifteen and twenty thousand persons, mostly Chicanos, attended the march to protest U.S. involvement in Southeast Asia and the disproportionate percentage of Chicano casualties in the war. The event, organized by past-president of the UCLA student body, Rosalio Muñoz, was widely supported by Chicano organizations and leaders throughout the Southwest. Moratorium organizers kept the police fully informed of their activities and designated monitors to maintain order during the march. The Los Angeles County sheriff's deputies, in turn, were to clear the parade route and direct traffic.

The march was to begin at Belvedere Park and follow a scheduled parade route with the ultimate destination being Laguna Park. The plan was disrupted, however, when, according to the Sheriff's Department, within five blocks marchers began to hurl rocks and bottles at deputies and marchers took over the entire width of the street in violation of the permit, which limited them to half of the street. The sheriff also asserted that a liquor store was looted and windows were broken at 2:34 P.M. and a second store was looted at 3:25 P.M. At 3:10 the situation was declared "critical" and sheriff's deputies moved in without warning to disperse all crowds.

What ensued was an all-out assault by sheriff's deputies on the marchers who had settled peacefully at Laguna Park to listen to music and various speakers. The Sheriff's Department reported that forty officers were injured and twenty-five cars damaged. Although these figures are probably exaggerated, they pale in comparison to the damage inflicted by the deputies themselves. Tear gas was freely used and crowds were attacked viciously and indiscriminately. Hundreds of civilians, many of them women, children, and elderly persons, were injured. The exact number is unknown but more than four hundred persons were arrested. The following is a vivid eyewitness account that appeared in *La Raza*, an East Los Angeles community newspaper:

> The marchers proceeded peacefully down Atlantic Blvd., watched by curious people on the sidewalks who have not fully grasped what "Chicano Power" means. While marching on Whittier Blvd. near Eastern Ave., the marchers were hit with bottles from the overpass. The overpass is part of the Long Beach Freeway that runs parallel to Eastern Ave., North and South. Some of the marchers were cut.
>
> The march proceeded West on Whittier Blvd. It was a hot summer day and some of the marchers fainted along the way, but they were quickly taken care of by medical crews that were assigned to station wagons.
>
> Two blocks before Laguna Park, a scuffle occurred between Sheriff's deputies and the marchers. No one seems to know how or why it started, but it was quickly quieted by the monitors.
>
> It took almost one hour for all the marchers to file into Laguna Park, rest their tired aching feet, and find a place on the lawn. Many families began to open up their picnic baskets and have a late lunch. Others were searching for refreshments to cool off.

This is where the trouble started. Many Chicanos went to a liquor store to buy sodas and beer. The owner of the liquor store was swamped with business. He attempted to close his doors in order to deal with the customers inside. In fact, he succeeded in doing so.

The sheriff's station in East L.A. (where in the past two years six Chicanos have "supposedly" committed suicide) claims to have received a call from the owner asking for their assistance in calming the people coming into the store (the store owner denies calling the sheriff's station). The sheriffs responded to the call by sending more units into the area. Next they moved in numerous police units across the street from Laguna Park. Obviously, this drew the attention of some of the people in the park, especially since there were about 40-50 sheriff deputies standing behind their cars. The deputies then formed a parallel formation and with their billy-clubs started advancing. No warnings about illegal assemblies or such. At that time, the Chicano Moratorium security personnel came in to keep peace and they would have been able to do so if the sheriff's deputies had gone back to their cars, but instead of retreating, they attacked not only the monitors, but the people who were peacefully hearing the speakers. They indiscriminately fired tear gas capsules into unaware crowds of Chicanos who were sitting on the grass. Shoes, purses and lost children on the field stood as symbols of the inhumanity expressed by the deputies.

As chaos ensued, children were lost from their parents, fathers who came to the front to defend their children were beaten, bloodied and arrested! Chicanos and Chicanas everywhere were crying in amazement over what they were seeing.

Men were kicked, struck in the chest and stomach and brutally beaten over the head. They were then dragged unconsciously to awaiting police cars. Our people rallied time after time and pushed the perros back with stones and fists but sticks, stones and fists cannot stand against guns, clubs, and tear gas missiles. After an hour or two of fighting, the Metropolitan Police from Los Angeles City reinforced the sheriffs. The Metro Police are trained to deal with demonstrations. They hit first and ask questions later.

Men, women and children were indiscriminately tear-gassed. The fighting spread into the side street and spilled onto Whittier Blvd. A few police cars were set on fire but Chicanos paid dearly for it. (Morales 1972, pp. 102-3)

CHICANO-POLICE CONFLICT: AN ASSESSMENT

Conflict with law enforcement agencies has been a persistent feature of the Chicano experience in American society. According to Armando Morales, one could say that from a historical perspective, "the conflict began when the Southwest Mexicans told the Anglos *Mi casa es su casa* (my home is your home) and the hospitable invitation was taken literally" (Morales 1972, p. 91).

Encounters with law enforcement agencies have continued, but the nature of these incidents has changed over time. Whereas the riots of the 1940s involved direct confrontation between racial-ethnic groups and were termed "communal" riots (Janowitz 1969) most incidents today are "commodity" riots and involve the destruction or looting of businesses (many of them Anglo owned). Rather than being a direct confrontation between Chicanos and Anglos, commodity riots entail a confrontation between them and the police. Yet the difference between communal and commodity riots may be more apparent than real, reflecting a more sophisticated form of racial-ethnic conflict. In the 1940s Chicanos were perceived as having made economic progress at the expense of the dominant group and Anglo hostility was vent directly at this group (Morales 1972, p. 94). Such hostility undoubtedly continues but is now expressed by the police, the Border Patrol, the courts, and the mass media, which are predominantly white and reflect the interests of Anglo-American society.

Police abuse of Hispanics increased at a dramatic rate during the 1970s and reached a peak in 1976-1977 when in Texas alone sixteen Hispanics died while in police custody (Sotomayor 1982, p. 29). According to the Community Relations Division of the U.S. Justice Department, nine of the ten major civil disturbances in the country during 1980 occurred when a police officer abused a citizen. The pervasiveness of the problem led the director of the Community Relations Division to conclude that there is "an undeclared war between minorities and police, an unnecessary war" (ibid.).

In 1978 the Mexican-American Legal Defense and Education Fund wrote to the attorney general complaining of a widespread increase in official violence against Chicanos and providing detailed documentation of fifty-six incidents of abuse taken from over one hundred reported cases of official violence (MALDEF 1978a). In the two years previous to the report alone, law enforcement officers had killed at least sixteen Chicanos and physically abused many more. Representatives of MALDEF urged the Justice Department to address this pressing issue and to vigorously prosecute civil rights violations.

Most policemen who abuse Chicanos go unpunished. Of the fifty-six MALDEF cases, police were convicted in only six of the homicides by state courts and in only two by federal courts (National Hispanic Conference 1980, p. 63). When convictions are obtained, sentences are often extremely lenient. Darrell Cain, the patrolman who killed Santos Rodríguez, for example, was sentenced to five years in prison (Sotomayor 1982, p. 31). Rodríguez, twelve years old, stopped and questioned about a service station robbery, was killed as Cain, playing "Russian roulette," placed a loaded .357-magnum revolver to his head and pulled the trigger.

Because of the reluctance of local and federal agencies to bring criminal charges against police officers, there has been an increase in the number of civil suits filed against individual officers, police departments, and cities. The cost of litigation, however, is often prohibitive, especially because many victims of police abuse are poor or working-class.

Undocumented workers are especially vulnerable. They lack requisite resources and familiarity with the legal and judicial system. More importantly, they are unlikely to report incidents of abuse for fear of retaliation or deportation. Mr. Juan Gutiérrez, in testimony presented before the National People's Hearing and Inquiry into Police Crimes in the United States, noted that in 1979 "ten totally unjustified murders by police or INS officers were committed against people in the border area, some of whom were shot in the back from helicopters, others killed while arrested and in handcuffs, and one shot on the Mexican side of the border" (Committee on the Judiciary 1984, p. 1566). The *Sacramento Bee* and *Stockton Record* reported that for many years U.S. border patrolmen have chased undocumented workers into local rivers and watched them drown. At least twelve deaths have been reported in the past decade (Bárbaro 1984a). When asked by reporters why agents do not carry ropes or life rings, Western Regional Commissioner Harold Ezell responded that "ropes and life rings would only encourage them to run into the water, thinking they'll be saved if they get into trouble" (ibid.).

One of the most disturbing aspects of the growing conflict between minorities and police is that law enforcement has become increasingly polarized and militant in defense of their actions. In response to community outcry over the shooting of ten persons in Dallas, including five Hispanics and four blacks, Police Chief Billy Prince responded that eleven of the thirteen Dallas police officers shot since 1979 were shot by members of minority groups (Bárbaro 1984b). Many attempts have been made to justify police violence on the grounds that they too are being subjected to increasing violence and abuse. Yet, available evidence indicates that while there has been an increase in the absolute number of police officers killed, the rate of officers killed per 100,000 authorized police personnel has not increased (Takagi 1979, p. 31). The death rate for male civilians aged 10 and over killed by police has increased (ibid., p. 33). Other occupations, moreover, such as mining and construction have been found to be two or three times more dangerous than police work (ibid., p. 32).

Captain William J. Newman, director of the Dallas Police Department Internal Affairs Division, blames much police violence on the victims themselves. He maintains that there would be less police abuse if:

> People would only learn to get arrested. People should learn to submit to police officers....Not insult them, but submit with dignity, and if the officer is wrong then settle in court. People shouldn't try to battle it out with the officer in the street, because in almost every case, the citizen is the one who is going to come out losing. (Sotomayor 1982, p. 35).

Rather than attempting to obtain justice, police departments and cities often assume a defensive posture and seek to protect the officer (ibid., p. 32). In McAllen, Texas, the American Civil Liberties Union filed suit against a dozen officers and forced the city to release video tapes of the police beating and kicking defenseless inmates. Unfortunately, attacks on the police are often perceived as attacks on the city so that police and local city councils align themselves against the community. The problem will not be resolved until police officers know that they will be held responsible for their actions and punished for abusing their position. Vilma Martínez, president and general counsel of MALDEF, noted in a letter to the United States attorney general that the prevalence of official violence against Chicanos:

> reflects a widespread law officer mentality that equates a gun and badge with being the local embodiment of the supreme authority of the law. In many of these cases, the state judicial system has proved unconcerned or inadequate to punish the perpetrators of violence. The quality of the response by local prosecutors, judges, and jurors in many cases reflects the rampant prejudice against Mexican-Americans in many parts of the Southwest. (MALDEF 1978a)

6

Gangs or Barrio Warriors?

INTRODUCTION

The mobilization of bias was so rampant during the 1940s that terms such as "zoot-suiter," "pachuco," and "gang member" became interchangeable with "Mexican" or "Mexican-American." As a result, youth gangs came to be seen as endemic to Chicano culture. This view persisted despite the protestations of more sympathetic social scientists. Emory S. Bogardus, for example, noted:

> Not all zoot-suiters are members of gangs, only a small percentage. Not all gangsters are Mexican-Americans, only a small fraction. Not all Mexican-American youth are gang minded, only a small proportion. (Bogardus 1943, p. 55)

The zoot suit was made popular by motion picture stars and worn not only by Mexican-Americans but by Anglo, black, and Filipino youth, especially those who were part of the jitterbug "dance cult" (ibid.). Beatrice Griffith (1948, pp. 73-74) similarly observed that the 1.3 percent increase in delinquency among Mexican-American boys between 1941 and 1942 was actually less than the increase for all boys in Los Angeles County (3.5 percent). Ruth Tuck, on the other hand, found that although residents of the barrio of Descanso made up 12 percent of the population of San Bernardino, they accounted for 28 percent of all juvenile arrests (Tuck 1946, p. 213). Although Tuck fails to consider that Chicanos are younger than the population as a whole and that there is therefore a higher proportion of Chicano youth, she does acknowledge that "the prejudices, conscious or unconscious, of law enforcement officers provide further impetus to frequent arrest" (ibid.). The practice of hanging out on street corners, consistent with the village pattern of recreation followed by elders in the *colonia*, made

Mexican-American boys especially vulnerable to police harassment and arrest (ibid.). Nonetheless, Tuck concluded that "the *colonia* has no entrenched gang organizations, little recidivism, and juvenile delinquency chiefly of a casual and accidental type" (ibid., p. 216).

Formal recreational facilities were extremely limited in the barrio, and so there was little alternative to socializing in the streets. But in the United States, youth were expected to stay off the streets and the police and social workers shared the belief of the dominant class that "idleness, under any circumstances, was morally wrong" (Adler 1974, p. 146).

Negative attitudes toward Chicano street youth were also common among the more "respectable" segments of the Mexican-American community. During the U.S. government riots, *La Opinión*, the major Spanish-language daily in Los Angeles, warned that "wrongdoers would incite the mobs of servicemen to continue invasions of the barrios" and that "idlers would be beaten" (ibid., p. 155). It added that, unfortunately, "*pagaron justos por pecadores*" ("the innocent paid for the guilty") (*La Opinión*, June 5, 1943, p. 8).

Historian Manuel P. Servín similarly concluded that the zoot-suit era eroded significant gains made by Mexican-Americans in the pre-World War II period. Mexicans had made inroads by demonstrating that they were good workers, by producing respectable movie stars like Gilbert Roland and Dolores del Rio, and by the establishment of a very good Spanish press "as exemplified by *La Opinión*" (Servín 1966, p. 333). Jobs that were previously denied were now open and Mexicans could enter swimming pools and restaurants that had been off-limits. According to Servín, just as Mexican-Americans were gaining acceptance as Americans,

> a minority of the wartime Mexican-American youths, the Pachucos or Zootsuiters, reacted in a most un-Mexican-like manner. Dressed outlandishly, as they followed the styles of less acceptable minorities, they quickly undid the hard-earned reputation of the Pre-war Mexican. Rejecting their own culture, the bizarrely attired Pachucos attacked the United States service men in a rat-pack manner and, regardless of justification or guilt, gave the Mexican community— which incidently seemed to condemn the Pachucos as much as the North American [community]—an undeserved reputation for lawlessness, cowardice, and disloyalty. (Ibid., p. 334)

Although Servín's analysis does little to advance our understanding of the pachuco experience, it reveals a great deal about the prevailing mentality within the so-called respectable Mexican community. The mobilization of bias served to effectively divide the Chicano community. Just as the *ricos* had often sided with the Anglo during the land grab in the nineteenth century, so did many respectable Mexicans seek to dissociate themselves from the zoot-suiters. Servín thus not only blames pachucos for their own oppression but also for retarding the progress that had already been made by the Mexican-American respectable class. As the pre-World War II period came to an end, "instead of being acknowledged for his behavior, his hard working habits, and his bravery, he was mistakenly identified with the Pachuco and deprived of a well-deserved recognition" (ibid.).

The view of Chicanos as criminals has its origin in the *bandido* image that evolved during the nineteenth century, but it was not until the 1940s that Chicano criminality came to be closely associated with Chicano youth gangs and, eventually, with drugs. With the possible exception of the social bandits, Chicano criminality in the past was viewed largely as an individual phenomenon and one that was not necessarily linked to youth. The riots of the 1940s served to crystalize the view not only that delinquency was rampant among Chicanos but also that youth gangs constituted a significant social problem in the barrio. Ruth Tuck noted, however:

> Contrary to popular impression, *pachucos* were never organized. They were just boys who hung around street corners and formed shifting, informal allegiances. At the height of the *pachuco* jitters, Descanso's *colonia* never had more than twenty-five boys who might be considered confirmed in anti-social activities, and they more often fought among themselves than elsewhere. (Tuck 1946, p. 141)

It was the police and the press that created the Chicano "crime wave," a belief that still persists.

This chapter critically examines the issue of Chicano youth crime and focuses specifically on juvenile gangs. What is the relationship between youth gangs and the Chicano community? Are they an accepted feature of barrio life, as suggested by some social scientists, or a deviant adaptation? How do members of youth groups view themselves relative to society at large and the barrio? Are gangs unique to Chicano experience or a universal feature of urban society? What is the relationship among gangs, drugs, and prisons in the barrios of the Southwest? Are gangs a stage of juvenile development that is eventually outgrown or a stepping stone to adult crime?

THE PACHUCO EXPERIENCE IN HISTORICAL PERSPECTIVE

Even a cursory examination of the sociological literature on youth gangs would reveal that such groups have been a persistent feature of urban life in the United States since the 1920s, especially among lower income groups and racial/ethnic minorities.

One of the first large-scale studies of urban gangs was Frederick Thrasher's analysis of 1,313 gangs in the city of Chicago. Such groups were, according to Thrasher, "largely a phenomenon of the immigrant community" (Thrasher 1927, p. 193). It was not until the 1940s that youth gangs were identified exclusively as a Mexican problem. Ruth Tuck (1943, p. 313) commented that in the past Mexican gangs were not considered much of a menace. More recently, Alfredo González concluded on the basis of an extensive analysis of Mexicano/Chicano gangs in Los Angeles, that prior to 1941 the existence of Chicano gangs was not acknowledged and there was little concern with this issue (1981, p. xi). But within two years Mexican youth crime became one of the most pressing problems of the day.

Juvenile gangs were common in all large cities since the 1920s and in Los Angeles they had been in existence since at least 1900. McWilliams (1968, p. 239) argues, moreover, that pachuquismo was part of the general pattern found among American boys of "hanging out" with other youth. These associations were typically based on shared interests:

> The boys in the "gang" may go to the same school, live in the same neighborhood, or have the same hobbies. There is, however, a difference in the degree to which the members of various "gangs" feel a sense of solidarity. . . . A "gang" of Mexican boys in Los Angeles is held together by a set of associations so strong that they outweigh, or often outweigh, influences as the home, the school, and the church. (Ibid., p. 239)

The Chicano gang was unique only in that it was more tightly knit than other city gangs. The common experience of discrimination made for greater cohesion and, according to McWilliams, "nothing makes for cohesiveness more effectively than a commonly shared hostility" (ibid., p. 241). Because Chicano youth are not welcome in many sections of Los Angeles, they "create their own world and try to make it as self-sufficient as possible" (ibid.).

Pachuquismo was a response not only to prejudice and discrimination but to intergenerational conflict. Chicano youth were considered

American by Mexicans, especially their parents and grandparents, and Mexican by Americans. One of the most tragic aspects of the 1943 riots is that most victims were not aliens or foreigners but second- and third-generation American citizens who, though not totally assimilated or accepted, had adopted the American style of dress. The zoot suit, after all, was not a traditional Mexican costume; it was American. By adopting the zoot suit, or "drapes" as they were called by Chicano youth, Chicano adolescents were conforming, or perhaps overconforming, to American fashions and, to some extent, rejecting their Mexicanness. Yet, at the same time the pachuco also symbolized the rejection experienced by Mexican-American adolescents at the hands of American society. As Octavio Paz observed:

> The *pachuco* tries to enter North American society in secret and daring ways, but he impedes his own efforts. Having been cut off from his traditional culture, he asserts himself for a moment as a solitary and challenging figure. He denies both the society from which he originated and that of North America. . . . The *pachuco* is the prey of society, but instead of hiding he adorns himself to attract the hunter's attention. Persecution redeems him and breaks his solitude: his salvation depends on his becoming part of the very society he appears to deny. (Paz 1961, p. 17)

McWilliams similarly notes that zoot suits "are often used as a badge of defiance against the outside world and, at the same time, as a symbol of belonging to the inner group" (1968, p. 243).

Not only the dress but the language of the pachuco revealed the intermixing of Mexican and American cultural influences.[30] The argot of pachucos, their *caló*, was an innovative Americanization of the Spanish language and Mexicanization of English. Griffith described it as "a mélange, composed of *caló*, hispanicized English, anglicized Spanish, and words of pure invention" (Griffith 1948, p. 55). Perhaps what was most distinctive about the dialect was its flexibility and creativity. Pachucos took "delight in the fun and prestige of inventing new words" (ibid., p. 56).

Paz maintained that the apparel of the pachuco was "impractical" (Paz 1961, p. 15), but zoot suits were comfortable and practical. Carey McWilliams concluded:

> The costume is certainly one of the most functional ever designed. It is worn by boys who engage in a specific type of activity, namely, a style of dancing which means disaster to the average suit. The

trouser cuffs are tight around the ankles in order not to catch on the heels of the boy's quickly moving feet. The shoulders of the coat are wide, giving plenty of room for strenuous arm movements; and the shoes are heavy, serving to anchor the leg to the dance floor as he spins his partner around. There is nothing esoteric about these "sharp" sartorial get-ups in underprivileged groups, quite apart from their functional aspect. (McWilliams 1968, pp. 242-43)

Thus, although the newspapers saw the zoot suit as a "badge of crime" and depicted their wearers as gangsters and hoodlums, the pachucos were very much an American urban phenomenon and their activities (i.e., dancing, dressing in style, and speaking a distinctive dialect) were similar to those of other American adolescents. The problem was that they were carried out by youth who were not considered American but Mexican.

Simply in turning to peers for comfort and recognition, rather than to family, Chicano adolescents were conforming to the American norm. Pachuquismo was at once an attempt to blend into and to reject American society. Intergenerational conflict had been common among immigrant groups but there were several factors that made the Chicano experience unique. First, and perhaps most importantly, although Chicanos were considered the latest arrival, they were not immigrants but residents of an area that was once Mexican territory, often referred to as "occupied Mexico." The American Southwest after all had been acquired as a result of military conquest. This colonial legacy and the history of conflict that has characterized relations between Chicanos and the dominant society (see chapter 1) has had a profound impact on the Chicano experience.

Secondly, the fact that Mexicans were brown (predominantly Indian and mestizo), whereas European immigrants were white, set them apart not only culturally but physically. Ruth Tuck observed that the Mexican was slow to attain economic and social parity and that this was "due in no small part to the fact that the predominantly Indian blood of the Mexican makes him easy to segregate and discriminate against" (Tuck 1943, p. 314). Racism thus provided the ideological justification for the separation of the races. Mexican anthropologist Manuel Gamio argued that prejudice against Mexicans was not a new or recent phenomenon but one that dated back to the initial contact of white Americans with American Indians and Mexicans in the frontier regions that were subsequently annexed to the United States:

It is natural that they should have called them Mexicans and made social discriminations with regard to them first, as was done with German or Italian immigrants. But the second or third generation of Germans or Italians became Americans in appearance and customs, and the social discrimination disappeared, whereas the Mexicans, though they might be American citizens of the second or third generations, nevertheless remained or were kept apart socially, and were almost always called "Mexicans." (Gamio 1930, p.53)

A distinction was made between lighter skinned Mexicans who were thought to be Spanish, or white, and darker ones who were Indian or mixed. Many Mexicans sought to bypass racism and discrimination by passing as Spanish or Hispanic. Gamio was led to the following important conclusion relative to the failure of Chicanos to assimilate:

The only enduring conquest is racial conquest, since any other after a time is not conquest but exclusion. If racial prejudice had not existed in the United States, there would be at present no citizens nominally American but really Mexican, for they would long ago have become part of the nation racially. Moreover, the Mexican border states would have at present a population predominantly American. (Ibid., pp. 55-56)

Although some Mexican-Americans sought to be accepted and assimilated, American society was slow to incorporate them, especially if they were dark and had Indian features. The autobiographical documents collected by Gamio revealed "very few cases of Mexican immigrants who have entered into the life of the United States and come to feel themselves an integral part of it" (Gamio 1931, p. 225). Those few who were relatively assimilated, moreover, had no Indian blood or appearance (ibid.).

A third factor distinguishing the Chicano experience from that of European immigrants was the proximity to Mexico. European immigrants were far removed from their homeland, but both spatially and culturally Chicanos remained close to their native roots. Typically, the second or third immigrant generation assimilated into American society. The proximity to Mexico, however, meant a continuous Mexican first generation and this, as much as any other factor, helps to explain the resistance to assimilation.

Within this context the emergence of pachuquismo in the 1940s can be viewed as a collective response not only to prevailing prejudice and discrimination but also to intergenerational conflict. Rejected by the dominant society that saw them as foreign and nonwhite, misunderstood by parents and grandparents, and accepted neither as Mexicans nor as Americans, Chicano youth turned to peers for approval and support. Pachuquismo was not a bizarre or pathological phenomenon but a cultural adaptation—an attempt to forge a distinctive identity and lifestyle.

CHICANO GANGS: SHARED AND UNIQUE CHARACTERISTICS

Although Chicano gangs share certain key features with other youth gangs, they also have a number of distinctive characteristics. Sociologist Joan Moore argues that the youth gang is a significant structure in urban barrios throughout the United States and that despite their differences such groups have a number of key features in common. Chicano gangs, according to Moore, are territorially based, so that the word for gang and for neighborhood are the same and there is rigid age-grading so that a new grouping or *klika* is established about every two years (Moore 1978, p. 35). "The gang and the klika remain salient lifelong membership and reference groups for some, but not all, members of the gang" (ibid.). Finally, she maintains that "all Chicano gangs are fighting gangs—and most, if not all, use drugs" and, consequently, "the gang is the principal context for both use and marketing of heroin" (ibid., p. 36). It is this last feature that perhaps most distinguishes Chicano gangs, for non-Chicano gangs tend to either engage in fighting or deal in drugs but not both.

The gang as a specialized structure within the barrio, like other structures such as the church, develops its own subculture. Moore isolates three points concerning this subculture. First, the behavior and activities of Chicano gangs represent a symbolic challenge or protest. From the zoot-suiters of the 1940s to the contemporary attire of *cholos* and the prevalence of graffiti *(placas)*, Chicano youth have offered a symbolic challenge not only to rival gangs but to the Anglo world (ibid., p. 38). This challenge is perhaps most strongly manifested through gang violence.

In addition to being a symbolic challenge, Chicano gangs are an example of innovative behavior. Moore notes:

> We use the word innovation in both its ordinary meaning and as a sociological term from Robert Merton. To sociologists, innovation occurs when normal means as to normal ends are inaccessible, and specialized means to those ends are developed. . . . The gangs are

innovative stylistically and symbolically. . . . Innovation, both symbolic and stylistic, also affected patterns of drug use. (Ibid., pp. 38-39)

Finally, Moore maintains that, surprisingly, Chicano gang subcultures have
been responsive to programs. Although gang-oriented programs have sought
to either destroy or radically alter the structure of the gang, Chicano gangs
have been opportunistic in utilizing city, county, and private agency
resources to advance their own ends (ibid., p. 42).

Although Moore's work is sympathetic and, in fact, ostensibly written from the perspective of *pintos* (Chicano convicts) (ibid., p. 6), the
underlying perspective developed by Moore is one of cultural pluralism.
According to Moore, "Sociologically, we argue that the pluralistic and in-
ductive approach will result in more realistic policies" (ibid., p. 176). The
basic model adopted is one of "blocked access to legitimate opportunities"
first proposed by Merton (1963, pp. 131-60) in his typology of deviant
behavior and further developed by Cloward and Ohlin (1960) and others.

Moore is not openly pejorative, but by linking gangs, drugs, and
prison experiences to one another and to the sociocultural context of the
barrio, the implication clearly is that gang life is endemic to Chicano culture.
Moore, for example, traces the roots of urban gangs to less organized
sociability groups in rural areas:

> There is some hint about the precursors of Chicano urban gangs in
> the portrayals of young male sociability groups in the small rural
> towns of South Texas (Madsen 1964; Rubel 1966). The *palomilla*
> (literally, "flock of doves") are a group of young men who cheerfully
> go from one village to another, drinking, dating, and raiding. Fights
> are a considerable part of the fun. (Moore 1978, p. 42)

Although Moore rejects the notion that urban gangs are simply cultural
importations from Mexico or from rural areas, her analysis suggests that
activities such as drinking and fighting are a deeply ingrained and acceptable feature of Mexican/Chicano culture.

Moore develops a fourfold typology of careers in the barrio, which
includes three so-called square types (nongang members) and one deviant
type. The first two types are squares who live in the barrio. One is the
new immigrant who lives in the community but does not engage in deviant
activities and for whom "the work role is highly salient" (ibid., p. 158).
The second is native to Los Angeles but he cannot make it in the Anglo
system and lives in the barrio more by default than by choice. Finally,

there is the square who is successful and leaves to enter the dominant society. These three square types are contrasted with the barrio-oriented deviant whose primary reference is the gang during adolescence and the *pinto-tecato* (prisoner-junkie) network in adulthood.

One of the most disturbing aspects of the typology is that it does not permit Chicanos to be "normal." A person is thus, either "square" or "deviant." Perhaps what is most sorely lacking in Moore's analysis is any recognition of large segments within the barrio eschewing gang violence and denouncing gang warfare. The parents of gang members themselves would not typically condone illicit and illegal activities.

In 1943 sociologist Emory S. Bogardus noted that out of approximately thirty-six thousand school-age youth of Mexican descent in the County of Los Angeles, no more than seven hundred fifty to a thousand were involved in gang activities (Bogardus 1943, p. 57). There were, according to Bogardus, forty to seventy juvenile gangs and a handful of adult gangs. For Bogardus these gangs were part of the total picture of gangs of various racial and ethnic backgrounds, not a uniquely Mexican phenomenon. Rejecting the biological theory of Chicano criminality prevailing at the time, he suggested:

> The underlying factors that explain the gang behavior of Mexican-Americans are not new except as they are modified by local conditions. . . . The gang behavior of the Pachucos may be traced back to the ways in which the culture and language of Mexican-American youth differs from the backgrounds of other youth in the same region. When these children enter school at the age of six, they speak Spanish and they act in ways that are strange to the other children. . . . They are ostracized and made to feel inferior. (Ibid., p. 60)

This pattern continued so that by adolescence many Chicano youth were alienated not only from the school and Anglo society but from their parents as well. Parents were baffled by the excessive freedom granted children in this country (ibid.). The emergence of Chicano gangs was thus, according to Bogardus, a response to social conditions and cultural conflict experienced by underprivileged Mexican-American youth.

Alvin Rudoff, on the other hand, has sought to explain delinquency and gang behavior among Chicano youth as stemming from familial and cultural values endemic to their culture. The cultural emphasis on *envidia* (envy), *falso* (hypocrisy), and *machismo* (manliness), for example, serves to impede not only normative acculturation but the treatment process for incarcerated delinquents. Crime, delinquency and, presumably, gang behavior result from the cultural emphasis on aggressive and violent behavior. Beginning during adolescence and continuing throughout his lifetime, the male is socialized to be a macho, measured by sexual prowess and physical strength and courage (Rudoff 1971, p. 226).

Celia Heller similarly felt that many boys get into trouble with the police simply by conforming to the cultural role of protector and guardian for younger brothers and sisters (1966, p. 35). Delinquent Mexican-American youth, rather than being deviant are in fact overconforming to a cultural pattern (ibid., p. 76).

Like Bogardus, Beatrice Griffith saw the emergence of Chicano gangs as being broadly based on poverty, poor housing, and the economic and social discrimination found among underprivileged youngsters (1948, p. 51). Consequently, it was not uncommon for boys from other ethnic and racial backgrounds to be absorbed into pachuco gangs:

> You find youths of Scotch-Irish Protestant, Jewish or Italian, Russian or Negro backgrounds who have learned to speak Spanish with Pachuco emphasis, wear the traditional Pachuco clothes and haircuts, and otherwise become lost in the group. (Ibid.)

The cultural value of machismo also played a critical part in the development of pachuco gangs. Personal honor and integrity are critical to the maintenance of a macho image:

> A boy who feels his honor has been impugned doesn't go to his teacher at school, or to his Scout Master or club leader; he takes the matter into his own hands. Or if he takes it up with his friends, they in turn may well decide he has been wronged sufficiently seriously to justify their assistance. (Ibid., p. 50)

Machismo was measured by the mutual respect accorded gang members:

> The respect individual members have for each other is commensurate with the ability to "take it" and not "chicken out." For machismo represents the large male ego that every Mexican-American, young or old, is endowed with. Machismo makes a boy swear big round oaths as a youngster, join the paratroopers or marines when he is older, seek dangerous positions in battle, "drop" his girl on the dance floor if he has sufficient provocation, and take any and all dares. (Ibid.)

While not utilizing the term machismo, Ruth Horowitz (1983) also sees the Mexican cultural emphasis on manhood, male dominance, and honor as critical to understanding Chicano gangs in Chicago. In *Honor and The American Dream*, she argues that solidarity, male dominance, virginity, motherhood, and respect are important symbols of family life (1983, p. 75). Whereas manhood is manifested by demonstrating independence, strength, control over the environment, and dominance over others, femininity is maintained by construction of "a sexual identity around the cultural symbols of motherhood, virginity, and male domination" (ibid., p. 13). Honor is contingent on one's ability to command deference from other persons. Within this honor-bound subculture that emphasizes manhood and interpersonal etiquette,

> any action that challenges a person's right to deferential treatment in *public*—whether derogating a person, offering a favor that may be difficult to return, or demonstrating lack of respect for a female relative's sexual purity—can be interpreted as an insult and a potential threat to manhood. Honor demands that a man be able physically to back his claim to dominance and independence. (Ibid., p. 81)

An insult to one's honor occurs when there is a perceived infringement of personal or collective space (i.e., gang territory). Impression management is critical to the development of self-image, reputation, and honor.

> The competition for honor among youths, unlike adults, results in a hierarchial ranking, a precarious and action-oriented ranking of reputation, or "rep," that depends on continuous confirmation by others of one's placement. Those young men measure themselves against a local code of personal honor. Whatever prestige or status they acquire through those means must be affirmed by their peers. (Ibid., p. 89)

The reputation of the individual and the gang is, thus, determined largely by the way insults and affronts to honor are negotiated.

Stumphauzer, Aiken, and Veloz maintain that "behavioral excesses" among Chicano youth in a high juvenile crime community in Los Angeles result from the emphasis placed on maintaining *la vida loca* ("the crazy life"). Delinquent behavior, they argue, "is being taught and learned throughout" the community (Stumphauzer, Aiken, and Veloz 1977, p. 76). The *loco* street dude defines himself as crazy and willing to do almost anything so as to gain approval from peers. He is fatalistic, seeks out dangerous situations, and tries to get maximum enjoyment out of life at the moment. "Mi vida loca usually has a violent connotation, meaning that the individual conducting his life accordingly is willing to put himself in maximum risk situations such as risks of personal freedom (as with con-flict with the police), or those situations in which the risk may involve the potential loss of his life (drug abuse, gang violence, etc.)" (ibid., p. 81). *Mi vida loca* and related gang values thus spring directly from Chicano cultural values.

Stumphauzer, Aiken, and Veloz applied the behavioral analysis model to East Los Angeles, which they termed a high juvenile crime community. When applied to individuals, the behavioral analysis model entails seven major points: (1) initial analysis of the problem; (2) clarification of the pro-blem; (3) motivational analysis; (4) developmental analysis; (5) analysis of self-control; (6) analysis of social relationships; and (7) analysis of the social-cultural-physical environment (ibid., p. 77).

The initial behavioral analysis of the community was conducted with law enforcement officers who patrol the area and sought to identify assets, deficits, excesses, and controlling variables of the youth population. The chief behavioral excess identified was the use of firearms by youth. Other behavioral excesses included assault, robbery, burglary, car theft, and rape. Some of the individual deficits were truancy, unemployment, and poor com-munity relations. The community as a whole was seen as lacking adequate jobs and job training for young members, structured programs for youths aged fifteen to eighteen, gang prevention programs, and programs to help parents in controlling the behavior of their children. Some of the behavioral assets identified were strong family bonds, competitive skills, artistic talents, and "smooth talking" ability (ibid.).

The researchers focused on a youth gang called "East Loma" or "E/L" in order to show how delinquency and gang-related behavior are being taught and learned. The gang dates back to the 1920s and is said to have originated in response to the absence of recreational facilities for youth and as a mechanism for self-protection from other groups, including the police and Border Patrol. The gang is estimated to have three hun-dred to four hundred members divided into various age cohorts or *klikas*. Although a girl's *klika* was abolished by the boys because it was believed to intensify gang violence, approximately one hundred fifty girls are close-ly associated with the gang. A member of the gang is easily identifiable:

By the proud and "cool" manner of walk and uniform: kaki pants, camp or prison jacket, plaid pendleton shirt, and head bandana or brim hat. Moreover, many of the gang members (vatos) are decorated with tatoos such as tear drop beside the eye, an insignia representing the barrio they belong to, or something dramatically announcing their life style as with "Mi Vida Loca." (Ibid., p. 80)

This preliminary analysis led Stumphauzer, Aiken, and Veloz to conclude that delinquency and gang-related behavior are being taught and reinforced through a multifaceted "learning program." It is truly an intergenerational phenomenon as *veteranos* indoctrinate new members to the lore of the group. Because gang behavior is learned and positively reinforced, it will not be extinguished by incarceration, removal of the individual from the community, or individual behavior therapy. When the individual returns to the community, he will encounter the same stimuli and reinforcement for delinquent activities. The pattern will be changed only through unified community intervention. According to the authors, "perhaps what is indicated is a banding together of a group of agencies and residents under a common analysis and intervention methodology with the express purpose of solving problems directly where they occur, in the natural environment" (ibid., p. 83).

The behavioral-ecological model of intervention with Chicano gang delinquents was tested in West Place (a pseudonym), which consists of five municipalities ranging in size from twenty-five to eighty thousand, by Chicano Services Incorporated (CSI), a private nonprofit community-based organization. According to Alan Hunsaker, the results of the analysis, although not conclusive, suggested a number of potentially effective community intervention strategies (Hunsaker 1981, p. 230). Behavioral excesses, deficits, and assets were assessed not only from the point of view of the community but that of gang members as well. From the perspective of gang members, West Place was deficient in providing jobs and job training programs, especially programs willing to work with gang members. By far the most outstanding example of behavioral excesses by agents of the community was police harassment and overreaction by police to minor incidents. An additional community excess mentioned was ethnic discrimination against Chicanos in general and gang members in particular. A community asset cited was the city's attempt to create a "mini-city hall" in the barrio (ibid., p. 231).

The community, on the other hand, viewed gang members as behaviorally deficient relative to school attendance and employment. Some of the behavioral excesses listed were the use of deadly force, gang violence, the use of graffiti in inappropriate places, and the use of psychoactive substances (ibid.). The community did, however, recognize assets such as their artistic ability and skill in customizing cars ("low-riders").

The change agent's intervention strategy included becoming an advocate for gang members relative to the job market and job training programs, and attempting to obtain direct funding for job recruitment and job training programs. It initiated a "Youth Leadership and Employment Training" class for gang members and developed techniques designed to identify and prevent behavioral excesses. Gang members were also offered modest commissions for submitting art work, essays, poems, and stories, which were published in the agency newsletter.

It is difficult to find fault with the behavioral-ecological model goal of eliminating behavioral deficits and excesses, and enhancing behavioral assets among gang members. The model correctly rejects the notion that desired changes in gang behavior will be brought about by increased law enforcement or removal of individual gang members from the community, and calls instead for direct community intervention. At first glance, it appears to go beyond cultural deficit models, which see gang behavior as endemic to Chicano culture. Unlike the perspective adopted by Joan Moore (1978), the behavioral-ecological model acknowledges that nondelinquent behavior is also being taught and learned in the barrio:

> Within the Eastside Loma community there is a fairly high probability that any given youngster will become a gang member. However, some do not. Some manage to live in this community without being a gang member or delinquent in any traditional sense. By conducting behavioral analyses of several of these non-delinquents we hope to determine precisely how and from whom they learned alternate, incompatible, non-criminal behaviors. (Stumphauzer, Aiken, and Veloz 1977, p. 82)

Despite these trappings, the model is grounded in a negative conception not only of Chicano gangs but of Chicano culture. If Chicano gangs are, in fact, an integral component of barrio culture and community life, it is difficult to escape the conclusion that behavioral intervention cannot be effected without at the same time also radically altering Chicano culture.

Although the model creates the illusion that its intervention strategies are based on an advocatory position on behalf of gang members, closer examination suggests that the model represents the interests of the dominant society. The goal of the change agent, after all, is to eradicate behavior defined as undesirable by law enforcement and the dominant society. Significantly, Stumphauzer, Aiken, and Veloz's initial behavioral analysis was conducted with law enforcement agents. When "community" persons are involved, they represent the segment of the community that stands to benefit most from the existence of a gang and delinquency "problem." There is also a class dimension: the change agents in the community are more closely aligned with the dominant class interests and ideology. Finally, although the behavioral analysis model recognizes the existence of nondelinquent behavior in the community, such behavior is clearly viewed as the exception rather than the rule. The vast majority of adolescents in the barrio are considered delinquent and as engaging in gang-related behavior. The pathological model dies hard in social science.

Unfortunately, the work of Stumphauzer and his associates is typical of the theories and paradigms of Chicano gang and delinquent behavior that have prevailed. In a review of the literature of Chicano gangs, Alfredo González is critical of what he terms the "correctional" perspective. Research on deviants has traditionally sought to get rid of deviant phenomena (Matza 1969, p. 15). According to González:

> The result is that such a correctional posture interferes with truly understanding the phenomenon because it is motivated by the purpose of eliminating it. The correctional posture entails studying or observing objects, and doing *your thing* on them or to them. The phenomenon itself and its accompanying milieu receive only cursory attention. (González 1978, p. 11)

Rather than attempting to understand Chicano gangs, this research tradition simply verified preconceived stereotypes and assumptions. González proposes that the correctional perspective be supplanted by a new "appreciative" framework. Whereas the correctional perspective viewed those being studied as objects, the new perspective treats them as subjects and assumes their definition of the situation:

> It is an appreciative perspective as opposed to a corrective perspective which will most legitimately lend itself to a deeper and more meaningful understanding of the Chicano gang. This understanding

should act to subvert certain philosophical and ideological biases as well as fallacies originated by exterior investigations. (Ibid., p. 19)

One of the most significant implications of the appreciative perspective is that it will provide a meaningful and relevant knowledge base that can be utilized by the community to develop action programs to deal with emergent problems and situations. All too often such programs, even when termed "community-based," are externally conceived and implemented. Funding is typically provided by federal, state, or local government and other agencies whose primary goal is not to understand Chicano gangs but to eliminate them.

Brazilian educator Paulo Freire has noted that one should be leary of generous liberal programs designed by oppressors to "help" the oppressed to liberate themselves. The Chicano community, including gang members, must learn to recognize and to reject "false generosity": "In order to have the continued opportunity to express their 'generosity,' the oppressors must perpetuate injustice as well. An unjust social order is the permanent fount of this 'generosity,' which is nourished by death, despair, and poverty" (Freire 1970, p. 29). In the end, solution of the so-called gang problem and other issues facing the Chicano community will come only from Chicanos themselves for, as Freire observed, "only power that springs from the weakness of the oppressed will be sufficiently strong to free both" (ibid., p. 28) the oppressed and their oppressors.

José López argues that Chicano gangs are considered problematic by social scientists and representatives of the dominant order precisely because they are defined as unacceptable communities or forms of association (López 1978, p. 1). The family, according to López, has been the root of most social science theories of human behavior. Social scientists view the family as a legitimate and acceptable community. When individuals leave the family to engage in community activity, they may associate in acceptable communities such as the boy scouts or a college fraternity, or in unacceptable ones such as street gangs, secret societies, and mafias. It is commonly believed that "deviant" behavior leads individuals into unaccepted forms of association, but López holds that it is the other way around, that "communities are [first] identified as unacceptable, and [then] the behavior of its members is defined and studied as deviant" (ibid.). When a member of an acceptable group—say, a member of a college fraternity—commits a crime, the crime is attributed to the individual, but when a member of a gang or the Mexican Mafia commits a crime, the crime is automatically linked to the group. Terms such as "gang-related" or "ganglike" illustrate this process and are mechanisms by which bias is mobilized not only against Chicano gang members but, more significantly, against all Chicanos.

PRISON GANGS: THE MEXICAN MAFIA AND *NUESTRA FAMILIA*

The topic of organized crime has received considerable attention in recent years both in the mass media and among law enforcement personnel. Unfortunately, information on the topic is not only extremely limited but biased and generated by persons whose primary concern is to fight crime and eradicate such groups. José López observed that "most articles written on or about Mexican Mafia are written by informants, undercover agents, criminologists, and heads of correctional and law enforcement agencies" (López 1978, p. 8).

One of the few studies of the Mexican Mafia carried out by a person who was neither an informant nor formally affiliated with law enforcement was R. Theodore Davidson's *Chicano Prisoners: The Key to San Quentin*. Davidson went to San Quentin as a graduate student in anthropology to do field work on prison violence. As a participant-observer he got to know many of the prisoners well and befriended a number of them. Although Davidson claims to present an insider perspective on prisoner culture, it is important to keep in mind that his study was commissioned by prison administrators at San Quentin who "wanted to see if an anthropologist could determine what subcultural factors were responsible for Mexican-American prisoners being excessively violent and excessively reluctant to participate in rehabilitation activities" (Davidson 1974, p. 1).

Davidson distinguishes between two types of prisoners—"convicts" and "inmates." Convicts are hard-core prisoners who may interact with the prison staff but only to the degree that is absolutely necessary. They would never cooperate with the staff or snitch on a fellow convict. Most prisoners are not convicts.

> Inmates are willing to do just about anything to convince the staff that they have become rehabilitated. Concerned only for himself, the inmate has no sense of duty toward, unity with, or real concern for other prisoners. Inmates frequently report on the illegal and rule-

breaking activities of convicts, so it is understandable that convicts think of inmates in terms such as rats, snitches, and punks. (Ibid., p. 48)

The third, deepest, and most covert level of prisoner culture is the family level. Without understanding this level, it is not possible to understand the real prisoner culture or, as Davidson puts it, to "delve into hitherto unmentioned depths" (ibid., p. 55). Because almost all prisoners on the third level are Chicanos, a full understanding of this level can be attained only by first understanding Chicano prisoners. It is for this reason that Chicano prisoners are said to hold the "key" to comprehending prisoner culture. More specifically, the third level, according to Davidson, is controlled by the Mexican Mafia, or *Familia*. The norms and values espoused by this organization epitomize the convict code. Underlying the strength, integrity, and organizational success of the family is the cultural emphasis on machismo:

> Family actions accord with the highest ideals of *machismo*; they are honest and moral when viewed from within the prisoner culture. . . . Chicanos have a firmly established reputation for their willingness and ability to engage in violence. With its strong emphasis on the ideals of *machismo*, the seriousness of most of its activities, and the necessity to maintain secrecy, Family has increased that reputation. . . . With Family, the pattern of violence is even more extreme than among Chicano prisoners. . . . Family violence does not stop half-way—with the knifing of an opponent; it goes all the way—to the death of the non-family individual. (Ibid., pp. 82-83)

Prospective members must demonstrate their machismo beyond doubt. A prerequisite to admission to *Familia*, according to Davidson, is evidence not only of having killed someone but of having done so in a macho manner (ibid., p. 86). One cannot, for example, have killed someone in the back.

The idea that Chicano prisoners are honorable, honest, righteous, and manly, and that the Mexican Mafia is a powerful super-secretive organization is a seductive one. It is, after all, a romanticized and idealized conception of deeply cherished cultural values. Yet, more careful scrutiny suggests that the view of Chicano culture espoused by Davidson is negative, if not openly condescending. Davidson appears to view drug use as endemic to Chicano culture and holds, for example, that "marijuana is culturally accepted by the majority of Chicanos—much like the teen-age and later use of cigarettes are in the Anglo culture" (ibid., p. 66). Heroin may not be as widely approved, but the use of heavy drugs is accepted by many Chicanos, and within the peer group it is defined as *muy macho*. Using and selling drugs become a way of retaining one's manhood in an Anglo-dominated society. Finally, even if apprehended, "doing time in prison as a real convict, although an unpleasant experience, is a very *macho* thing" (ibid., p. 68). Perhaps what is most disturbing about Davidson's analysis is the implication that being in prison is not really that bad and that some Chicanos may actually prefer to be in prison, for it is here that they can more readily wield power and retain their sense of masculinity.

Another difficulty with Davidson's *Chicano Prisoners* is that in a not too subtle way it may promote racism and intensify racial conflict between blacks and Chicanos. From reading Davidson, one comes to think that perhaps the oppressor of Chicanos is not Anglo society but blacks. Whereas Chicano cultural values are viewed as being consonant with the convict code, black values are antithetical to the code. Davidson proposes a Chicano-black continuum, according to which Chicanos as a whole are most convictlike and blacks most inmatelike, with Anglo prisoners occupying an intermediate position between the two ends of the continuum.

Because of their conception of machismo, "manliness," for example, few Chicanos would be pressured into homosexual activity or assume the passive role in such a relationship. The few Chicano "broads" found in San Quentin are almost always involved with Chicanos, although they may occasionally have sex with an Anglo. The Chicano "broad"who has sex with an Anglo is held in low esteem, but the one who gets involved with a black is most subject to ridicule and contempt. "In those cases, not only was the act an insult to the group image, it also was a gross insult to Chicano *machismo* to assume the non-*macho* female role with a black, because Chicanos generally regard the blacks as representing the antithesis of the ideals of *machismo*" (ibid., p. 77).

The black conception of manliness is very different and is so extensive and eclectic that it permits a wide range of acceptable behaviors:

> Most blacks take manly pride in the ability to handle themselves well verbally. This includes a pride in the ability to talk oneself out of an undesirable situation. Consequently, there is little concern about being held accountable for what one says. . . . This ability is directly linked to a second quality from which many blacks take manly pride—the pragmatic ability to personally get ahead of and/or manipulate others. (Ibid., p. 79)

This produces what appears to be contradictory behavior: blacks will often say things that are in conflict with their private actions. This ideology, Davidson contends, makes it difficult for them to attain unity or to function as real convicts (ibid.).

Perhaps what makes Davidson's analysis of interracial conflict between black and Chicano prisoners so insidiously pernicious is that it is presented as a positive "insider" characterization of Chicano culture. Although racism may be prevalent among Chicanos, it should not be extolled either as a virtuous trademark or a positive cultural trait. The presence of white supremacy groups such as the Aryan Brotherhood would suggest that racism is no less prevalent among white prisoners. We should not forget, after all, that Davidson himself is Anglo and that this might somehow color his perception.

There are additional methodological and conceptual problems with Davidson's *Chicano Prisoners*. Although he maintains that he was able to present an insider perspective by penetrating to the inner depths of the Mexican Mafia and that "my shoes were my office," it seems incredulous that hard-core members of a super-secret organization would bare their souls to an Anglo social scientist, especially one who was commissioned by the administration to find out why Chicanos are so violent and uncooperative with the staff. What is perhaps most ironic is that such cooperation is completely at odds with the convict code. What appears more likely is that those convicts who served as informants told him only those things that they wished to reveal or, perhaps more accurately, what they thought he wanted to hear. This point appears especially relevant in the context of the racial conflict between blacks and Chicanos described by Davidson. One cannot help wondering whether Chicano prisoners were more likely to reveal antiblack attitudes in the presence of a white researcher because this was a story that he would find more palatable. How would Chicanos have responded to a black or a Chicano anthropologist?

Ironically, Davidson notes that two common stereotypes of Chicanos held by the prison staff is that they are reluctant to participate in rehabilitation activities and that they are liars and cannot be trusted by the staff (ibid., p. 61). Joan Moore has similarly observed that Chicano prisoners are distrustful of academic research, whether it be quantitative or qualitative. The use of informants, in fact, is seen as being similar to the use of informants by law enforcement (Moore 1978, p. 4). Moore adds that "there are many good reasons for them to con the researcher into believing that he/she is getting what he/she wants" (ibid., p. 5).

Finally, probably the most serious omission is Davidson's failure to consider other prison gangs such as the Aryan Brotherhood and the Black Guerilla Family. Davidson refers to the Mexican Mafia as "Family," or "Baby Mafia" (a term that he says is no longer used), but, incredibly, does not acknowledge the existence of two conflicting Chicano gangs within the California prison system. It is only in the Postscript, almost as an afterthought, that he notes that as of 1972, "the unity of Family, as a single organization, no longer exists" (Davidson 1974, p. 194) and that there are now two factions—*Familia* and Mafia-EME (the Spanish pronunciation for the letter "M").

In October 1977 a study of prison gang activities and their impact on the community was initiated by the California Board of Corrections at the request of Secretary of Health and Welfare Mario Obledo (Kahn 1978).[31] Obledo had expressed concern over the apparent rise of organized crime within the California prison system. Although much had been written on the topic, materials were scattered and a comprehensive overview of gang activities was not available. Because of the classified nature of much of the material and the fear that an extensive disclosure would interfere with possible criminal prosecution of pending cases, the depth and scope of the study was necessarily limited.

One of the most significant conclusions of the report is that it demonstrated that criminal behavior is not limited to any single racial or ethnic group. Chicanos, blacks, and Anglos are involved in organized and syndicated criminal activities. It is also clear that the roots of such gangs are not in prisons per se but in the community. Many prison gang members were also youth gang members. The East Los Angeles barrio of Maravilla, for example, was thought to be critical to the formation of the Mexican Mafia (EME). Prisons may not cause prison gangs but they are the catalyst for their formation. Prisons, after all, are dangerous places that are understaffed and cannot guarantee the safety of inmates, and the main reason for the formation of prison gangs is protection against physical assault. Thus, the absence of safe facilities almost forces prisoners to affiliate with prison gangs.

The four major prison gangs isolated by the Kahn report are the Aryan Brotherhood (AB), Black Guerilla Family (BGF), *Nuestra Familia* (NF) and Mexican Mafia (MM or EME). Other gangs include the Texas Syndicate, Common Revolution in Progress (CRIPs), and the Vanguards (U.S. Department of Justice 1985, p. 92).

The Aryan Brotherhood is believed to have originated in the late 1960s in San Quentin and Folsom prisons and is said to have been preceded by a group known as the "Bluebirds." The primary goal of the group is to protect white inmates against attacks and to promote white racism. Some, but certainly not all, members are recruited from outlaw "Biker Clubs." Listed among its activities are the distribution of narcotics, bank robberies, and murder. A strong "antiauthority" theme is found among the membership, which is estimated to range between two hundred seventy-five and five hundred. The organization is loosely structured and leadership is accorded those with strength and criminal ability. The governing unit of AB is a three-man commission and a nine-man council. Entrance into the group is by election and a "blood in, blood out" oath is taken by new members. It is alleged to have a written constitution, although it has not been found by law enforcement officers. The group operates on the streets, but its primary activities take place within the prison system. Interestingly, the Aryan Brotherhood has been loosely associated with the Mexican Mafia in various illegal activities.

For a long time, AB was considered the weakest and most poorly organized of the prison gangs, but recent evidence suggests that it has gained strength and power. A special report on organized crime published by the *San Francisco Chronicle* concluded that the Aryan Brotherhood "has become a significant national crime organization allied to the Mafia" and that the ultimate goal of the organization is to take control of traditional organized crime (Wallace 1984, p. 1). During the previous ten years alone, more than two dozen members were killed as a result of combat with rival gangs and internal struggles (ibid).

The Black Guerilla Family (BGF), the prison counterpart of the Black Liberation Army found on the streets, is believed to have been formed in the late 1960s or early 1970s. Included among its primary goals are cultural unity, group protection, and the promotion of armed revolution. According to prison officials, the BGF "attract exceptionally violent black convicts who are interested in the destruction of the 'white establishment' and are dedicated to the armed overthrow of the government" (U.S. Department of Justice 1985, p. 101). Although most members are black, there are a few nonblack members. In fact, contrary to Davidson's thesis, the organization is loosely allied with *Nuestra Familia* and in conflict with EME and the AB. Activities are guided by a rigid paramilitary structure:

> Each prison has an organization which is directed by Holliday through a central committee and five generals. Assignments are carried out by lieutenants and soldiers for their unit captain. (Kahn 1978, p. 10)

There are regular group discussions on Marxist political theory, and recruitment programs include not only combat training but ideological indoctrination as well. Also contradicting Davidson's contention that blacks cannot attain unity is the practice of requiring new members to pledge their commitment to Family by taking a "death oath":

> IF EVER I SHOULD BREAK MY STRIDE,
> OR FALTER AT MY COMRADE'S SIDE,
> THIS OATH WILL KILL ME!
>
> IF EVER MY WORD SHOULD BE UNTRUE,
> SHOULD I BE SLOW TO MAKE A STAND,
> OR SHOW FEAR BEFORE THE HANGMAN,
> THIS OATH WILL KILL ME!
>
> SHOULD I MISUSE THE PEOPLE'S TRUST,
> SHOULD I SUBMIT EVER TO GREED OR LUST,
> THIS OATH WILL KILL ME!
>
> SHOULD I GROW LAX IN DISCIPLINE
> IN TIME OF STRIFE, REFUSE MY HAND,
> THIS OATH WILL SURELY KILL ME!!!!
>
> (Ibid., p. 11)

Nuestra Familia (NF) developed in response to the activities of the Mexican Mafia. The locale of its origin is disputed, with some sources saying it began in Soledad in 1967, and others in San Quentin in 1968. What is clear is that it was established to provide protection for Chicano inmates who were being pressured by the Mexican Mafia (EME) for such things as canteen items and homosexual favors. A group of northern Chicanos reputedly formed their own alliance on September 16, 1968, after "a San Quentin EME stole shoes belonging to a Northern Hispanic inmate and wore them openly in the yard, daring the Northern group to act" (U.S. Department of Justice 1985, p. 93).

Whereas EME draws its membership primarily from urban areas in southern California, especially Los Angeles (or "Los"), NF members tend to come from rural communities in the north and are often referred to as "farmers" by the Mexican Mafia. The organization is said to be a "blood in-blood out" group, which carries a lifelong membership. Individuals who do not conform to the expectations of the group may be targeted for death and, according to estimates of law enforcement agents, their "hit list" may exceed two hundred persons at a given time. Like the Black Guerilla Family, members are required to swear to an oath:

IF I GO FORWARD, FOLLOW ME.
IF I HESITATE, PUSH ME.
IF THEY KILL ME, AVENGE ME.
IF I AM A TRAITOR, KILL ME.

(Kahn, 1978, p. 12)

In addition to providing protection for members, the group seeks to control the sale and distribution of narcotics in prison and has attempted to establish a sophisticated organization to accomplish this end. *Nuestra Familia* is unique in having a written constitution, an exposition of its complex paramilitary organizational structure, bylaws, and an operations manual. Members are trained in its structure and rules, and must take written proficiency examinations. The leader (i.e., *Nuestra* general) is in charge of some ten captains, with each captain, in turn, being in command of a regiment. At the bottom of the hierarchy are soldiers who are organized into squads depending on their reliability. Some of the more critical sections of the constitution are found in Article II:

Section I: The primary purpose or goals will be for the betterment of its members and the building up of the organization *on the outside* into a strong and self-supporting familia [emphasis added].

Section II: All members will work solely for that objective and put all personal goals and feeling aside until said fulfillment is accomplished.

Section III: A familiano will not be released from his obligations towards the organization because he is released from prison. But will be expected to work twice as hard to see that a familia is established and work in hand with the organization already established behind the [prison] walls....

Section IV: A familiano will remain a familiano member until death or otherwise discharged from the organization, he will always be subject to put the interest of the organization first and always above everything else in prison or out.

Section V: An automatic "death" sentence will be put on a familiano that turns traitor, coward, or deserter. Under no other circumstance will a brother familiano be responsible for spilling the blood of a brother familiano; to do so will be considered an act of treason. (Ibid., pp. 13-14)

Familia soldados are expected to sacrifice their personal interests for those of the organization. Profits from illegal activities in the community are to go into the *Familia* bank until there is enough money for the organization to purchase its first business. Although *Familia* is a super-secret organization, it makes and keeps written records. Law enforcement officials claim to have accumulated a great deal of information about its operations. In January 1982, for example, twenty-five alleged key members and leaders of NF were indicted in Fresno, California, for violation of the Federal Racketeer Influences and Corrupt Organizations (RICO) statutes. All subsequently pleaded guilty and twenty-one received prison sentences ranging from fifteen to forty years. The number of *Familia* members is estimated at four hundred. Law enforcement pressure has caused problems for the organization and NF is currently attempting to reestablish itself.

The Mexican Mafia (EME) is the oldest of the prison gangs and was reputedly formed in 1957 at the Deuel Vocational Institution. Initially, it was composed of so-called hoodlum elements who specialized in stealing canteen items, collecting loans, and selling drugs. In return for their services, members were offered protection from other prisoners. Many members of the organization were reportedly members of youth gangs in "Los," especially the barrio Maravilla. These youth gang members are said to have organized in prison to create EME. Eventually its criminal activities were expanded to the streets. A large number of killings in Los Angeles County in recent years have been attributed by law enforcement agents to the Mexican Mafia and yearly arrests of members for narcotics, assaults, and parole violations are said to number in the hundreds. Membership is estimated to be between one hundred fifty and two hundred hardcore members with some one thousand associates and sympathizers. Like NF, EME has attempted to get involved in legitimate activities on the streets and is said to have had considerable success at infiltrating local community organizations.

EME is considered one of the strongest and most feared prison gangs and has been blamed by prison officials for more than a hundred killings. The goals of the organization are to gain power by controlling such illicit in-prison activities as narcotics traffic, provision of special clothing (starched and pressed denims), ducats or canteen privileges, loansharking, gambling, and male prostitution (Ault 1977b, p. 7). On the streets it is also involved in robberies, burglaries, and the sale of narcotics. The Mexican Mafia reputedly has only one leader or "godfather," along with several captains, lieutenants, and *soldados en armas* (ibid.). It is reported to be a highly organized, well-structured, and very sophisticated organization that utilizes violence to attain its ends.

Although violence among rival gangs reached a peak between 1969 and 1972, there has been a recent resurgence of violence, especially between blacks and Chicanos. In San Quentin alone, five prisoners were killed in a period of only five weeks (García 1984, p. 1). Prison authorities blamed the violence on prison gangs, racial hatred, and a deteriorating physical structure that makes security difficult to maintain (ibid., p. 10). At least one death, however, resulted from negligence by prison authorities:

> Guards going against prison regulations allowed a Mexican-American gang leader and a black gang leader to walk unrestrained on a prison tier in hopes that they would negotiate a truce between the gangs. Somehow . . . the Mexican-American obtained a knife and fatally stabbed the 22-year-old Louis Montgomery, the black gang leader, . . . before the prison guards could stop the attack. (Ibid.)

Black prisoners were outraged, holding that only Montgomery was handcuffed and that he had been "set up," but prison officials maintained that neither prisoner was restrained (ibid.).

Although prison gangs are not a new or recent phenomenon, media and law enforcement interest in the problem has greatly intensified. When the activities of such groups were confined to prisons, the problem was a distant one for most Americans, but as their activities were perceived as spreading into the community the problem became more relevant and direct.

Without minimizing the seriousness of prison gangs and gang violence, it is imperative that the problem be kept in perspective. It is especially important to remember that almost all of our knowledge in this area is based on statements of law enforcement agents or their informants. These statements are accepted uncritically by the media, sensationalized, and then presented to the public as "independent" reports and exposés. The hierarchy of credibility is such that this view is not seen as biased or as representing a particular perspective, but as an accurate reflection of reality. Thus, the law enforcement view is legitimized and bias is mobilized against Chicanos.

Despite the claims of law enforcement officials that criminal behavior is not restricted to any particular ethnic group and that all major cultural groups are involved in organized crime, their primary focus is clearly on Chicano and, to a lesser extent, black gangs both inside and outside prison.

Kahn's *Report on Prison Gangs in the Community* (1978), for example, noted that the roots of prison gangs are to be found in the community and then proceeded to show the importance of Maravilla gang members in the formation of the Mexican Mafia and the prevalence of gang-related deaths in East Los Angeles. The Aryan Brotherhood, on the other hand, is depicted as an "outlaw" gang composed of misfits and "bikers"; a fringe group whose members "espouse a crude white supremacist philosophy and favor swastika tatoos and paraphernalia associated with Nazism" (Wallace 1984, p. 1). The point simply is that the Mexican Mafia and *Nuestra Familia* are seen as closely linked to the Chicano community, but white gangs are somehow independent of white society. There is similarly no attempt to link the Aryan Brotherhood with Anglo youth gangs. The discrepancy is not benign, for it reinforces the view that Mexican/Chicano culture is somehow deviant or pathological. Finally, whereas Chicano prison gangs are seen as infiltrating legitimate Chicano community organizations, no such infiltration is alleged to occur within Anglo groups and organizations.

The mass media have been especially effective in mobilizing bias against Chicanos. The *Progress Bulletin* in Pomona, California, for instance, presented a series of five articles on the Mexican Mafia and *Nuestra Familia*, highlighting their activities in the local area. Two of the headlines read: "Gang Crime Threat in Valley" (Ault 1977a) and "Prison Gang Members Out on Valley Streets" (Ault 1977b). The series was introduced by the following Editor's Note:

> This is the first in a series of five articles reporting on activities of the Mexican Mafia and La Nuestra Familia, two violent prison gangs operating in the valley. Law enforcement authorities fear this type of violent crime may increase since California's determinate sentence law went into effect July 1, and may result in the freeing of more gang members from behind prison bars. (Ault 1977a, p. 1)

Although the articles ostensibly were focusing on "prison gangs" rather than on Chicanos per se, no mention was made of other gangs. Thus, just as the word "pachuco" or "zoot-suiter" became interchangeable with "Mexican" in the 1940s, gang and gang violence have become virtually synonymous with Chicano.

Finally, it is important to emphasize that no matter how powerful Chicano and black gangs are alleged to be, they are still prison gangs and occupy a subordinate position within the hierarchy of organized crime. The

Bureau of Organized Crime and Criminal Intelligence (1982-83) distinguishes between traditional organized crime and non-traditional organized crime. Traditional organized crime is said to be a multimillion-dollar industry involved in a variety of illegal activities such as bookmaking, extortion, loansharking, labor racketeering, narcotics trafficking, fraud, pornography, and receiving stolen property. Yet, perhaps the two most distinguishing characteristics of traditional organized crime are that it has had considerable success in infiltrating legitimate business enterprises and protecting its membership from criminal prosecution.

If Chicanos and blacks have gained in power relative to other prisoners, perhaps it is because their representation within prison has also increased. In California the distribution of male felons newly received from court has changed dramatically over the years. In 1960 the distribution was 60.6 percent white, 16.7 percent Chicano, and 20.8 percent black. In 1980 only 38.6 percent were white, whereas 25.5 percent were Chicano and 34.1 percent black (Department of Corrections 1980, p. 14). The proportion of Chicano felons actually decreased slightly between 1960 (16.7 percent) and 1970 (16.3 percent). Thus, Chicano representation increased dramatically between 1970 and 1980. Essentially the same pattern is found among female felons: in 1960 the distribution was 67.6 percent white, 4.9 percent Chicana, and 25.7 percent black. By 1980 the proportion of white women in prison had declined to less than 50 percent (44.9). Chicanas had increased to 15.7 percent and black women to 35.7 percent of the total prison population (ibid., p. 27). Increased power within prison thus reflects decreasing power and increased vulnerability in society at large.

Mafia, after all, is not a sophisticated social movement but a primitive or archaic form of social protest. Eric Hobsbawm sees mafia as being similar to social banditry, although somewhat more complex:

> [They are similar] insofar as their organization and ideology are normally rudimentary, insofar as they are fundamentally "reformist" rather than revolutionary— except, once again, when they take some of the forms of collective resistance to the invasion of the "new" society. (Hobsbawm 1959, p. 5)

Yet, mafias are also more permanent and more powerful, and rather than being individual revolts, are an institutionalized system of law standing outside the official legal system (ibid., pp. 5-6). Mafia, moreover, "tends to develop in societies without effective public order" (ibid., p. 32).

GANGS OR BARRIO WARRIORS?

The history of the oppressed is replete with examples clearly demonstrating that their subordination is maintained as much by indirect symbolic control and manipulation as by the use of physical force and coercion. Once the process is set in motion, the struggle for liberation becomes as much a struggle for cultural self-determination as for economic and political equality; as much a struggle against oneself, as against the oppressor. As Robert Blauner observed:

> Culture and social organization are important as vessels of a people's autonomy and integrity; when cultures are whole and vigorous, conquest, penetration, and certain modes of control are more readily resisted . . . . America's third world groups, Africans, Indians, and Mexicans, are all conquered peoples whose cultures have been in various degrees destroyed, exploited, and controlled. (Blauner 1972, pp. 67-78)

One of the principal functions of racism is precisely that it serves to deny the humanity of persons of color and legitimate their subordination (ibid., p. 68).

Social science theories and perspectives on Chicano deliquency and gang behavior have played an important part in this process of social control. Ultimately, most of these theories have served to reinforce the image of Chicanos as criminal or deviant, and to blame Chicanos for their own subordination. Rather than focusing on economic, political, and cultural exploitation, the theories have looked to internal defects in Chicano youth or culture as key explanatory variables. Drawing on the work of Thomas Kuhn, Alfredo González has commented on the conservatizing role of scientific theory itself; he calls for the rejection of such traditional approaches and the development of new theories "realistically reflective of the Chicano community" (González 1978, p. 18). Gangs, according to González, should be viewed "with as little negative or positive imputation as possible" (ibid., p. 17). José López goes a step further and suggests that Chicano gangs have some very positive functions and are an integral part of the Chicano community:

> The Chicano youth gang serves as a means for youth to express their worth, their identity, and their sense of security when other community vehicles are either not available to them or reject them. . . . The

Chicano youth gang, therefore, is a vital and necessary part of the Chicano community—to preserve its culture. To attack and destroy the Chicano youth gang will surely result in the death of the Chicano community and all its cultural riches. (López 1978, p. 9)

Perhaps it is appropriate that one of the most insightful analyses of barrio warfare should come not from a social scientist but from a "homeboy," Gus Frias, from the barrio Rock Maravilla, or "Rock Mara." Although he pursued higher education, he remained closely tied to the barrio. Frias, author of *Barrio Warriors: Homeboys of Peace* (1982), attended the University of Southern California and Hastings Law School, and was one of the founders of the California Coalition to End Barrio Warfare. Although *Barrio Warriors* is a personal statement on barrio warfare by a person who has witnessed much violence among Chicanos and an attempt to avert additional bloodshed by communicating with the young homeboys of the barrio, it is filled with valuable insights and alternative solutions to a pressing problem that social scientists have been unable to deal with effectively. Like González and López, Frias notes that social scientists have approached the study of homeboys from a negative Anglo-ethnocentric perspective that labels them not only deviant but "sociopathic criminal gang members" (Frias 1982, p. 9). Society is threatened because the homeboy has defiantly refused to assimilate in the American melting pot:

From the way he dresses, the way he walks, the language he uses, and the car he drives, this person has created a unique form of expressing Chicano resistance to institutionalized American racism. . . . As a result, the homeboy element has become a target. The goal of powerful Anglo forces is to inculcate internal Chicano self-destruction. Through all the social means of communication, particularly the news media and the educational system in the schools, they've inculcated in the young homeboy's mind, self-depreciation, destructive values, false loyalties, reprisal killing, violence for fun, negative Machismo, and drug addiction. (Ibid)

From reading Frias it is clear that the word "gang" is inherently negative and that research utilizing such terminology, despite its trappings, is bound to produce negative conclusions (see, for example, California Council on Criminal Justice 1986). Frias is careful to avoid the word "gang"; instead, he uses the terms "homeboys" and "barrios." "Barrio" is used to designate a person's home territory or turf, and one's "homeboys" or "homies" are fellow *carnales*, or brothers, from the same barrio. The barrio of Maravilla in "East Los" covers seven and a half miles and contains over thirteen splinter barrios:

> Each of its splinter barrios possesses a unique anatomical structure, one in which as the individual gets older, his promotion to a higher stage in the barrio's structure is pugnaciously or automatically granted. (Ibid., p. 15)

The barrio functions not only as a source of identity and pride, as symbolized by *plaqueazos* (ornate Chicano writing showing a homeboy's nickname or a barrio's acronym), but as a way of defining the territory of the barrios. Yet, as with prison groups, the most basic function of barrio affiliation is protection against attacks from other barrios. Each barrio seeks to demonstrate that it is the biggest, baddest, and toughest, and that it will stand up to other barrios. There are both positive and negative elements within the barrio, however:

> The negative homeboy is called the Vato Loco. This is the weak person who is a victim of Anglo Society and who doesn't care about anyone or anything. He does not hesitate to kill his own Raza. . . . He lives a crazy life—La Vida Loca. He helps produce, sell, and consume deadly drugs in our barrios. He doesn't care about La Raza's future . . . .
>
> The positive homeboy is called the Barrio Warrior. A Barrio Warrior is a brave, honest person who dedicates his/her life to help bring unity, peace and justice to our Raza. He is a person of courage who is an excellent example of strict discipline. . . . He is a believer who believes in himself and the powerful destiny of La Raza. (Ibid., p. 11)

The key to ending barrio warfare, according to Frias, is education and the development of more barrio warriors who become educated but return to their barrios to serve as positive role models for younger homeboys and as agents of social change. The point simply is that there is no necessary link between the lifestyle of the barrio homeboy and barrio warfare. One is a positive source of identity and cultural pride; the other, a negative manifestation of the same pride that leads to self-destruction or fratricide. The key is to transform the pride in the barrio into a positive sense of pride and unity among all Chicanos—that is, to develop Chicanismo or *carnalismo* (i.e., brotherhood):

However, for the young confused homeboy, Chicanismo has lost its universality. Instead, he has narrowed its meaning to encompass advocacy of superficial barrio territory. This is often influenced and determined by the same adverse forces founded to destroy him. Barrio pride which is synonymous with Chicano pride has been obfuscated and in some cases completely distorted. Therefore, many weak-minded homeboys have fallen prey to its irrationality and have become victims of manipulated barrio terror. . . . Love is confused with hatred, and justice with death. (Ibid., pp. 10-11)

Some members of the Chicano gang culture stick together as they work their way through college. Courtesy Professor H. McGuire, San Diego City College. From his *Homeboys in College.*

7

A Theoretical Perspective on Gringo Justice

THEORETICAL MODELS AND THE CHICANO: AN OVERVIEW

From the discussion of social science theories of Chicano crime and delinquency in the previous chapter, it is clear that Chicanos generally have not fared well in such characterizations. Most social science theories have been based, directly or indirectly, on pathological models that attribute crime, delinquency, and conflicts with the legal and judicial system to internal deficiencies in Chicano cultural and familial values. The challenge facing contemporary social scientists is not to avoid discussion of such issues but to develop perspectives that are not only less pejorative but that emanate from within Chicano culture and reflect a Chicano worldview.[32]

Before proposing such a perspective, however, a brief overview of three of the major prevailing theoretical models will be presented. Much of the criminological literature, especially the early literature, was based on an order-consensus, or assimilationist, model of society. This model was challenged in the late 1960s and early 1970s by a conflict model of society. Basically two variants of the conflict model emerged. One, the colonial model, rejected the view of Chicanos as an immigrant group and saw them instead as a conquered people; the other, the Marxist model, traced their subordination and that of other racial-ethnic groups to the oppressive nature of capitalism. Both are structural discrimination theories in that they "locate the source of minority disadvantage in the social structure of the society as a whole" (Barrera 1979, p. 184), but they differ in important respects.

ORDER-PLURALISTIC AND CONFLICT MODELS

The order-pluralistic, or assimilationist, model is based on a consensus view of society.[33] Cooperation and harmony are the natural order of

216

society and the United States is seen as being truly a melting pot of diverse interests. Law is, thus, an expression of common interests and exists for the benefit of all members of society.

This is undoubtedly the oldest and most widely held perspective and provides the ideological underpinnings for much criminological theory and thought. According to Richard Quinney, "The ideas of the early sociologists directly influenced the school of legal philosophy that became a major force in legal thought—sociological jurisprudence" (1970, p. 30). Roscoe Pound was, perhaps, the leading exponent of this view. Pound maintained that law can be seen as a barometer that measures the "moral consciousness" of society at a given time. The primary function of law, thus, is to adjust and to resolve conflicting interests. In a pluralistic society the interests of society as a whole, rather than those of special interest groups, are reflected in the law:

> Looked at functionally, the law is an attempt to satisfy, to reconcile, to harmonize, to adjust these overlapping and often conflicting claims and demands, either through securing them directly and immediately, or through securing certain individual interests, or through delimitations or compromises of individual interests, so as to give effect to the greatest total of interests or to the interests that weigh most in our civilization, with the least sacrifice of the scheme of interests as a whole. (Pound 1943, p. 39)

Because law is an expression of common interests, or a compromise of conflicting interests, deviance, crime, and protest are the result of system imbalance, disorganization, or anomie.

When applied to racial-ethnic groups, the model stresses the assimilation and integration of these groups into the great melting pot. According to the model:

1. American society is composed of diverse racial-ethnic groups integrated into an orderly, cohesive "melting pot" of diverse interests.
2. The entrance of these diverse groups into American society is on an individual and voluntary basis.
3. Immigrant groups generally come from less industrialized and less developed nations and are lacking the skills necessary to compete effectively in modern society.
4. Immigrants enter society at the bottom of the socio-economic ladder, but their economic position is markedly better than it was in their country of origin.

5. New arrivals are initially at a disadvantage economically, socially, and politically, but their ultimate fate is assimilation and integration into the host society.
6. The keys to gaining parity for immigrant groups are education and
   acculturation to the values and culture of the dominant group and
   rejection of more traditional cultural and familial values.
7. Groups who do not attain parity are those that for one reason or
   another have failed to assimilate and to take advantage of the opportunities afforded in our open, pluralistic society (Mirandé 1985,
   pp. 186-87).

Deviance and crime are common among recent immigrants because
they often live in poverty and squalor, and because they have not been
fully integrated into American society. Their cultural and familial values
are, therefore, at odds with those of the dominant society. Despite its liberal
rhetoric, the order-pluralistic model is ultimately a cultural deficiency
theory.[34] Since most immigrant groups have been able to be upwardly
mobile, in a sense to "pull themselves up by their own bootstraps," the
continuous subordination of other groups is attributed to deficiencies within
the group itself. Chicanos have not made it economically and engage in
deviant and criminal behavior, according to this perspective, because they
have been unable or unwilling to assimilate. Chicano culture, moreover,
is seen as an impediment to assimilation and integration.

The order-pluralistic, melting-pot model remained largely unchal-
lenged until the late 1960s when the conflict view began to gain prominence
and recognition. The conflict perspective rejected the underlying premises
of the order-pluralistic model, and proposed that law was not a compromise
of diverse interests or the codification of shared societal interests, but rather
the imposition of some interests at the expense of others. Specifically, it
argued that groups with power are able to gain control of governmental
processes and enact laws that allow them to maintain their position of power
and advance their interests:

> Society is characterized by diversity, conflict, coercion, and change,
> rather than by consensus and stability.... Law incorporates the
> interests of specific persons and groups; it is seldom the product of
> the whole society. Law is made by men, representing special interests,
> who have the power to translate their interests into public policy.
> Unlike the pluralistic conception of politics, law does not represent

a compromise of diverse interests in society, but supports some interests at the expense of others. (Quinney 1970, p. 35)

Power groups control not only the creation of law but also its administration, and are instrumental in shaping public perceptions and conceptions of crime. They control the mass media, the police, task force reports, and other agencies that help to formulate public conceptions of crime. From this perspective, the pluralistic-order model itself is an ideological tool employed by representatives of the power structure (e.g., the police, legal scholars, and social scientists), which legitimates the exploitation of the weak by the strong. The broad acceptance of the pluralistic view throughout society indicates that this has been an effective and powerful mechanism of social control. It is so effective, in fact, that the masses do not believe they are being controlled and hold that the legal system represents all, rather than just some, interests.

COLONIAL AND MARXIST MODELS

Colonial and Marxist theory are both variants of the conflict model. They are structural theories and reject both the order-pluralistic immigrant group model and cultural deficiency theories. These theories emerged in response to the conservatizing and assimilationist bent of social science and criminological perspectives.

The internal-colony model refuted the most basic assumptions of the order-pluralistic, assimilationist model.[35] American society, it argued, is not really a melting pot or a nation made up exclusively of voluntary immigrants. Chicanos, blacks, and native Americans, after all, did not immigrate to the United States. Their initial entry into American society was forced and involuntary. Like Third World peoples colonized by European nations, these groups too were colonized, but their colonization occurred within the territorial boundaries of the United States. They are, thus, internal colonies. The internal-colony model holds the following tenets:

1. American society is composed of diverse racial-ethnic groups, but rather than being integrated into an orderly and cohesive "melting pot," the society is characterized by the subordination of some groups by others who benefit from their subordinate status.
2. While Europeans immigrated individually and freely, the entrance of certain racial-ethnic minorities was not only forced and involuntary but en masse.

3. Although it is frequently asserted that internally colonized groups come from less-advanced, underdeveloped nations, some groups have in fact come from older, advanced civilizations which in many ways were superior.
4. Internally colonized people enter the society at the bottom of the socioeconomic and political ladder, and their subordination is maintained through a variety of mechanisms.
5. Internally colonized groups make up a dependent and secondary colonial labor force that receives lower wages and few, if any, of the benefits received by workers in the primary labor force. They are dependent rather than free labor.
6. The subordination of internally colonized groups is not only economic and political but cultural as well. The dominant group seeks to render their culture dependent and to eradicate their language, thereby facilitating control of the colonized group.
7. Although the cultures of internally colonized people have been rendered dependent, they have not been eradicated, and such groups have not been assimilated or integrated into the dominant society.
8. The dominant group permits a certain amount of upward mobility for individual members of internally colonized groups who are either more Caucasian in appearance and/or willing to adopt the values and culture of the dominant group. Ironically, such individuals are accepted largely to the extent that they are perceived as *not* identifying with or representing the interests of the colonized group. (Mirandé 1985, pp. 188-89)

Chicanos are, accordingly, a colonized people. They were not only conquered militarily and forcefully incorporated into the United States but had a foreign language and culture imposed upon them.

Although internal colonialism and Marxism are both structural theories and subsumable under the conflict model, they differ in the relative emphasis placed on race and class oppression. At the risk of oversimplification, it could be said that internal colonialism sees racism as the primary basis for the economic, political, and cultural exploitation of Chicanos and other racial-ethnic groups, whereas Marxism sees economic forces as being responsible for their exploitation. Marxist critics contend, moreover, that internal colonialism is a limited, nonprogressive perspective.[36] By focusing on racial and cultural oppression, the model diverts attention from the root cause of racism and inequality—capitalism. Capitalism exploits working-class persons of all colors, it is argued, not just racial and ethnic minorities. According to the Marxist perspective:

1. Capitalism is inevitably oppressive and based on the exploitation of some groups by others.
2. Racial minorities constitute an exploited underclass within American society.
3. The basic cause of the exploitation of racial-ethnic minorities is economic rather than racial or cultural.
4. Racism will end only when capitalism is destroyed and a classless society is established.
5. Paradigms which focus on racial-cultural exploitation are misguided because they are dealing with the effects rather than the root causes of such exploitation.
6. By assuming that all whites are oppressors and all people of color oppressed, one is blinded to the fact that the white proletariat are oppressed and some people of color are oppressors or would-be oppressors.
7. The issue is ultimately not one of race or culture but one between the oppressors (capitalists) and the oppressed (proletariat). (Ibid., pp. 189-90)

One of the major criticisms leveled at the internal-colony model is that its emphasis on race and culture would inevitably result in a race war (G. González 1974, p. 157). Decolonization will come only when all Chicanos, regardless of economic status, are unified. When extended to a Third World perspective, the mobilization of all persons of color against white oppression is said to be an integral component of the colonial model. Marxism, on the other hand, seeks solidarity and mobilization among all workers against the capitalist class.

SYNTHESIS AND INTEGRATION OF THE MODELS

One of the most unfortunate consequences of the ongoing debate between internal colonialists and Marxists is that the models have often been assumed to be inherently incompatible, mutually exclusive. Proponents of either model have argued for its superiority, and there have been few attempts to uncover similarities, commonalities, or points of convergence between the models. A very different position, advanced here, is that the models are not only compatible but complementary, and that racial and economic oppression are very much intertwined.

It is my contention that any theory must take into account the fact of colonization of Chicanos. This is not to suggest that colonialism is the only or the "correct" perspective, but rather that colonization is an essential historical fact that cannot be ignored. Just as any theory of black oppression must consider the legacy of slavery, so any perspective on the Chicano must be cognizant of its colonial legacy. One can acknowledge colonization, however, and still be open to other models or theories, such as Marxism, which might well enhance our understanding of the Chicano experience. Colonialism should, therefore, be the starting point rather than the concluding point of a theory of Chicano oppression.

I hold, in fact, that a full understanding of the Chicano experience cannot be gained without also recognizing the importance of capitalism for perpetuating the subordination of racially oppressed groups. Imperialism and capitalism have had a profound impact on Chicanos, and have radically altered the relationship between Mexico and the United States. The North American invasion of Mexico and the acquisition of its northern territory resulted from an expansionist capitalistic system. Chicanos provided much of the cheap labor used in the mines, farms, ranches, railroads, and factories. Indeed, Mexican labor contributed immensely to the development of American capitalism in the nineteenth and twentieth centuries. Racism, moreover, was used to legitimate the economic exploitation of persons of color.

Some scholars have attempted to merge or synthesize the colonial and Marxist models, arguing that they are compatible. [37] One of the first to recognize the need for such a synthesis was Robert Blauner in *Racial Oppression in America* (1972). He noted that no one had proposed a theory that successfully integrated Marxist and colonial theory. Blauner envisions but himself falls short of proposing a new theoretical synthesis:

> This suggests a major defect of my study. It lacks a conception of American society as a total structure beyond the central significance that I attribute to racism. . . . Racial oppression and racial conflict are not satisfactorily linked to the dominant economic relations nor to the overall distribution of political power in America. The failure of Marxism to appreciate the significance of racial groups and racial conflict is in part responsible for this vacuum, since no other existing

framework is able to relate race to a comprehensive theory of capitalist development. (Blauner 1972, p. 13)

Blauner notes, moreover, that neither Marxism nor colonialism by themselves are able to adequately grasp the complexity of racial oppression in advanced capitalistic societies.

Despite its shortcomings, *Racial Oppression in America* laid the foundation for the mergence of the colonial and Marxist models. Blauner held that labor and its exploitation should be seen as the initial cause of contemporary race relations, and that this division of labor was still manifested in the privileged position of whites within the occupational and economic structures of present-day multiracial societies (ibid., p. 29). Colonial labor, moreover, was critical to the development of Western capitalism:

> Capitalism and free labor as Western institutions were not developed for people of color; they were reserved for white people and white societies. In the colonies European powers organized other systems of work that were noncapitalist and unfree. (Ibid., p. 58)

European immigrants and persons of color were both exploited by capitalism, but white labor differed from colonial labor. European immigrants worked largely within the free capitalistic system, whereas persons of color constituted a dependent and unfree labor force. White immigrants worked mostly within the industrialized modern sectors and were able to be upwardly mobile economically, politically, and socially (ibid., p. 62). Thus, within a generation or two they were integrated into American society.

Tomás Almaguer has sought to further develop the complex interrelationship between race and class exploitation. Almaguer contends that racism is much more than an epiphenomenon or a manifestation of false consciousness, as some Marxists would suggest. Like Blauner, he proposes that racism has a structural component and a material basis. In both Mexico and the United States, "race was not only to provide the central source of ideological justification of the colonial situation, but it also became the central factor upon which classes in colonial society were to develop outwardly and take their form" (Almaguer 1975, p. 74). Chicanos first served as an exploited underclass and as an unfree labor force used to develop American capitalism. Subsequent to 1940, according to Almaguer, they were gradually incorporated into the lowest segments of the working class.

Almaguer rejects the view that racism will be eliminated automatically by doing away with the class basis of Chicano oppression. Racism will end only when we begin to recognize that the white working class benefits, in the short run at least, from racial exploitation and racism itself has a material basis. He concludes by suggesting:

> What is needed is an honest appraisal of the many ways in which the working class has become segmented and divided. An assessment of racial minorities within the working class is but one step in this direction. It is only when oppressed peoples begin to seek out the commonalities—as well as differences—in their oppression that we can hope to build those political alliances that will be both meaningful and ultimately effective. (Ibid., p. 95)

Perhaps the most complete and successful attempt to integrate Marxist and colonial theories is Mario Barrera's *Race and Class in the Southwest* (1979). Barrera acknowledges that Chicanos were a dependent and unfree labor force during the nineteenth century and throughout much of the twentieth century. Yet, because many Chicanos today are part of the working class, and some have even been incorporated into the middle and professional classes, there is a need for a more complex theory that captures the reality of the contemporary situation. What Barrera proposes is a modification of the internal colonial model, taking into account the operation of both class and colonial interests. Social classes are assumed to be the most general structural elements in society. Chicanos, according to Barrera, are found in all social classes but because of class segmentation they constitute a subordinate segment within each class. Persons within a particular class share certain interests with other members of that class, regardless of ethnicity:

> A Chicano in the subordinate segment of the working class is still a member of that class, and has interests in common with all members of the working class, for example, in higher wages, better working conditions, the right to bargain collectively, and, ultimately, the establishment of a classless society. These interests are in opposition to those of other classes, particularly the capitalistic class. (Barrera 1979, p. 214)

But because of institutional discrimination, Chicanos, regardless of their class position, also share a number of interests in common (i.e., colonial interests), such as ending discrimination:

> The different Chicano segments also constitute an internal colony in the sense that they share a common culture, at least in part, and

this may be reflected in a shared interest in such things as bilingual-bicultural programs in the schools. (Ibid., p. 216)

TOWARD A THEORY OF GRINGO JUSTICE

Although Barrera, Almaguer, and Blauner have done much to integrate Marxist and colonial theories and to enhance our understanding of class and racial oppression, these works have significant limitations. One limitation is their almost exclusive concern with political economy. Political economy is important, but social science paradigms cannot continue to ignore the role of culture in shaping the behavior of Chicanos.

The conflict and tension that have historically characterized relations between Chicanos and Anglo society, though rooted in political economy, extend well beyond it. In addition to being a conflict between economic and political systems, it has been a conflict between competing cultures, values, legal and judicial systems, and worldviews. Barrera, for example, purports to subscribe to the internal-colony model, yet perhaps what is most lacking in his conceptualization is a clear vision of Chicano culture. His theory is, in the end, a mergence of two structural discrimination theories (i.e., internal colonialism and Marxism):

> Barrera completely discards deficiency theories and concludes that bias theories are not so much wrong as incomplete in that they fail to identify the origins of racism, but he does not present a positive cultural theory of the Chicano experience. One is therefore led to conclude either that Chicanos have no culture, other than a common interest in things like bilingual education and *Cinco de Mayo* parades, or that culture is epiphenomenon. (Mirandé 1985, p. 220)

There is a need for a new synthesis that will reflect the dynamic interrelationship between structure and culture. This new synthesis would recognize that there is a sense in which race transcends class and that Chicanos are subjected to differential and unequal treatment both between and within social classes. The proposed perspective is unique not so much in seeking to integrate Marxist and colonial theories, for that has already been attempted, but in incorporating both structural and cultural explanations.

Although Anglo society and economic oppression have impinged on the Chicano, Chicano culture is not totally dependent on Anglo culture. Chicanos, after all, have a very rich cultural legacy that was in existence long before the American invasion and even before the landing of the Pilgrims. If we are to gain a full understanding of Chicanos, we must, therefore, consider the impact of culture. This does not mean that structural forces are not important, but rather that our culture, identity, and sense of self-worth are not epiphenomenal or simply a response to structural oppression.

The perspective is unique also in extending beyond political economy and examining the relationship of Chicanos to the legal and judicial system. Most of the more recent theoretical developments in Chicano scholarship have been confined to political economy. [38] The result has been a somewhat unidimensional and limited view of the Chicano experience. It is necessary to consider the impact of all institutions that impinge upon Chicanos.

It is unfortunate, on the other hand, that works that have focused on Chicanos and the legal and judicial system have tended either to subscribe to cultural deficiency models or to be descriptive and fairly devoid of theory. Books such as Paredes's (1958) *"With His Pistol in His Hand,"* Morales's (1972) *Ando Sangrando* (I Am Bleeding), Castillo and Camarillo's (1973) *Furia Y Muerte*, and Samora, Bernal, and Peña's (1979) *Gunpowder Justice* are significant contributions to the literature, but they are largely descriptive, not theoretical. If they have a common theoretical orientation, perhaps it is an implicit or unstated form of the colonial model.

The perspective on gringo justice proposed here differs from the bulk of the criminological literature in rejecting the correctional perspective. It does not, in fact, seek to explain Chicano criminality or gang behavior. In a manner consistent with sociological labeling and conflict theory, it attempts, instead, to trace the development and differential application of Anglo judicial and criminal norms. Theoretical perspectives that seek to explain why Chicanos are more criminally prone, it is argued, have answered the question a priori and are inherently pathological. They are bound, in other words, to attribute the *bandido* image to a deficit in the Chicano, whether it be biological, psychological, or cultural. Even works with the best of intentions, such as *Homeboys* (Moore 1978) or *Chicano Prisoners* (Davidson 1974), ultimately have tended to link Chicano criminality to some defect in the Chicano.

The cultural clash that has characterized relations between Anglos and *mexicanos* since the initial contact between the two groups is an essential component of the proposed framework. Mexican culture, after all, was Catholic, feudal, traditional, communal, and person-oriented, whereas Anglo-American culture was Protestant, capitalistic, modern, individualistic, and materialistic. According to Carey McWilliams, Anglos have always been considered gringos to the *mexicano;* and to the American, Mexicans, or "Meskins," have always been "greasers" (1968, p. 115). These pejorative terms capture the mutually reinforcing hostility between the two groups. The conflict did not diminish with increased contact; "in fact, tensions mounted through the nineteenth century and into the twentieth" (Rosenbaum 1981, p. 7). The ease and swiftness of the victory over Mexico, moreover, intensified the North American contempt for the Mexican (McWilliams 1968, p. 129). According to McWilliams, the first impressions that Americans had of Mexicans, especially the lower classes and *cholos*, were very unfavorable and provided the outlines for present-day stereotypes of the Mexican (1968, p 131). T. J. Farnham's characterization, published in 1855, typifies the prevailing attitude:

> The Spanish population of the Californias [is] in every way a poor apology of European extraction; . . .incapable of reading or writing, and knowing nothing of science or literature, nothing of government but its brutal force, nothing of virtue but the sanction of the Church.... Destitute of industry themselves, they compel the poor Indian to labor for them, affording him a bare savage existence for his toil, upon their plantations and the fields of the Missions. In a word, the Californians are an imbecile, pusillanimous, race of men, and unfit to control the destinies of the beautiful country. (Farnham 1855, pp. 358-59, 363)

Manuel Ramírez has argued that from the onset European and indigenous Mexican or mestizo cultures were characterized by very different worldviews. The basic tenets of the European worldview were:

1. The technological and economic development of a culture or society are synonymous with the degree of psychological development of its members. This belief states that countries which are technologically underdeveloped are populated by peoples who are not psychologically sophisticated and/or who are pathological.
2. The second tenet concerns the equation of psychological development with religious ideology—the greater the adherence to European-Christian beliefs by a culture or a nation, the more civilized, sophisticated, and well adjusted its inhabitants or members are assumed to be.
3. The third tenet concerns the belief in genetic superiority... nurtured by the Darwinian theory of evolution.... Specifically, peo-

ple of Northern and Western European stock are believed to be genetically superior to the native peoples of the Americas and to Blacks.
4. The fourth tenet of the European world view holds that certain cultures and belief systems are superior to others. European cultures are believed to be superior to non-European cultures. (Ramírez 1983, pp. 5-6)

The tenets of the mestizo worldview, on the other hand, were:

1. Knowledge obtained from living and surviving the challenges of life makes every individual's philosophy of life valuable and makes every person a potential teacher.
2. The Indian cultures view the person as an open system which both affects and is affected by his/her surroundings. Harmony with the environment, both physical and social, is thus of primary concern....
3. The third tenet of the mestizo world view ... speaks to the importance of openness to diversity; the ultimate criterion for achieving knowledge and sophistication in life is acceptance and respect for the beliefs of all cultures and religions.... It is this acceptance of diversity which facilitated the development of bicultural/ multicultural identities and ways of life by... people in the Americas.
4. The fourth tenet of the mestizo world view concerns the advantages of pluralistic socialization—the more a person is willing to learn from the knowledge, life experiences, and life meanings of other peoples' religions and cultures, the more he/she has opportunity to incorporate these into his/her own personality and, in turn, make use of these additional resources to become more flexible and adaptable in meeting the diverse demands of life. (Ramírez 1983, pp. 8-9)

Although Ramírez's intent is to develop a psychology of the Americas, his conceptualization is useful for understanding the cultural clash between Anglos and *mexicanos*, and the pervasiveness of the correctional perspective in sociological and criminological literature. Chicanos, after all, have been perceived and evaluated according to the tenets of the European worldview not only by Anglo-American society as a whole but by social and behavioral scientists as well. Theoretical perspectives do not develop in a vacuum; they tend to reflect the worldview of the prevailing social order.

Like Ramírez in psychology, I have identified the need for developing a Chicano perspective on sociology and social science:

> Over the years social scientists have demonstrated an inordinate concern with the Mexican/Chicano people.... *Raza*, however, has not fared very well in social-science depictions. When compared to middle-class, Anglo Protestant and Judaic values, Chicano cultural, familial, and religious values have been found wanting.... The Chicano people have been viewed as inferior and as lacking those characteristics essential to success in modern, urban, American society. A persistent theme is that Anglo culture is modern, individualistic, futuristic, and achievement-oriented; in contrast, Chicano culture is traditional, collectivistic, backward, and lacking in achievement. (Mirandé 1985, p. 201)

Chicanos, moreover, have often been viewed as criminal and violent, and their aberrant behavior has been attributed to genetic, psychological, or cultural deficiencies.

These theoretical constructs enable us to reinterpret the cultural conflict as a clash of worldviews. The American invasion and subsequent military victory were a vindication for American culture and the Anglo worldview. The United States was technologically and economically more advanced and its citizens therefore judged themselves superior to the backward Mexicans. This attitude was so pervasive that the Mexican was considered incapable of taking proper care of the vast and rich territory that had been under Mexican control. Although Mexicans were technically Christians, their religion incorporated many elements of indigenous religions and was perceived not as European Catholicism but as a pagan and idolatrous brand of Christian Mexicanism (see Grebler, Moore, and Guzman 1970, pp. 449-50; Orozco 1980, p. 37). This antipathy was buttressed by the belief that Europeans were genetically and culturally superior to the native peoples of the Americas.

Differences in cultures and worldviews dictated very different orientations toward property and land. Whereas *mexicanos* lived in a pastoral economy, Anglo society was organized around individualistic capitalism. Attitudes toward the land varied in the two systems:

> For peasants, land is one of the givens of the world. Like family, religion, or seasonal change, land is part of the total environment that sustains the community and gives it focus and direction. Bourgeois society, as historian Eric Hobsbawm points out, requires

> a transformation of land tenure and ownership: "land [has] to be turn-
> ed into a commodity, possessed by private owners and freely pur-
> chasable and saleable by them." (Rosenbaum 1981, p. 11)

Under capitalism, land was not there simply to be used; it was a commodity that could be bought, sold, and hoarded. It also produced other com-modities such as crops, livestock, and minerals, which could be sold or exchanged in an open market (ibid., p. 12).

There were also important differences between the American and Mexican systems of land tenure. Perhaps the most significant difference was that under Hispanic/Mexican law communal or collective land owner-ship was widely recognized, whereas Anglo-American law only acknow-ledged individual ownership. *Mexicano* landownership also was never ab-solute but conditional, and could be revoked if the conditions of the grant were not observed. Under Spanish law, for example, if land was not cultivated for two years, ownership reverted to the crown. In short, land grants gave the grantees permission to use the land under certain specified conditions. An underlying premise of the land grant system was that each family was to be awarded only sufficient land for its own use. All other lands and natural resources were to be held in common by an entire village or community.

Given this pastoral heritage where personal identity and sense of self-worth were determined largely by one's relation to the land, it is ironic that Chicanos today are predominantly an urban, landless people. Whether wealthy rancheros or lowly *campesinos*, they were an agrarian people in the nineteenth century. At the present time, approximately 80 percent of the Chicano population resides in urban areas and most of this population occupies lower-status working-class jobs. Most Chicanos are, therefore, part of a landless, urban proletariat.

In restrospect, the Treaty of Guadalupe Hidalgo looms significant, for although it supposedly protected civil and property rights of displaced Mexican citizens, in reality it brought into question the validity of their land titles. In addition, there was no provision in the treaty or in Anglo-American law for communal ownership of land. Unlike Native Americans whose collective claim to the land was recognized by treaty, Chicanos were to fend for themselves as individuals. Thus, although Native Americans have experienced extensive prejudice, discrimination, and poverty, their claim to the land has enabled them to retain a certain amount of sovereignty and cultural autonomy. They have, for example, retained their own tribal governments and judicial systems (see Deloria and Lytle 1983). Indian institutions, however, have had to adapt to changing realities. Deloria and Lytle note:

> Had the tribes abandoned their old ways and wholeheartedly adopted the new institutions of the intruders, we would have no identifiable Indian today. On the other hand, if they had absolutely resisted any changes, we most probably would not have Indians today either.... Consequently, tribes everywhere adjusted cautiously and did their best to keep what was good in the old culture while adopting those things that helped them deal with new realities and new people. (1983, p. xi)

The differences between the Indian experience and the Chicano experience parallel differences between classic and internal colonialism. Classic colonialism entails acquisition of a distant land; internal colonialism that of contiguous territory. Whereas the classic colony is recognized formally and legally, the internal colony is not. The Treaty of Guadalupe Hidalgo accorded displaced Mexicans all the rights of United States citizens and declared them equal under the law, according to the principles of the American Constitution, without at the same time honoring these guarantees. It therefore transformed Chicanos into a de facto colony:

> The informality of internal colonization makes it more insidious and oppressive, however, because the existence and legitimacy of native institutions and culture are not recognized. The culture, values, and language of Chicanos thus have had no formal or legitimate standing within American society.... Although Chicanos may have formal and legal equality, they are informally excluded from full participation in the educational, economic, and political system. (Mirandé 1985, pp. 4-5)

The Indian tribal and judicial system, on the other hand, was significantly altered, but it was not totally disregarded or destroyed.

The political and economic downfall of the Chicano, particularly the displacement from the land, set a process in motion—barrioization—that was to have a critical impact not only on the Chicano people but on their relationship with the dominant society. As Chicanos became part of the urban proletariat in the twentieth century they became increasingly concentrated in barrios, *colonias*. Within every large city and almost all smaller communities in the Southwest one could find a Mexican section or Mextown. For instance, in Santa Barbara:

> During the last quarter of the nineteenth century the processes of barrioization and Americanization created a new reality for Mexican people in Santa Barbara. As the Anglo capitalist economic order became dominant during the 1870s, Chicano workers tied to the dying pastoral economy experienced increasing privation. This impoverishment was reflected in the general appearance of the residentially segregated and isolated barrio of Pueblo Viejo. Made politically powerless through various methods of disenfranchisement and gerrymandering and without political leaders, the Chicanos were defenseless within a dominant society that regarded them as foreigners. (Camarillo 1979, pp. 77-78)

Similarly, in Los Angeles Mexicans were discouraged from settling in other parts of the city and established their own communities in the flat lowlands along the Los Angeles River (Romo 1983, p. viii).

Although segregation played a part in barrioization, the process was much more extensive. As Chicanos were displaced from the land and as they lost economic and political power, they became superfluous. By being separated and isolated, they were, in effect, eliminated from the social and political milieu of the dominant society. The "Mexican problem" could now be dealt with more effectively, for Chicanos had become invisible (Mirandé 1985, p. 19). To the Chicano, on the other hand, barrios offered a certain sense of security and insulation. The East Los Angeles barrio, for example, "became a haven for a Mexican population which faced discrimination in housing, employment, and social activities in Anglo parts of the city" (Romo 1983, p. viii).

The isolation of Chicanos in barrios and Indians on reservations is reminiscent of Philip Slater's discussion of the "toilet assumption." According to Slater, Americans subscribe to the idea that social problems and other undesirable situations will go away if they can be put out of sight (1971, p. 15). The prevailing approach taken is basically "out of sight, out of mind." Rather than seeking to eliminate poverty, blighted areas are bulldozed in the name of urban renewal. When the problem rises to the surface again, society is shocked and angered, and calls in the emergency plumber (ibid.). Crash programs or special commissions are established to provide instant solutions. Unfortunately, such solutions typically are aimed at the effects, rather than the root causes, of the problem. Conflict between Chicanos and law enforcement agencies, for example, is very much symptomatic of their political, economic, and cultural oppression. Although much can be done to improve relations between law enforcement and the Chicano community, an ultimate solution will require addressing these more basic, root causes of the problem.

Because Mexicans have historically been a source of cheap and dependent labor, the American attitude toward this group has been predictably ambivalent. The fact that Mexicans were willing to work long hours at low wages, the proximity to Mexico, and the perception that most would return to their native land, made the Mexican an ideal worker. Although Mexicans were not integrated into the economic, political, and cultural life of the community, their labor was essential to American capitalism. Barrioization facilitated political and economic control. Mexican labor would be readily available without any need for the assimilation or integration of the Chicano. Chicanos could be kept not only in their own neighborhoods but in poor housing and inferior, segregated schools. A high drop-out rate and the continual influx of undocumented workers guaranteed a vast pool of cheap labor. Law enforcement and the prevailing system of gringo justice, moreover, insured that Chicanos would be kept in their place.

Cultural and physical isolation coupled with the hostile relationship between barrios and the outside world has worked to intensify barrio identity and pride, at times to the detriment of a larger identification with Chicanismo or *carnalismo*. It is precisely because they are a landless people that barrio identification looms so large in the lives of Chicanos. Chicanos may not own land and it may be difficult for them to identify with the community as a whole, because it is generally Anglo owned and controlled, but identification with their barrio gives them a great deal of ethnic identity and pride. Similarly, for many Chicano youth, membership in a barrio club or group provides the same sense of pride, self-worth, and legitimation that other youths receive from athletic teams, fraternities and sororities, or the Boy Scouts. John C. Quicker, for example, has likened "homegirls" (i.e., Chicana gangs) to working-class sororities. "Gangs" do not exist in the conventional sense as separate, aberrant forms of association:

> Gangs are not unique groupings of adolescents, distinct and separate from other forms of adolescent organizations. Gangs, at least Chicana gangs, share many values and are organizationally very similar to another well-known adolescent group—the Girl Scouts.... In fact,

they may be more similar than different from more "acceptable" organizations. (Quicker 1983, p. 53)

Also critical to the proposed perspective is the premise that the legacy of conquest, the proximity of the border, and the history of economic and political dependence of Mexico on the United States have had a profound impact on the Chicano experience. The border, as has been demonstrated, has subjected Chicanos to a form of double oppression as well as harassment by both local and state law enforcement agencies and the Border Patrol. Social science theories, unfortunately, have not really attached sufficient importance to the border. It is my contention that the "border experience" should occupy a central role in any conceptualization of the Chicano experience, for there is a sense in which Chicanos, try as they may, cannot divorce themselves from their Mexican roots. Despite efforts to merge into the melting pot by establishing themselves as "Mexican-Americans," "Americans of Mexican descent," or just plain "Americans," the United States has been reluctant to incorporate them. Because of their distinctive language and racial and cultural features, to many Americans they somehow remained "Mexican" and "foreign." The point simply is that the destiny of the Chicano is very much linked not only to Mexico but to the economic and political dependence of that nation on the United States.

The pachuco and the *cholo* experience, in fact, reflects a continual attempt by Chicano youth to forge a distinctive cultural identity. Critical to this unique identity is the premise that Chicano youth were considered Americanized by the older generation but treated as "Meskins" by the schools and Anglo society. Because there has been no legitimate place for Chicano barrio youth in American society, they have found it necessary to develop their own culture and lifestyle.

While immigrant groups have tended to blend into the American melting pot, the proximity of Mexico and the demand for cheap and dependent labor have resulted in a perpetual Mexican first generation. This, coupled with the fact that Mexicans were distinct culturally and physically, and that they constituted a dependent and exploited labor force, has facilitated the perpetuation of racism and discrimination. Individual Chicanos could be upwardly mobile and enter the professional or petty bourgeois class, but to the Anglo they remained Mexicans, for as Manuel Gamio (1930, p. 53) observed, prejudice against Mexicans dates back to the first contact of white Americans with Mexicans and Indians on the frontier. Also, individual Chicanos have recently made economic, educational, and political progress, but Chicanos as a people have not. American society has always permitted a limited mobility for Chicanos as "individuals," but not for Chicanos as a group. Barrios remain ethnic enclaves, physically, socially, and economically isolated from the dominant society. They remain inhabited almost exclusively by *mexicanos*, especially the poor and recent arrivals from Mexico, and have a preponderance of poverty, unemployment, substandard housing, Anglo ownership of property, externally owned and controlled businesses and industry, inferior schools, drug and inhalant abuse, barrio warfare, youth groups (i.e., "gangs," from the perspective of the dominant society), and community/police conflict.

Although Chicanos lack ownership of land, there is a sense in which barrios are reservations where Chicano culture is nurtured and preserved. They constitute a fictive land base. At the same time that many of the social problems facing Chicanos, such as barrio warfare and police abuse, are most strongly manifested in homogeneous Chicano neighborhoods, the barrio also holds the key to the liberation of the Chicano people. The pride and energy that has mobilized barrios against one another must be channeled toward obtaining economic and political power for the community as a whole, not simply for individual Chicanos. All too often, individual success for Chicanos occurs at the expense of, or in lieu of, community welfare. An essential first step in attaining liberation, then, is for Chicanos to gain control of their own communities and to obtain collective political and economic power. Although Chicanos are predominantly a landless, urban people, their cultural roots are deeply embedded in an agrarian past. Significantly, urban barrios are not "asphalt jungles"; they retain a distinct rural ambience within urban centers. Land is still important to the Chicano and the land question needs to be more adequately addressed by social science theories. Collective ownership of land will be difficult to attain, but control over community centers and parks, schools, and local governments can be more readily effected.

In retrospect, gringo justice ultimately has been but an extension of the economic and political system. The American invasion resulted in the military defeat of Mexico and acquisition of what is today the American Southwest, but the water, land, property, and cultural rights of displaced Mexican citizens were to be protected by provisions of the Treaty of Guadalupe Hidalgo. Instead, the legal and judicial system became a mockery; a vehicle for legitimating a massive land grab that left Chicanos landless and transformed them into an unfree, dependent labor force. The view of Chicanos as bandits emerged as they responded to such abuses and went outside of law to attain justice. Whether as "greasy *bandidos*" in the nineteenth century, pachucos in the 1940s, or contemporary *cholos* or gang members, the image persists unabated.

A basic thesis of this book is that Chicanos have been labeled bandits and criminals because they have not passively accepted their economic and political exploitation. Pachucos of the 1940s and contemporary "barrio warriors" have been termed violent, lawless, and dangerous precisely because they are seeking to form and express a unique sense of cultural identity and pride. They are a threat to society not because they are violent—barrio warfare occurs among Chicanos themselves—or criminal, but because they reject both Anglo society and the gringo system of justice.

Notes

1. The term "Chicano" is used here to designate a person of Mexican descent living in the United States on a relatively permanent basis, regardless of citizenship or place of birth. Like *pocho* (assimilated Mexican) and *cholo* (low-life Mexican), in the past it has had pejorative connotations when used in both Mexico and the United States. In the 1960s "Chicano" was self-consciously selected by participants in *el movimiento* ("the movement") as the preferred term, not only because it was symbolic of ethnic nationalism and pride but because it captured the reality of the Mexican experience within the United States. "Mexican" was discarded because it failed to distinguish between Mexicans living north and south of the border; "Mexican-American" was not adopted, because it connoted middle-class respectability and greater identification with and integration into American society. Inasmuch as it was popularly believed that "Chicano" was derived from the Aztec word for *mexicano* (i.e., *Meschica* or *Meshicano*), the term was unique in linking Chicanos with their Indian heritage while distinguishing them from Mexicans living in Mexico. The term, however, does not appear to have had its anticipated unifying effect and *mexicano* is still the preferred term of "public" self-reference (see Limón 1981, p. 205). "Like 'nigger' in all-black in-group settings, 'Chicano' may express closeness and group solidarity when it is performed within the group" (ibid., p. 206), but there has been reluctance to accept it as a term of public self-reference, especially in Texas and among the middle, or more "respectable," social classes.

Although "Chicano," "Mexican-American," "Mexican," and *mexicano* have different connotations, they are denotatively the same. The word "Chicano" is used throughout this book to denote persons of Mexican descent living within the territorial boundaries of the United States. This usage, however, is merely for convenience and is not intended to suggest that Chicanos are somehow not also *mexicanos*. Rather than seeking to determine which is the best or most desirable label, the focus here is on the "Chicano experience"; in other words, on the experience of Mexicans with American society and the gringo system of justice.

2. More extensive discussion of Anglo attitudes toward Mexicans during the nineteenth century can be found in Arnoldo De León (1983), *They Called Them Greasers: Anglo Attitudes Toward Mexicans in Texas, 1821-1900;* James Ernest Crisp (1976), "Anglo-Texan Attitudes Toward the Mexican, 1821-1845"; and Robert F. Heizer and Alan J. Almquist (1977), *The Other Californians: Prejudice*

237

and Discrimination under Spain, Mexico, and the United States to 1920.

3. Although Rendon is a journalist, *Chicano Manifesto* contains some valuable insights on the treaty.

4. This is not to suggest that all Anglos who broke the law were considered heroes or that all Chicanos who did so were labeled bandits, for social banditry is a complex phenomenon that transcends racial groups. Richard White distinguishes between organized opposition to vigilantes and social banditry. Social bandits did not represent an organized opposition to vigilantes. "They, too, arose where law enforcement was distrusted, where criminal was an ambiguous category, and where the legitimacy of vigilantism was questioned. Where social banditry occurred, however, the vigilantes and their opponents did not form two coherent groups, but instead consisted of numerous, mutually hostile factions" (White 1981, p. 389). What distinguishes social bandits from ordinary criminals is the presence of a large number of persons who are themselves law-abiding, but who identify with and are willing to support them "on grounds other than fear, profit, or expediency" (ibid.). There were both Anglo and Chicano social bandits, hence the emergence of the *"bandido* image" extends well beyond social banditry. What is unique about the *bandido* image is that not just some individuals, but a whole group, were labeled bandits.

5. Although xenophobia prevailed in the early 1940s, concern with the problem of Mexican crime has been a persistent feature of American society since the takeover of Mexico's northernmost territories.

6. *Cholo* is used here in a pejorative context to refer to the "low-life" colonizers of Alta California. Pitt notes that in encouraging colonization, California acquired a number of petty thieves and political prisoners from northern Mexico (1966, p. 6). The genteel elite Californios *(gente de razón)* were quick to dissociate themselves from these "scoundrels." In its contemporary usage, *cholo* designates a young street dude whose style of dress and speech is patterned after the pachucos of the 1940s.

7. For further discussion of the Spanish and Mexican land grants see, Knowlton (1980), Van Ness and Van Ness (1980), McBride (1923), Westphall (1983), Brayer (1949), Keleher (1964), Pearson (1961), Cortés (1974), Robinson (1948), Hoffman (1862), Ellison (1927), Jones (1850), Leonard (1970), Ortiz (1980), Ebright (1980), Cowan (1977), Bowden (1971), and Avina (1932).

8. The biographical sketches of Catron and Elkins are taken primarily from Brayer (1949, p. 167) and Keleher (1964, pp. 147-51).

9. For a discussion of labeling and social conflict theories, see Lemert (1951 and 1967), Becker (1966), Douglas (1970), Schur (1971), Filstead (1972), and Rubington and Weinberg (1973).

10. David Pierce Barstow's account is somewhat different. According to Barstow, Cannon, in his drunken condition, "reached in his hand to apologize for pushing the door in" and "she stabbed him to the heart with this knife" (Recollections of David Pierce Barstow, 1849-51, pp. 7-8).

11. The location of the bridge where Juanita was hanged has been disputed. According to Sinnott, "A careful consideration of many items of evidence leads the writer to the conclusion that the hanging was from the Durgan Bridge" (Sinnott 1977, p. 49).

12. For additional discussion see, Brent (1976) and Robinson (1976).

13. Correspondence concerning the Texas Rangers in the Office of the Adjutant General of Texas indicates that in this early period (1838-1842), the Rangers were poorly organized and lacked supplies and horses (Adjutant General of Texas, 1838-1865).

14. See, for example, Ford (1963), Gillett (1925), Hughes (1964), Greer (1952), Jennings (1930), and Sterling (1959).

15. For an interesting discussion of Anglo machismo on the frontier, see Paredes (1967, pp. 73-74).

16. Lea (1968, vol. 1, p. 285) refers to the ranch as the *Cachattus*. Webb (1965, p. 264) also calls it the *Cachattus* or *Las Curchas*, whereas the name used by Samora, Bernal, and Peña (1979, p. 49), *Las Cucharas* (the spoons), makes more sense in Spanish. Spanish names often suffered in translation. Enrique Mindiola, grandson of the owner of the ranch, also identified it as *Las Cucharas* in a letter to Webb (Walter Prescott Webb Papers, General Correspondence, 1962-63).

17. Latta (1980, p. 305) points out that the records of the Texas Rangers do not show a Harry Love.

18. See Schaefer (1965, pp. 287-323); Crichton (1928); and Beckett (1962).

19. It is not clear whether Renteria was truly a bandit or a Mexican revolutionary: the term "bandit" tends to be used indiscriminately when applied to Mexicans. Pancho Villa, for example, is often termed a bandit, rather than a revolutionary leader or a general. Significantly, Hinkle refers to Renteria as "a well known, desperate, and vindictive villista bandit leader" (1970, p. 25).

20. As early as 1853, the mounted customs inspectors were established by the secretary of the treasury to guard against smugglers and illegal entrants (Myers 1971, p. 15). The mounted inspectors were relieved of their immigration duties in 1891, however, by the special inspectors of immigrants who were to patrol border crossings.

21. For a more detailed discussion of these problems, see, García (1980, pp. 106-38).

22. For discussion of the Bracero Program, see Galarza (1964), Craig (1971), Copp (1963), Anderson (1961), and Jones (1946).

23. In his analysis of the American G.I. Forum, Carl Allsup presents a less condemning view of *What Price Wetbacks?* Allsup notes that the focus of the G.I. Forum's anti-*mojado* stance primarily became the Mexican-American who "bore the effect of illegal labor; the Mexican-Americans lost jobs or were forced to work for depressed wages. Many had to leave their homes and subject their families to the cruelties of the migrant trail" (Allsup 1982, p. 110).

24. Recently, for example, four marines from Camp Pendleton in northern San Diego County were arrested for nighttime raids and armed robberies against illegal aliens. Lance Cpl. Stephen Dale Gardner was accused of going into the hills and hunting "beaners," as he called them (Associated Press 1984, p. B-6).

25. For an overview of immigration policy, see Samora (1975) and Bustamante (1972), Gómez-Quiñones (1981), Hoffman (1974, pp. 5-23), Cardoso (1980), and Cornelius and Montoya (1983).

26. The bill was approved in the Senate by a wide margin (80-19) but died in the House during the 97th Congress. The bill was introduced again on February

22, 1983, but it was not until October 1986 that a compromise measure was approved by both houses of Congress.

27. For a law enforcement view of the history of the police, see the U.S. President's Commission on Law Enforcement and the Administration of Justice (1967b, pp. 3-7). A more critical perspective can be found in *The Iron Fist and the Velvet Glove: An Analysis of the U.S. Police* (Center for Research on Criminal Justice 1977).

28. The only in-depth analysis of the Los Angeles police riots (1970-1971) is Armando Morales's (1972) classic work *Ando Sangrando* ("I am bleeding"). Much of the factual information presented here is taken from this source.

29. In comparison, the media were shocked by the Kent State shootings in which four white students were killed and nine wounded (Morales 1972, front jacket cover).

30. Although zoot-suiter and pachuco are often used interchangeably, there are important differences between the two terms. The zoot-suit craze appears to have been started by Filipino youth, and many pachucos did not sport zoot suits. George C. Barker defines "pachuco" as a unique language or argot which originated among youth from El Paso, Texas and Juárez, Mexico and spread to Los Angeles, Tucson, and other Southwest cities (1950, p.13). The development of this argot, or *caló*, in turn, can be traced to *grifos* (marijuana smokers) and members of the Mexican underworld. What is significant is that this argot goes back to at least the early 1930s and precedes the zoot-suiters of the 1940s.

31. The overview of the four major prison gangs presented here is taken primarily from Kahn (1978) and U.S. Department of Justice (1985).

32. For a more detailed discussion of these and related issues, see Mirandé (1978, 1982, 1985).

33. A more extensive discussion of the models can be found in Quinney (1970, pp. 29-35).

34. See Barrera (1979, pp. 176-79).

35. See Fanon (1963, 1967), Memmi (1965), Blauner (1972), Moore (1970), Almaguer (1971), Acuña (1972), Barrera, Muñoz, and Ornelas (1972), and Barrera (1979).

36. For a critique of internal colonialism, see González (1974), Almaguer (1975), Fernandez (1977).

37. A more elaborate treatment of these works is to be found in Mirandé (1985, chapters 9 and 10).

38. See, for example, Barrera (1979), Acuña (1981), Fernandez (1977), Camarillo (1979), and Almaguer (1974, 1975).

Bibliography

Manuscripts

Adjutant General of Texas. Biennial Report, 1915-1916. Texas State Archives, Austin. January 1, 1915-December 31, 1916.

Adjutant General of Texas. 1838-1865. "Correspondence Concerning the Texas Rangers, 1838-1865." The Walter Prescott Webb Collection, Eugene C. Barker History Center, University of Texas Archives, Austin.

Barstow, Alfred. 1849. "Statement of Alfred Barstow: A Pioneer of 1849." Dictation recorded for H. H. Bancroft, 1877. Bancroft Library Manuscript Collection.

Barstow, David Pierce. 1849-1851. "Statement of Recollections of 1849-51 in California." Dictation recorded for H. H. Bancroft, 1878. Bancroft Library Manuscript Collection.

Castro, Manuel de Jesús. 1836-1863. "Manuel de Jesús Castro Correspondence and Papers, 1836-1863." Bancroft Library Manuscript Collection.

Cox, S. S. 1960. "Laws of National Growth—Mexican Affairs." Speech of Hon. S. S. Cox, of Ohio. Delivered in the House of Representatives, March 19, 1860. Bancroft Library Manuscript Collection.

Hittell, John S. 1858. "Mexican Land-Claims in California." *Hutchings' California Magazine*, vol. 11, no. 10 (April 1858): 442-48. Stanford University Special Collections.

Huse, Charles E. 1876. "Sketch of the History and Resources of Santa Barbara City and County, California." Written and compiled by Charles E. Huse, Office of the Daily Press. Bancroft Library Manuscript Collection.

Jewett, George Enoch. 1849-1850. "George Enoch Jewett's Jounal, 1849-50." Bancroft Library Manuscript Collection.

Kingsbury, Gilbert D. 1859. "Letters of G. D. Kingsbury." Gilbert D. Kingsbury Papers, Eugene G. Barker History Center, University of Texas Archives, Austin.

Kirpatrick, Charles A. 1849. "Journal of Charles A. Kirpatrick, 1849." Bancroft Library Manuscript Collection.

Lugo, Don José del Carmen. 1877. "Vida de un Ranchero." Dictado por Don José del Carmen Lugo. Natural de la Alta California donde nació en el año de 1813 en el Pueblo de Los Angeles. Escrito por D. Tomás Savage para la Bancroft Library, año de 1877. Bancroft Library Manuscript Collection.

Robertson, George L. 1864. "Letter of George L. Robertson to His Sister." George
    L. Robertson Papers, 1855-1874. Eugene C. Barker History Center, Univer-
    sity of Texas Archives, Austin.
Ruiz, Manuel. 1942. Manuel Ruiz Collection. Stanford University Special Collec-
    tions, Manuscript no. 295.
Webb, Walter Prescott. The Walter Prescott Webb Collection. Eugene C. Barker
    History Center, University of Texas Archives, Austin.

Public Documents

Bevans, Charles I. 1972. *Treaties and Other International Agreements of the United
    States of America, 1776-1949*, vol. 9. Department of State Publications 8615.
    Washington, D.C.: U.S. Government Printing Office.
Bureau of Organized Crime and Criminal Intelligence. 1982-83. *Organized Crime
    in California, 1982-83*. Sacramento: State of California Department of
    Justice.
California Council on Criminal Justice. 1986. *State Task Force on Criminal Justice*.
    Final Report. Sacramento.
Chargin, Judge Gerald S. 1969. A Public Record, In the Superior Court of the
    State of California in and for the County of Santa Clara Juvenile Division.
    Statements of the Court. September 2, 1969. Susan K. Strahm, Official Court
    Reporter.
Comisión pesquisidora de la frontera del norte. 1875. "Reports of the Committee
    of Investigation: sent in 1873 by the Mexican Government to the Frontier
    of Texas." Translated from the Official Edition made in Mexico. New
    York: Baker & Godwin Printers.
Department of Corrections. 1980. *California Prisoners, Summary Statistics of Felon
    Prisoners and Parolees*. Sacramento: Offender and Information Services.
Hoffman, Ogden. 1862. *Report of Land Cases Determined in the United States
    District Court for the Northern District of California*. June term, 1853, to
    June term, 1858, inclusive, vol. 1. San Francisco: Numa Hubert Publisher.
    Reprinted by Yosemite Collections, 1975.
Jones, William Carey. 1850. *Report on the Subject of Land Titles in California*,
    made in pursuance of instructions from the Secretary of State and the
    Secretary of the Interior, together with a translation of the principal laws
    on that subject and some other papers relating thereto. Washington,
    D.C.: Gideon and Co., Printers.
Kahn, Brian. 1978. *Prison Gangs in the Community: A Briefing Document for
    the Board of Corrections*. Sacramento: California Board of Corrections.
Lohman, Joseph D., and Misner, Gordon E. 1966. *The Police and the Communi-
    ty: The Dynamics of Their Relationship in a Changing Society*. A Report
    Prepared for the President's Commission on Law Enforcement and the Ad-
    ministration of Justice. Washington, D.C.: U.S. Government Printing
    Office.
Miller, Hunter. 1937. *Treaties and Other International Acts of the United States*

of America. Vol. 5, Doc. 129. Washington, D.C.:   U.S. Government Printing Office.

National Center on Police and Community Relations, School of Police Administration and Public Safety, Michigan State University. 1967. *A National Survey of Police and Community Relations*, Field Survey V, prepared for the President's Commission on Law Enforcement and the Administration of Justice. Washington, D.C.:   U.S. Government Printing Office.

National Hispanic Conference on Law Enforcement and Criminal Justice. 1980. "A Report from the National Hispanic Conference on Law Enforcement and Criminal Justice," (July 28-30). Washington, D.C.:   U.S. Department of Justice, Law Enforcement Assistance Administration.

National Institute of Law Enforcement and Criminal Justice. 1979. *A Community Concern: Police Use of Deadly Force*. U.S. Department of Justice, Law Enforcement Assistance Administration. Washington, D.C.:   U.S. Government Printing Office.

People v. Zammora et al. October 4, 1944. District Court of Appeal, Second District, Division I, California. *Pacific Reporter*, 2nd series, vol. 152, pp. 180-216. St. Paul, Minn.:   West Publishing Co., 1945.

President's Commission on Immigration and Naturalization. 1953. *Whom We Shall Welcome*. Washington, D.C.:   U.S. Government Printing Office.

Statutes at Large and Treaties of the United States of America. March 3, 1851. "An Act to Ascertain and Settle the Private Land Claims in the State of California." December 1, 1845 to March 3, 1851, vol. IX, chap. 41, pp. 631-34. 31st Congress, 2nd Session. Boston: Little, Brown and Company.

Statutes at Large and Treaties of the United States of America. March 3, 1891. "An Act to Establish a Court of Private Land Claims." December 1889 to March 1891, vol. XXVI, chap. 539, pp. 854-62. 51st Congress, 2nd Session. Washington, D.C.:   U.S. Government Printing Office.

United States Statutes at Large. August 3, 1882. "An Act to Regulate Immigration." December 1881 to March 1883, vol. XXII, chap. 376, pp. 214-15. 4th Congress, 1st Session. Washington, D.C.:   U.S. Government Printing Office.

United States Statutes at Large. August 4, 1942. "Agreement Between the United States of America and Mexico Respecting the Temporary Migration of Mexican Agricultural Workers." vol. 56, part 2, pp. 1759-69. 77th Congress, 2nd Session. Washington, D.C.:   U.S. Government Printing Office.

United States Statutes at Large. June 27, 1952. "An Act to Revise the Laws Relating to Immigration, Naturalization, and Nationality; and for Other Purposes." vol. 66, chap. 477, pp. 163-281. 82nd Congress, 2nd Session. Washington, D.C.:   U.S. Government Printing Office.

U.S. Commission on Civil Rights. 1970. *Mexican Americans and the Administration of Justice in the Southwest*. Washington, D.C.:   U.S. Government Printing Office.

U.S. Commission on Civil Rights. 1981. *Who Is Guarding the Guardians: A Report on Police Practices*. Washington, D.C.:   U.S. Government Printing Office.

U.S. Congress Senate Committee on Immigration. 1928. "Restriction of Western Hemisphere Immigration." A bill to subject certain immigrants, born in countries of the Western Hemisphere, to the quota under the immigration laws. Washington, D.C.:   U.S. Government Printing Office.

U.S. Congress Senate Immigration Commission (Dillingham Commission). 1911. *Reports of the Immigration Commission.* 42 vols. Wathington, D.C.:   U.S. Government Printing Office.

U.S. Department of Justice, Immigration and Naturalization Service. 1978. *The Border Patrol.* Washington, D.C.:   U.S. Government Printing Office.

U.S. Department of Justice, Immigration and Naturalization Service. 1982. *1982 Annual Report of the Immigration and Naturalization Service.* Washington, D.C.:   U.S. Government Printing Office.

U.S. Department of Justice, Immigration and Naturalization Service. 1984. *1984 Statistical Yearbook of the Immigration and Naturalization Service.* Washington, D.C.:   U.S. Government Printing Office.

U.S. Department of Justice, Office of Legal Policy, 1985. *Prison Gangs: Their Extent, Nature and Impact on Prisons.* Federal Justice Research Program. Washington, D.C.:   U.S. Government Printing Office.

U.S. House of Representatives. 1849-1850. "California and New Mexico." Message from the President of the United States, transmitting information in answer to a resolution of the House of the 31st of December, 1849, on the subject of California and New Mexico. House Ex. Doc. 17. 31st Congress, 1st Session.

U.S. House of Representatives. 1860a. "Difficulties on Southwestern Frontier." House Ex. Doc. 52. 36th Congress, 1st Session.

U.S. House of Representatives. 1860b. "Troubles on Texas Frontier." House Ex. Doc. 81. 36th Congress, 1st Session.

U.S. House of Representatives, Committee on the Judiciary. 1984. *Police Misconduct.* Hearings before the Subcommittee on Criminal Justice. Serial no. 50, parts 1 and 2. 98th Congress, 1st Session, Washington, D.C.:   U.S. Government Printing Office.

U.S. National Commission on Law Observance and Enforcement (Wickersham Commission). 1931. No. 10, *Report on Crime and the Foreign Born.* No. 6 in Patterson Smith Series in Criminology, Law Enforcement and Social Problems. 1968. Montclair, N.J.:   Patterson Smith.

U.S. President's Commission on Law Enforcement and the Administration of Justice. 1967a. *The Challenge of Crime in a Free Society.* Washington, D.C.:   U.S. Government Printing Office.

——.1967b. *Task Force Report: The Police.* Washington, D.C.:   U.S. Government Printing Office.

U.S. Senate. 1919. "Investigation of Mexican Affairs." Committee on Foreign Relations, Senate Document 285. 66th Congress, 2nd Session.

Villalpando, Manuel. 1977. *A Study of the Impact of Illegal Aliens on the County of San Diego on Specific Socio-Economic Areas.* San Diego: San Diego County Human Resources Agency.

Newspapers

Alta California. 1851. "Foreign Miners Tax." March 7:1.
Associated Press (AP). 1976. "3 Indicted in Torture of Aliens." *The Arizona Republic*, August 29:B-1.
Associated Press (AP). 1977a. "First Border Watch Fruitless for Klan." *The Press*, Riverside, Calif., October 26:A-1.
——. 1977b. "Illegal Aliens Said Hell Under 'Dismal' State." *The Press*, Riverside, Calif., November 11.
——. 1977c. "Illegal Aliens Seized Tops Million Mark." *Press-Enterprise*, Riverside, Calif., November 24:A-3.
——. 1984. "Marine Fights War Against Illegal Aliens." *The Press-Enterprise*, Riverside, Calif., March 22:B-6.
Ault, Tony. 1977a. "Gang Crime Threat in Valley." *Progress Bulletin*, Pomona, Calif., July 31:1, 2.
——. 1977b. "Prison Gang Members Out on Valley Streets." *Progress Bulletin*, Pomona, Calif., August 1:1, 7.
Bárbaro, Kay. 1984a. "Sin pelos en la lengua." *Hispanic Link Weekly Report* 2. March 5:2.
——. 1984b. "Sin pelos en la lengua." *Hispanic Link Weekly Report* 2, September 17:2.
Bell Blawis, Patricia. 1977. "Torturers of Mexicans Acquitted." *People's World*, October 29:4.
El Clamor Público. 1856. Los Angeles, April 26:1.
El Paso Times. 1976a. "Arizona: Illegal Aliens Stripped, Stabbed, Burned." August 22:8-A.
——. 1976b. "Alien Torture Indictments Returned." August 31:3-A.
Galveston Daily News. 1893. May 21:7.
García, Francisco. 1984. "San Quentin Violence Worst Since 1970s." *Deadline*, Berkeley, Calif., July 20:1, 10.
La Opinión. 1943a "La Barriada en Estado de Alarma." Los Angeles, June 5:1, 8.
——. 1943b. "Alarma en el Barrio Mexicano." Los Angeles, June 6:1.
Law, Galen. 1977. "U.S. Intervention is Sought in Alien-Torture Acquittals." *The Arizona Republic*, October 11:B-1.
Los Angeles Daily News. 1943. June 8:3.
Los Angeles Times. 1943. June 8:1.
McMurtrie, Douglas Crawford. 1943. *A Report in April 1848, on the Discovery of Gold and Other Minerals in California, and on the People, Commerce, Agriculture, Customs, Religion, Press, etc. of the New Pacific Territory.* Reproduced from the *New York Herald*, August 19, 1848. Edited by Douglas C. McMurtrie. Evanston, Ill.
Negri, Sam. 1977. "FBI Probes Alien-Torture Case for Civil Rights Act Violations." *Arizona Republic*, October 19:B-1, B-2.
New York PM Magazine. 1943a. June 9:3.
——. 1943b. June 11:4.

San Angelo Standard. 1889. (September 21):1.

San Francisco Chronicle. 1985. "13-Year-Old Mexican Shot by a U.S. Guard." April 20:12.

Scripps Howard News Service. 1986. "Immigration Reform Bill Signed." *Press-Enterprise,* Riverside, Calif., November 7:A-3.

Sutherland, Tucker. 1978. "State of Texas Executed the First Woman in 1863." *San Angelo Standard-Times,* September 24:1C.

Tinsley, Jesse, and Ahlgren Jr., Frank. 1983. "Illegal Aliens Create Crime Problem in El Paso." *Special Report: The Border. El Paso Herald-Post.* Summer: 94.

United Press International (UPI). 1977. "Barrio Club to Monitor Klan." *The Press,* Riverside, Calif., October 24:A-8.

Wallace, Bill. 1984. "A Prison Gang's Link with Organized Crime." *San Francisco Chronicle,* August 27:1, 6.

Books

Acuña, Rodolfo. 1972. *Occupied America: The Chicano's Struggle Toward Liberation.* San Francisco: Canfield.

———. 1981. *Occupied America: A History of Chicanos,* 2d ed. New York: Harper & Row.

Allsup, Carl. 1982. *The American G.I. Forum.* Austin: University of Texas Press.

American G.I. Forum of Texas, Texas State Federation of Labor (AFL). 1954. *What Price Wetbacks?* Austin: Allied Printing.

Anders, Evan. 1982. *Boss Rule in South Texas: The Progressive Era.* Austin: University of Texas Press.

Anderson, Henry P. 1961. *The Bracero Program in California.* Berkeley: UCB School of Public Health.

Austin, Stephen. 1926. *The Austin Papers.* Ed., Eugene C. Barker. Austin: University of Texas Press.

Balderrama, Francisco E. 1982. *In Defense of La Raza: The Los Angeles Mexican Consulate and the Mexican Community 1929 to 1936.* Tucson: University of Arizona Press.

Barker, Eugene C. 1949. *The Life of Stephen F. Austin.* Austin: Texas State Historical Association.

Barrera, Mario. 1979. *Race and Class in the Southwest: A Theory of Racial Inequality.* Notre Dame: University of Notre Dame Press.

Becker, Howard S. 1966. *Outsiders.* New York: Free Press.

Beckett, V. B. 1962. *Baca's Battle.* Houston: Stagecoach Press.

Beers, George A. 1875. *Vasquez; or, the Hunted Bandits of the San Joaquin.* New York: Robert M. DeWitt, Publisher.

Blauner, Robert. 1972. *Racial Oppression in America.* New York: Harper and Row.

Bogardus, Emory S. 1934. *The Mexican in the United States.* Los Angeles: University of California Press.

Bowden, J.J. 1971. *Spanish and Mexican Land Grants in the Chihuahuan Acquisition.* El Paso: Texas Western Press.

Brayer, Herbert O. 1949. *William Blackmore: The Spanish-Mexican Land Grants of New Mexico and Colorado, 1863-1878,* vol. 1. Denver: Bradford-Robinson.

Camarillo, Albert. 1979. *Chicanos in a Changing Society: From Mexican Pueblos to American Barrios in Santa Barbara and Southern California, 1848-1930.* Cambridge: Harvard University Press.

Cardoso, Lawrence A. 1980. *Mexican Emigration to the United States, 1897-1931.* Tucson: University of Arizona Press.

Castillo, Pedro, and Camarillo, Albert, eds. 1973. *Furia y Muerte: Los Bandidos Chicanos.* Los Angeles: Aztlán Publications, Monograph no. 4, UCLA Chicano Studies Center.

Castro, Tony. 1974. *Chicano Power: The Emergence of Mexican America.* New York: Saturday Review Press/E.P. Dutton & Co., Inc.

Center for Research on Criminal Justice. 1977. *The Iron Fist and the Velvet Glove: An Analysis of the U.S. Police,* 2nd ed. San Francisco: Garrett Press.

Cleland, Robert Glass. 1941. *The Cattle of a Thousand Hills: Southern California, 1850-1870.* San Marino, Calif.:   The Huntington Library.

Cloward, Richard A., and Ohlin, Lloyd E. 1960. *Delinquency and Opportunity: A Theory of Delinquent Gangs.* New York: Free Press.

Cornelius, Wayne A., and Anzaldúa Montoya, Ricardo, eds. 1983. *America's New Immigration Law: Origins, Rationales, and Potential Consequences.* Monograph Series, 11. Center for U.S.-Mexican Studies, University of California, San Diego.

Cortés, Carlos, E., ed. 1974. *Spanish and Mexican Land Grants* (The Chicano Heritage). New York: Arno Press Reprint Edition.

——, ed. 1976. *Mexicans in California After the U.S. Conquest* (The Chicano Heritage). New York: Arno Press Reprint Edition.

Corwin, Arthur F. 1978. *Immigrants—and Immigrants: Perspectives on Mexican Labor Migration to the United States.* Westport, Conn.:   Greenwood Press.

Cowan, Robert G. 1977. *Ranchos of California: A List of Spanish Concessions 1775-1822 and Mexican Grants 1822-1846.* Los Angeles: Historical Society of Southern California.

Craig, Richard B. 1971. *The Bracero Program: Interest Groups and Foreign Policy.* Austin: University of Texas Press.

Crichton, Kyle S. 1928. *Law And Order, Ltd. The Rousing Life of Elfego Baca.* Santa Fe: New Mexican Publishing Corporation.

Davidson, R. Theodore. 1974. *Chicano Prisoners: The Key to San Quentin.* New York: Holt, Rinehart and Winston.

De León, Arnoldo. 1983. *They Called Them Greasers: Anglo Attitudes Toward Mexicans in Texas, 1821-1900.* Austin: University of Texas Press.

Deloria, Vine, Jr., and Lytle, Clifford M. 1983. *American Indians, American Justice*. Austin: University of Texas Press.

Douglas, Jack D. 1970. *Deviance and Respectability*. New York: Basic Books.

Ebright, Malcolm. 1980. *The Tierra Amarilla Grant: A History of Chicanery*. Sante Fe: The Center for Land Grant Studies.

Ellison, Joseph. 1927. *California and the Nation, 1850-1869*. Berkeley: University of California Press. Reprinted by Kraus Reprint Co., 1974.

Endore, Guy. 1944. *The Sleepy Lagoon Mystery*. Los Angeles: The Sleepy Lagoon Defense Committee.

Fanon, Frantz. 1963. *The Wretched of the Earth*. New York: Grove Press.

———. 1967. *Black Skin, White Masks*. New York: Grove Press.

Farnham, T. J. 1855. *Life, Adventures, and Travels in California* ("Pictorial Edition"). New York: Nafis and Cornish.

Fehrenbach, T. R. 1968. *Lone Star: A History of Texas and the Texans*. New York: Macmillan.

Fernandez, Raul. 1977. *The United States-Mexico Border*. Notre Dame: University of Notre Dame Press.

Filstead, William J. 1972. *An Introduction to Deviance*. Chicago: Markham.

Ford, John S. 1963. *Rip Ford's Texas*. Edited with an introduction and commentary by Stephen B. Oates. Austin: University of Texas Press.

Freire, Paulo. 1970. *Pedagogy of the Oppressed*. Translated by Myra Bergman Ramos. New York: Herder and Herder.

Frias, Gus. 1982. *Barrio Warriors: Homeboys or Peace*. Los Angeles: Díaz Publications.

Galarza, Ernesto. 1964. *Merchants of Labor: The Mexican Bracero Story*. Santa Barbara: McNally & Loftin, West (3d ed., 1978).

Gamio, Manuel. 1930. *Mexican Immigration to the United States*. Chicago: University of Chicago Press.

———. 1931. *The Mexican Immigrant: His Life Story*. Chicago: University of Chicago Press.

García, Juan Ramón. 1980. *Operation Wetback: The Mass Deportation of Mexican Undocumented Workers in 1954*. Westport Conn.:   Greenwood Press.

Geiger, Maynard, O.F.M. 1965. *Mission Santa Barbara, 1782-1965*. Santa Barbara: Heritage Printers.

Gillett, James B. 1925. *Six Years With the Texas Rangers, 1875 to 1881*. M.M. Quaife, ed. New Haven: Yale University Press.

Ginger, Ann Fagan, ed. 1967-1968. *Civil Liberties Docket*, vol. XIII. Berkeley: The National Lawyers Guild.

Grebler, Leo, Moore, Joan W., and Guzman, Ralph C. 1970. *The Mexican American People*. New York: Free Press.

Greer, James Kimmins. 1952. *Colonel Jack Hays: Texas Frontier Leader and California Builder*. New York: E.P. Dutton & Co.

Griffith, Beatrice. 1948. *American Me*. Boston: Houghton Mifflin.

Griswold del Castillo, Richard. 1979. *The Los Angeles Barrio, 1850-1890:   A Social History*. Berkeley: University of California Press.

Gurr, Ted Robert. 1970. *Why Men Rebel.* Princeton, N.J.:   Princeton University Press.

Heizer, Robert F., and Almquist, Alan J. 1977. *The Other Californians: Prejudice and Discrimination under Spain, Mexico, and the United States to 1920.* Berkeley: University of California Press.

Heller, Celia S. 1966. *Mexican America Youth: Forgotten Youth at the Crossroads.* New York: Random House.

Hinkle, Stacey C. 1970. *Wings Over the Border: The Army Air Service Armed Patrol of the United States-Mexican Border 1919-1921.* Southwestern Studies, Monograph no. 26. El Paso: Texas Western Press.

Hobsbawm, Eric J. 1959. *Primitive Rebels: Studies in Archaic Forms of Social Movements in the 19th and 20th Centuries.* New York: Praeger.

——. 1969. *Bandits.* London: Weidenfeld and Nicolson.

Hoffman, Abraham. 1974. *Unwanted Mexican Americans in the Great Depression.* Tucson: University of Arizona Press.

Horowitz, Ruth. 1983. *Honor and the American Dream.* New Brunswick, N.J.:   Rutgers University Press.

Hoyle, M. F. 1927. *Crimes and Career of Tiburcio Vasquez, the Bandit of San Benito County and Notorious Early California Outlaw.* Hollister, Calif.:   Evening Free Lance.

Hughes, William J. 1964. *Rebellious Ranger: Rip Ford and the Old Southwest.* Norman: University of Oklahoma Press.

Huse, Charles Enoch. 1977. *The Huse Journal: Santa Barbara in the 1850's.* Ed., Edith Bond Conkey (translated by Francis Price). Santa Barbara: Santa Barbara Historical Society.

Interchurch World Movement of North America. 1920. *The Mexican in Los Angeles: Los Angeles City Survey.* Reprinted 1970 by R. and E. Research Associates.

Jennings, N. A. 1930. *A Texas Ranger.* Dallas: Turner Co.

Johnson, Kenneth F., and Ogle, Nina M. 1978. *Illegal Mexican Aliens in the United States.* Washington, D.C.:   University Press of America.

Jones, Robert C. 1946. *Los braceros mexicanos en los estados unidos durante el período bélico: El programa Mexicano-estadounidense de prestación de mano de obra.* Washington, D.C.:   Unión Panamericana, Oficina de Información Obrera y Social.

Keleher, William A. 1964. *Maxwell Land Grant,* revised ed. New York: Argosy—Antiquarian (first published by the Rydal Press, 1942).

Kiser, George C., and Kiser, Martha Woody, eds. 1979. *Mexican Workers in the United States: Historical and Political Perspectives.* Albuquerque: University of New Mexico Press.

Kostyu, Frank A. 1970. *Shadows in the Valley: The Story of One Man's Struggle For Justice.* Garden City, N.Y.:   Doubleday.

Lasswell, Mary. 1958. *I'll Take Texas.* Boston: Houghton Mifflin.

Latta, Frank F. 1980. *Joaquín Murrieta and His Horse Gangs.* Santa Cruz, Calif.:   Bear State Books.

Lea, Tom. 1957. *The King Ranch*, 2 vols. Boston: Little, Brown.

Lemert, Edwin M. 1951. *Social Pathology*. New York: McGraw Hill.

———. 1967. *Human Deviance, Social Problems, and Social Control*. Englewood Cliffs, N.J.:   Prentice-Hall.

Leonard, Olen E. 1970. *The Role of the Land Grant in the Social Organization and Social Processes of a Spanish-American Village in New Mexico*. Albuquerque: Calvin Horn Publisher.

Lieberman, Jethro K. 1968. *Are Americans Extinct?* New York: Walker and Company.

McBride, George McCutchen. 1923. *Land Systems of Mexico*. American Geographical Society Research Series no. 12. New York: American Geographical Society.

McMurtry, Larry. 1968. *In a Narrow Grave: Essays on Texas*. Austin: Encino Press.

McWilliams, Carey. 1968. *North From Mexico*. New York: Greenwood.

Madsen, William. 1973. *The Mexican-Americans of South Texas*, 2d. ed. New York: Holt, Rinehart and Winston.

Matza, David. 1969. *Becoming Deviant*. Englewood Cliffs, N.J.:   Prentice-Hall.

Mazón, Mauricio. 1984. *The Zoot-Suit Riots: The Psychology of Symbolic Annihilation*. Austin: University of Texas Press.

Meier, Matt S., and Rivera, Feliciano. 1972. *The Chicanos: A History of Mexican Americans*. New York: Hill and Wang.

Meining, Donald William. 1969. *Imperial Texas: An Interpretive Essay in Cultural Geography*. Austin: University of Texas Press.

Memmi, Albert. 1965. *The Colonizer and the Colonized*. Translated by Howard Greenfeld. New York: Orion Press.

Merton, Robert K. 1963. *Social Theory and Social Structure*, rev. ed. Glencoe, Ill.:   Free Press.

Mirandé, Alfredo. 1985. *The Chicano Experience: An Alternative Perspective*. Notre Dame: University of Notre Dame Press.

Moore, Joan W. (with García, Robert, García, Carlos, Cerda, Luís, and Valencia, Frank). 1978. *Homeboys: Gangs, Drugs, and Prison in the Barrios of Los Angeles*. Philadelphia: Temple University Press.

Moquin, Wayne (with Charles Van Doren). 1971. *A Documentary History of Mexican Americans*. New York: Praeger.

Morales, Armando. 1972. *Ando Sangrando (I am Bleeding):   A Study of Mexican-American Police Conflict*. La Puente, Calif.:   Perspectiva.

Morales, Patricia. 1981. *Indocumentados mexicanos*. Mexico City: Editorial Grijalbo, S.A.

Morgan, Patricia. 1954. *Shame of a Nation: A Documented Story of Police-State Terror Against Mexican-Americans in the U.S.A.* Los Angeles: Committee for Protection of Foreign Born.

Myers, John Myers. 1971. *The Border Wardens*. Englewood Cliffs, N.J.:   Prentice-Hall.

Nadeau, Remi. 1974. *The Real Joaquin Murieta: Robin Hood Hero or Gold Rush Gangster?* Corona del Mar, Calif.: Trans-Anglo.

Nance, Joseph Milton. 1963. *After San Jacinto: The Texas Mexican Frontier, 1836-1841.* Austin: University of Texas Press.

——. 1964. *Attack and Counter-Attack: The Texas-Mexican Frontier, 1842.* Austin: University of Texas Press.

North, David S., and Houstoun, Marion F. 1976. *The Characteristics and Role of Illegal Aliens in the U.S. Labor Market: An Exploratory Study.* Washington, D.C.: Linton & Company.

Orozco, E. C. 1980. *Republican Protestantism in Aztlán.* Glendale, Calif.: Petereins Press.

Ortiz, Roxanne Dunbar. 1980. *Roots of Resistance: Land Tenure in New Mexico, 1680-1980.* Monograph no. 10. Los Angeles: UCLA Chicano Studies Research Center and American Indian Studies Center.

Paredes, Américo. 1958. *"With His Pistol in His Hand": A Border Ballad and Its Hero.* Austin: University of Texas Press.

Parker, William H. 1957. *Parker on Police.* Ed. O. W. Wilson. Springfield, Ill.: Charles C. Thomas.

Parkes, Henry Bamford. 1969. *A History of Mexico,* 3d ed. Boston: Houghton-Mifflin.

Paz, Octavio. 1961. *The Labyrinth of Solitude.* Translated by Lysander Kemp. New York: Grove Press.

Pearson, Jim Berry. 1961. *The Maxwell Land Grant.* Norman: University of Oklahoma Press.

Perkins, Clifford Alan. 1978. *Border Patrol* (assisted by Nancy Dickey and edited with an Introduction by C. L. Sonnichsen). El Paso: Texas Western Press.

Perrigo, Lynn. 1971. *The American Southwest: Its Peoples and Cultures.* Albuquerque: University of New Mexico Press.

Pierce, Frank C. 1917. *A Brief History of the Lower Rio Grande Valley.* Menasha, Wisc.: George Banta Publishing Co.

Pitt, Leonard. 1966. *The Decline of the Californios: A Social History of the Spanish Speaking, 1846-1890.* Berkeley: University of California Press.

Quicker, John C. 1983. *Homegirls: Characterizing Chicana Gangs.* San Pedro, Calif.: International Universities Press.

Quinney, Richard. 1970. *The Social Reality of Crime.* Boston: Little, Brown.

Rak, Mary Kidder. 1938. *Border Patrol.* Boston: Houghton Mifflin. Reprinted 1971 by R and E Research Associates, San Francisco.

Ramírez, Manuel, III. 1983. *Psychology of the Americas: Mestizo Perspectives on Personality and Mental Health.* New York: Pergamon Press.

Reisler, Mark. 1976. *By the Sweat of Their Brows: Mexican Immigrant Labor in the United States, 1900-1940.* Westport, Conn.: Greenwood Press.

Rendon, Armando B. 1972. *Chicano Manifesto.* New York: Macmillan.

Ridge, John Rollin (Yellow Bird). 1955. *Life and Adventures of Joaquín Murieta, the Celebrated California Bandit.* Norman: University of Oklahoma Press.

Roberts, Dan W. 1914. *Rangers and Sovereignty*. San Antonio: Wood Printing & Engraving Co.

Robinson, W. W. 1948. *Land in California*. Berkeley: University of California Press.

———. 1976. *PEOPLE VERSUS LUGO: Story of a Famous Murder Case and its Amazing Aftermath*. Los Angeles; Dawson's Book Shop, 1962. Pp. 1-51 in *Mexicans in California After the U.S. Conquest*, ed. Carlos E. Cortés. New York: Arno Press Reprint Series.

Rogers, Cameron. 1954. *A County Judge in Arcady*. Selected Private Papers of Charles Fernald, Pioneer California Jurist. Glendale, Calif.: The Arthur H. Clark Company.

Romo, Ricardo. 1983. *East Los Angeles: History of a Barrio*. Austin: University of Texas Press.

Rosenbaum, H. Jon, and Sederberg, Peter C., eds. 1976. *Vigilante Politics*. Philadelphia: University of Pennsylvania Press.

Rosenbaum, Robert J. 1981. *Mexicano Resistance in the Southwest*. Austin: University of Texas Press.

Rubinton, Earl, and Weinberg, Martin S. 1973. *Deviance, The Interactionist Perspective*, 2d ed. New York: MacMillan.

Ruiz, Manuel, Jr. 1974. *Mexican American Legal Heritage in the Southwest*. Los Angeles: Financial Center Building.

Samora, Julian, Bernal, Joe, and Peña, Albert. 1979. *Gunpowder Justice: A Reassessment of the Texas Rangers*. Notre Dame: University of Notre Dame Press.

Schaefer, Jack. 1965. *Heroes Without Glory, Some Goodmen of the Old West*, pp. 287-323. Boston: Houghton Mifflin.

Schur, Edwin M. 1971. *Labeling Deviant Behavior*. New York: Harper & Row.

Secrest, William B. 1967a. *Juanita: The Only Woman Lynched in the Gold Rush Days*. Fresno, Calif.: Saga-West.

———. 1967b. *Joaquín: Bloody Bandit of the Mother Lode*. Fresno, Calif.: Saga-West.

Silva Herzog, Jesús. 1960. *Breve historia de la revolución mexicana: los antecedentes y la etapa maderista*, vol. 1. Mexico City: Fondo de Cultura Económica.

Sims, Judge Orland L. 1967. *Gunfighters I Have Known*. Austin: Encino Press.

Sinnott, James J. 1977. *History of Sierra County: Volume 1, Downieville*. Downieville, Calif.

Slater, Philip. 1971. *The Pursuit of Loneliness*. Boston: Beacon.

Sleepy Lagoon Defense Committee. 1942. *The Sleepy Lagoon Case*. Los Angeles: Citizen's Committee for the Defense of Mexican-American Youth.

Steiner, Stan. 1970. "The Shrunken Head of Pancho Villa," pp. 208-29 in *La Raza*. New York: Harper & Row.

Sterling, William Warren. 1959. *Trails and Trials of a Texas Ranger*. Norman: University of Oklahoma Press.

Stowell, Jay S. 1921. "The Mexican at Work in the United States." *The Near Side of the Mexican Question*. New York: George H. Doran Company.

Taylor, Bayard. 1850. *El Dorado, or Adventures in the Path of Empire*, 4th ed. New York: George P. Putnam.

Thrasher, Frederick M. 1927. *The Gang: A Study of 1,313 Gangs in Chicago*. Chicago: University of Chicago Press.

Truman, Benjamin C. 1874. *Life, Adventures and Capture of Tiburcio Vasquez, The Great California Bandit and Murderer*. Los Angeles: Los Angeles Star Office.

Tuck, Ruth D. 1946. *Not With the Fist: Mexican-Americans in a Southwest City*. New York: Harcourt, Brace and Company.

Twitchell, Ralph Emerson. 1963. *Old Santa Fe: The Story of New Mexico's Ancient Capital*. Chicago: Rio Grande Press. (First published by the Rio Grande Press, 1925.)

Valdez, Luis, and Steiner, Stan, eds. 1972. *Aztlan: An Anthology of Mexican American Literature*. New York: Knopf.

Vigil, James Diego. 1974. *Early Chicano Guerilla Fighters*. La Mirada, Calif.:   Advanced Graphics.

Weaver, John. 1973. *The Brownsville Raid*. New York: Norton Publishers.

Webb, Walter Prescott. 1965. *The Texas Rangers*. Austin: University of Texas Press.

——. 1975. *The Texas Rangers in the Mexican War*. Austin: Jenkins Garrett Press.

Westphall, Victor. 1983. *Mercedes Reales: Hispanic Land Grants of the Upper Rio Grande Region*. Albuquerque: University of New Mexico Press.

Woodman, Lyman L. 1950. *Cortina: Rogue of Rio Grande*. San Antonio: The Naylor Company.

Articles

Adler, Patricia R. 1974. "The 1943 Zoot-Suit Riots: Brief Episode in a Long Conflict." Pp. 142-58 in *An Awakened Minority: The Mexican-Americans*, ed. Manuel P. Servin, 2d ed. Beverly Hills: Glencoe Press.

Almaguer, Tomás. 1971. "Toward the Study of Chicano Colonialism." *Aztlán: Chicano Journal of the Social Sciences and the Arts* 2 (Spring):   7-21.

——. 1974. "Historical Notes on Chicano Oppression: The Dialectics of Racial and Class Domination in North America." *Aztlán: Chicano Journal of the Social Sciences and the Arts* 5 (Spring-Fall):   27-56.

——. 1975. "Class, Race, and Chicano Oppression." *Socialist Revolution* 5 (July-September):   71-99.

Barker, George C. 1950. "Pachuco: An American-Spanish Argot and its Social Transactions in Tucson, Arizona." *University of Arizona Bulletin*, Social Science Bulletin no. 18, 21 (January):   1-38.

Barrera, Mario, Muñoz, Carlos, and Ornelas, Charles. 1972. "The Barrio as an Internal Colony." In *Urban Affairs Annual Reviews*, ed. Harlan H. Hahn, 6: 465-98. Beverly Hills: Sage.

Becker, Howard S. 1967. "Whose Side Are We On?" *Social Problems* 14 (Winter): 239-47.

Bogardus, Emory S. 1943. "Gangs of Mexican-American Youth." *Sociology and Social Research* 27 (September-October): 55-66.

Brent, Joseph Lancaster. 1976. "The Lugo Case: A Personal Experience. New Orleans, 1926." Pp. 1-69 in *Mexicans in California After the U.S. Conquest*, ed. Carlos E. Cortés. New York: Arno Press Reprint Edition.

Brooks, Robin. 1979. "Domestic Violence and America's Wars: An Historical Interpretation." Pp. 307-27 in *Violence in America: Historical and Comparative Perspectives*, ed. Hugh Davis Graham and Ted Robert Gurr. Beverly Hills: Sage.

Bustamante, Jorge A. 1972. "The Historical Context of Undocumented Mexican Immigration to the United States." *Aztlán: Chicano Journal of the Social Sciences and the Arts* 3 (Fall): 257-81.

——. 1977. "The Immigrant Worker: A Social Problem or a Human Resource." Pp. 165-83 in *Immigration and Public Policy: Human Rights for Undocumented Workers and Their Families*, ed. Antonio José Ríos-Bustamante. Anthology no. 2. Los Angeles: UCLA Chicano Studies Research Center.

——. 1981. "The Historical Context of Undocumented Mexican Immigration to the United States." Pp. 35-48 in *Mexican Immigrant Workers in the U.S.*, ed. Antonio Ríos-Bustamante. Anthology no. 2. Los Angeles: UCLA Chicano Studies Research Center.

Cumberland, Charles C. 1954. "Border Raids in the Lower Rio Grande Valley—1915." *The Southwestern Historical Quarterly* 57 (January): 285-311.

del Olmo, Frank. 1983. "Simpson-Mazzoli: Implications for the Latino Community." Pp. 123-26 in *America's New Immigration Law: Origins, Rationale, and Potential Consequences*, ed. Wayne A. Cornelius and Ricardo Anzaldúa Montoya. Center for U.S.-Mexican Studies, University of California, San Diego.

Eastland, Thomas B. 1939. "To California Through Texas and Mexico: The Diary and Letters of Thomas B. Eastland and Joseph G. Eastland, His Son." *California Historical Society Quarterly* 18 (June): 99-135.

Ellison, William H., ed. 1939. "'Recollections of Historical Events in California, 1843-1878, of William A. Streeter." *California Historical Society Quarterly* 18 (March, June, and September).

Friend, Llerena B. 1971. "W. P. Webb's Texas Rangers." *Southwestern Historical Quarterly* 74 (January): 293-323.

García, Mario T. 1976. "Merchants and Dons: San Diego's Attempt at Modernization, 1850-1860." (Reprinted from *The Journal of San Diego History*, vol. 21, no. 1., Winter 1975.) Pp. 52-80 in *Mexicans in California After the U.S. Conquest*, ed. Carlos E. Cortés. New York: Arno Press Reprint Edition.

Gómez-Quiñones, Juan. 1970. "Plan de San Diego Reviewed." *Aztlán: Chicano Journal of the Social Sciences and the Arts* 1 (Spring): 124-32.

———. 1981. "Mexican Immigration to the United States and the Internationalization of Labor, 1848-1980: An Overview." Pp. 13-34 in *Mexican Immigrant Workers in the U.S.*, ed. Antonio Ríos-Bustamante. Los Angeles: UCLA Chicano Studies Research Center.

———. 1982. "Critique of the National Question, Self-Determination and Nationalism." *Latin American Perspectives* 33 (Spring): 62-83.

González, Alfredo. 1978. "Towards an Understanding of Chicano Gangs." Paper Presented Before the National Association for Chicano Studies. Claremont, Calif.

González, Gilbert G. 1974. "A Critique of the Internal Colony Model." *Latin American Perspectives* 1 (no. 1): 154-61.

Harris, Charles H., III and Sadler, Louis R. 1978. "The Plan of San Diego and the Mexican-United States War Crisis of 1916: A Reexamination." *Hispanic American Historical Review* 58 (August): 381-408.

Hunsaker, Alan. 1981. "The Behaviorial-Ecological Model of Intervention with Chicano Gang Delinquents." *Hispanic Journal of Behavioral Sciences* 3 (no. 3): 225-39.

Janowitz, Morris. 1969. "Patterns of Collective Racial Violence." Pp. 412-44 in *The History of Violence in America: Historical and Comparative Perspectives*, ed. Hugh Davis Graham and Ted Robert Gurr. New York: Praeger.

Kiser, George, and Silverman, David. 1979. "Mexican Repatriation During the Great Depression." Pp. 45-66 in *Mexican Workers in the United States*, ed. George C. Kiser and Martha Woody Kiser. Albuquerque: University of New Mexico Press.

Knowlton, Clark S. 1980. "The Town of Las Vegas Community Land Grant: An Anglo-American Coup d-Etat." Pp. 12-21 in *Spanish & Mexican Land Grants in New Mexico and Colorado*, ed. John R. and Christine M. Van Ness. Santa Fe: The Center for Land Grant Studies.

Limón, José E. 1981. "The Folk Performance of 'Chicano' and the Cultural Limits of Political Ideology." Pp. 197-225 in *"And Other Neighborly Names": Social Process and Cultural Image in Texas Folklore*, ed. Richard Bauman and Roger D. Abrahams. Austin: University of Texas Press.

López, José M. 1978. "Chicano Youth Gangs, an Unaccepted Form of Hierarchical Community—Fact or Myth?" Paper Presented Before the National Association for Chicano Studies. Claremont, Calif.

McDonagh, Edward. C. 1949. "Status Levels of Mexicans." *Sociology and Social Research* 33 (July-August): 449-59.

McWilliams, Carey. 1943. "The Zoot-Suit Riots." *The New Republic* 108 (June 21): 818-20.

———. 1949. "California and the Wetback." *Common Ground* 9 (Summer): 15-20.

Martínez, Thomas M. 1969. "Advertising and Racism: The Case of the Mexican-American." *El Grito: A Journal of Contemporary Mexican American Thought* 2 (Summer): 3-13.

May, Ernest R. 1947. "Tiburcio Vásquez." *Historical Society of Southern California Quarterly* 29 (September-December): 122-35.

Mexican American Legal Defense and Education Fund (MALDEF). 1978a. "MALDEF Documents Official Abuse of Authority Against Mexican-Americans in Letter to Attorney General Griffen Bell." San Francisco.

——. 1978b. "Dallas Brutality Conference Displays Chicano Unity." *MALDEF* 8 (Summer): 1-8.

Mirandé, Alfredo. 1978. "Chicano Sociology: A New Paradigm for Social Science." *Pacific Sociological Review* 21 (July): 293-312.

——. 1982. "Sociology of Chicanos or Chicano Sociology?: A Critical Assessment of Emergent Paradigms." *Pacific Sociological Review*, 25 (October) 495-508.

Moore, Joan W. 1970. "Colonialism: The Case of the Mexican Americans." *Social Problems* 17 (Spring): 463-72.

Nackman, Mark E. 1975. "The Making of the Texas Citizen Soldier, 1835-1860." *Southwestern Historical Quarterly* 78 (January): 231-53.

Paredes, Américo. 1967. "Estados Unidos, México y El Machismo." *Journal of Inter-American Studies* 9 (January): 65-84.

Pound, Roscoe. 1943. "A Survey of Social Interests." *Harvard Law Review* 57 (October): 1-39.

Rosenbaum, Robert J. 1973. "Las Gorras Blancas of San Miguel County, 1889-1890." Pp. 128-33 in *Chicanos: The Evolution of a People*, ed. Renato Rosaldo, Robert A. Calvert, and Gustav L. Seligmann. Minneapolis: Winston Press.

Rudoff, Alvin. 1971. "The Incarcerated Mexican-American Delinquent." *Journal of Criminal Law, Criminology and Police Science* 62 (June): 224-38.

Samora, Julian. 1975. "Mexican Immigration." Pp. 60-80 in *Mexican-Americans Tomorrow*, ed. Gus Tyler. Albuquerque: University of New Mexico Press.

Schey, Peter A. 1983. "Supply Side Immigration Theory: Analysis of the Simpson-Mazzoli Bill." *La Raza Law Journal* 1 (Spring): 53-71.

Schlesinger, Andrew B. 1971. "Las Gorras Blancas, 1889-1891." *Journal of Mexican American History* 1 (Spring): 87-143.

Scott, Robin F. 1970a. "The Sleepy Lagoon Case and the Grand Jury Investigation." Pp. 105-15 in *The Mexican-Americans: An Awakening Minority*, ed. Manuel P. Servín. Beverly Hills: Glencoe Press.

——. 1970b. "The Zoot-Suit Riots." Pp. 116-24 in *The Mexican-Americans: An Awakening Minority*, ed. Manuel P. Servín. Beverly Hills: Glencoe Press.

Scruggs, Otey M. 1979. "Texas and the Bracero Program, 1942-1947." Pp. 85-97 in *Mexican Workers in the United States*, ed. George C. Kiser and Martha Woody Kiser. Albuquerque: University of New Mexico Press.

Servín, Manuel P. 1966. "The Pre-World War II Mexican-American: An Interpretation." *California Historical Society Quarterly* 45 (December): 325-38.

Sotomayor, Ernie. 1982. "Police Abuse: The Most Volatile Issue." *Perspectives: The Civil Rights Quarterly* 13 (Winter): 28-35.

Strickland, Barbara K. 1983. "Immigration Reform and Legal Rights: A Critical

Analysis of the Simpson-Mazzoli Bill." Pp. 103-12 in *America's New Immigration Law: Origins, Rationale, and Potential Consequences*, ed. Wayne A. Cornelius and Ricardo Anzaldúa Montoya. Center for U.S. Mexican Studies, University of California, San Diego.

Stumphauzer, Jerome S., Aiken, Thomas W., and Veloz, Esteban V. 1977. "East Side Story: Behavioral Analysis of a High Juvenile Crime Community." *Behavioral Disorders* 2 (February): 76-81.

Takagi, Paul. 1979. "Death by Police Intervention." Pp. 31-38 in *A Community Concern: Police Use of Deadly Force*. National Institute of Law Enforcement and Criminal Justice, U.S. Department of Justice, Law Enforcement Assistance Administration. Washington, D.C.: U.S. Government Printing Office.

Trujillo, Larry D. 1974. "La evolución del 'Bandido' al 'Pachuco': A Critical Examination and Evaluation of Criminological Literature on Chicanos." *Issues in Criminology* 9 (Fall): 43-67.

——. 1983. "Police Crimes in the Barrio." Pp. 199-242 in *History, Culture, and Society: Chicano Studies in the 1980s*, ed. Mario T. García, Francisco Lomelí, Mario Barrera, Edward Escobar, and John García. Ypsilanti, Mi.: Bilingual Press.

Tuck, Ruth D. 1943. "Behind the Zoot Suit Riots." *Survey Graphic* 32 (August): 313-16, 335.

Turner, Ralph H., and Surace, Samuel J. 1956. "Zoot-Suiters and Mexicans: Symbols in Crowd Behavior." *The American Journal of Sociology* 62 (July): 14-20.

Valdez, Luis. 1972. "Introduction: 'La Plebe'." Pp. xiii-xxxiv in *Aztlan: An Anthology of Mexican-American Literature*. New York: Random House.

Van Ness, John R., and Van Ness, Christine M. 1980. "Introduction." Pp. 3-11 in *Spanish and Mexican Land Grants in New Mexico and Colorado*. Santa Fe: Center for Land Grant Studies.

White, Richard. 1981. "Outlaw Gangs of the Middle Border: American Social Bandits." *Western Historical Quarterly* 12 (October): 387-408.

Wooster, Ralph A. 1971. "Wealthy Texans, 1870." *Southwestern Historical Quarterly* 74 (April): 24-35.

Wright, Doris Marion. 1940. "The Making of Cosmopolitan California: An Analysis of Immigration, 1848-1870." *California Historical Society Quarterly* 29 (December): 323-41.

Theses and Dissertations

Avina, Rose Hollenbaugh. 1932. "Spanish and Mexican Land Grants in California." Master's thesis, University of California, Berkeley.

Balderrama, Francisco Enrique. 1978. "En Defensa de la Raza: The Los Angeles Mexican Consulate and Colonia Mexicana During the Great Depression." Ph.D. dissertation, University of California, Los Angeles.

Cardoso, Lawrence A. 1974. "Mexican Emigration to the United States, 1800 to 1930: An Analysis of Socio-economic Causes." Ph.D. dissertation, University of Connecticut.

Copp, Nelson Gage. 1963. " 'Wetbacks' and Braceros: Mexican Migrant Laborers and American Immigration Policy, 1930-1960." Ph.D. dissertation, Boston University Graduate School.

Crisp, James Ernest. 1976. "Anglo-Texan Attitudes Toward the Mexican, 1821-1845." Ph.D. dissertation, Yale University.

Foster, Nellie. 1939. "The Corrido: A Mexican Culture Trait Persisting in Southern California." Master's thesis, University of Southern California.

Goldfinch, Charles W. 1949. "Juan N. Cortina, 1824-1892: A Re-Appraisal." Master's thesis, University of Chicago.

González, Alfredo. 1981. "Mexicano/Chicano Gangs in Los Angeles: A Socio-historical Case Study." Ph.D. dissertation, University of California, Berkeley.

Jones, Solomon James. 1969. "The Government Riots of Los Angeles, June 1943." Master's thesis, University of California, Los Angeles.

Kirstein, Peter Neil. 1973. "Anglo Over Bracero: A History of the Mexican Worker in the United States from Roosevelt to Nixon." Ph.D. dissertation, Saint Louis University.

Lipshultz, Robert J. 1962. "American Attitudes Toward Mexican Immigration, 1924-1952." Master's thesis, University of Chicago.

Mazón, Mauricio. 1976. "Social Upheaval in World War II: 'Zoot Suiters' and Servicemen in Los Angeles, 1943." Ph.D. dissertation, University of California, Los Angeles.

McKay, R. Reynolds. 1982. "Texas Mexican Repatriation During the Great Depression." Ph.D. dissertation, University of Oklahoma.

Mitchell, Richard G. 1927. "Joaquín Murieta: A Study of Social Conditions in California." Master's thesis, University of California, Berkeley.

Montejano, David. 1982. "A Journey Through Mexican Texas, 1900-1930." Ph.D. dissertation, Yale University.

Morefield, Richard. 1955. "The Mexican Adaptation in American California 1846-1875." Master's thesis, University of California, Berkeley.

Neal, Joe W. 1941. "The Policy of the United States Toward Immigration from Mexico." Master's thesis, University of Texas, Austin.

Peterson, Richard H. 1965. "Manifest Destiny in the Mines: A Cultural Interpretation of Anti-Mexican Nativism in California, 1848-1853." Master's thesis, San Francisco State University.

Reisler, Mark. 1973. "Passing Through Our Egypt: Mexican Labor in the United States, 1900-1940." Ph.D. dissertation, Cornell University.

Rocha, Rodolfo. 1981. "The Influence of the Mexican Revolution on the Mexico-Texas Border, 1910-1916." Ph.D. dissertation, Texas Tech University.

Scott, Robin Fitzgerald. 1971. "The Mexican-American in the Los Angeles Area, 1920-1950: From Acquiescence to Activity." Ph.D. dissertation, University of Southern California.

Tijerina, Andrew Anthony. 1977. "Tejanos and Texas: The Native Mexicans of Texas, 1820-1850." Ph.D. dissertation, University of Texas at Austin.

Index

Almaguer, Tomás, 223-25
Anglo attitudes toward Mexicans, 3-9, 28,
  55-66, 77, 79, 80-81, 94-95, 97,
  102, 130-31, 172-73, 226-29,
  234-35, 237n.
Ayres, Ed Duran, 160-61

Baca, Elfego, 77, 85-87
Badillo, Francisco, 65-66
bandido (image of Mexicans), 3, 17-26,
  51, 67, 72, 88, 109, 110, 134, 185,
  226, 235-36, 238n., 239n.
Barrera, Mario, 224-25
barrio warriors, 212-15
barrioization, 25-26, 29, 231-32
Blauner, Robert, 212, 222-23
Border Patrol
  abuses of, 21-23, 114, 181
  as agent of social control, 100-1
  as enforcer of employer interests,
    112-16
  establishment of, 106-8, 115, 139
  internal problems, 108, 112, 239n.
  Mexican view of, 114
  and Operation Wetback, 125-26
  overview of, 107-16
  parallels with Texas Rangers, 110-12
  predecessors of, 108-11, 126, 239n.
  See also immigration; undocumented
    workers
bracero program, 21, 50, 120-25, 127,
  141, 239n.
Bustamente, Jorge, 106

Chicano gangs
  explanations of emergence, 186-200
  and pachucos/zoot-suiters, 157, 159,
    163, 167, 183-90
  in prison, 200-4, 206-11
  redefinition of, 198-200, 212-15, 233-34
  unique features of, 190-92
  See also prison gangs

Chinese Exclusion Act of 1882, 103
cholo
  and *bandido* image, 236
  as cultural identity, 190, 234
  definition of, 238n.
  as "low-life" Mexican, 27
citizen soldier, 53, 71-72, 94
Comisión pesquisidora de la frontera del
  noter, 18, 46, 50, 75-76
conflict theory, 51-53, 218-19, 226, 238n.,
  240n.
  See also theoretical models
Cortez, Gregorio, 18, 77, 84-85
Cortina, Juan, 19, 89-93, 94
Court of Private Claims, 41-42
coyote, 106

Davidson, R. Theodore, 200-4, 226
de la Guerra, Pablo, 43
Díaz, José, 157
Dillingham Commission, 103-4, 131

East Los Angeles Riots, 2, 22
  See also Los Angeles police riots
El Plan de San Diego, 19-20, 95-97
Espíritu Santo grant, 31, 45, 89

Fernandez, Raul, 34
Figueroa, Alfredo, 148-49, 154-55
Flores, General Juan, 73, 75
Foreign Miners' Tax (1850), 58-59, 62
Frias, Gus, 212-15

Garza, Catarino, 93-95
Gentlemen's Agreement of 1907, 103, 139·
González, Alfredo, 186, 198, 212
Greaser Law (antivagrancy), 66
Greenfield, Alice, 159
gringo justice theory, 2, 25-26, 225-36

Hannigan, George, 22
Hobsbawm, Eric J., 75-76, 79, 88, 211

immigration
    attempts to regulate, 138-45, 239n.
    bracero program, 21, 50, 120-25, 127,
        239n.
    Operation Deportation, 116-20
    Operation Wetback, 21-22, 125-29
    patterns of migration, 102-7
    repatriation, 107-8, 116
    See also Border Patrol; undocumented
        workers
Immigration Act of 1917, 102, 105,
    120-21, 139
Immigration Act of 1921, 105, 139
Immigration Act of 1924, 105, 139
Immigration and Nationality Act of 1952
    (McCarran-Walter), 128-29, 140

"Juanita" of Downieville, 59-61, 238n.

Kenedy, Mifflin, 32, 51, 74-75
King, Richard, 32, 46, 51-53, 55, 74-75

labeling theory, 51-53, 151, 226, 238n.
Land Act of 1851, 31, 38-39, 43
land grants (Mexican/Spanish)
    differences with American system of
        land ownership, 34-38, 97-98,
        229-31
    loss of by Mexican residents, 27-34,
        39-49, 55-56, 235
    overview of, 238n.
    protected under Treaty of Guadalupe
        Hidalgo, 9-16, 18
Las Cuevas affair, 72-75, 239n.
Las Gorras Blancas, 19, 97-99
Las Vegas grant, 97-98
Lick Pier riot, 167-69
López, José, 199, 212
Los Angeles police riots, 2, 22, 146,
    173-82, 240n.

MALDEF (Mexican American Legal
    Defense and Education Fund), 1-2,
    143, 182

manifest destiny, 5, 55, 72
Maxwell land grant, 47-49
Mazón, Mauricio, 172-73
Mexican attitudes toward Anglos, 5-9, 56,
    59, 65-66, 77, 79, 81, 94-95, 97,
    226-29
Mexican Revolution, 93-96, 102-3
Milhiser vs. Padilla, 98
mobilization of bias, 23-24, 136, 163, 165,
    171, 183, 185, 200
Moore, Joan W., 190-92, 226
Murieta, Joaquin, 18, 77, 79, 80-84, 89

Operation Deportation, 21, 114-15, 116-20
"Operation Wetback," 21-22, 125-29
organized rebellions, 88-89, 109

pachuco (pachuquismo)
    argot, 187, 240n.
    differentiated from zoot-suiter, 240n.
    hysteria during the 1940s, 161-66
    and intergenerational conflict, 186,
        189, 234
    mobilization of bias toward, 163, 165,
        171
    as response to prejudice and
        discrimination, 186-190
    stripped of masculinity, 172
pachuquitas, 171-72
Paredes, Américo, 84-85, 226
patterns of Mexican migration, 102-7
People v. Zammora, 163
placas/plaqueazos, 190, 214
police
    abuse and misconduct, 22-24, 146-51,
        178-79, 180-82
    deployment practices, 151-53
    role in U.S. servicemen's riots, 168-70
    treatment of juveniles, 150-51
    See also Los Angeles police riots
prison gangs, 200-11, 240n.
Public Law 45, 123
    See also Bracero Program
Public Law 78, 124
    See also Bracero Program

Ramirez, Manuel, III, 227-29
relative deprivation, 54-55
repatriation, 21, 50, 108, 116-20

Rio Grande city riot, 93-94
robber barons, 44-49
Rodríguez, Chepita, 61-62
Rosenbaum, 88-89

Santa Fe Ring, 46-49, 238n.
Sleepy Lagoon case, 50, 146, 156-66,
    173-74
social bandits
    definition of, 75
    distinguished from vigilantes, 237-38n.
    overview of, 74-87
    as primitive protest, 55, 75-76, 211
    as response to Anglo domination, 2,
        18-19, 74-77, 84, 95
Stillman, Charles, 32, 44-45, 55
Swing, General Joseph M., 126

Texas Rangers (los rinches)
    abuses of, 2-3, 20-21, 23, 68-69, 72-74
    and American values, 69-72
    and Anglo machismo, 71-72, 239n.
    attempts to capture Catarino Garza,
        94
    establishment of, 67-68, 238n.
    and King Ranch, 72-74
    Mexican view of, 69
    role in Cortina War, 91-92
    role in Las Cuevas affair, 72-75, 239n.
Texas revolt, 6-9
theoretical models
    applied to gringo justice, 225-36
    conflict, 218-19, 240n.
    internal colonial, 219-20, 231, 240n.
    Marxist, 220-21, 240n.
    order-pluralistic, 216-18, 240n.
    synthesis and integration of, 221-25
Tijerina, Reies López, 19
Treaty of Guadalupe Hidalgo 2-3, 9-19,
    31, 34, 40-42, 45, 50, 56, 89, 98,
    100, 231, 235

undocumented workers
    attempts to regulate, 108, 127-29,
        138-45, 239n.
    and contradictions in U.S. capitalism,
        106

contributions to U.S. economy, 131,
    222
deportation of, 116-20, 125-29
and economic fluctuations, 21, 104,
    106, 108, 112-13, 116, 127,
    130-31
employer preference for, 104-5, 120,
    145, 233
impact on crime, 129-38
police abuse of, 100, 112, 114, 137,
    181
racism directed at, 104-5, 137, 239n.
as victims of crime, 136-38, 239n.
See also Border Patrol; Immigration
U.S. Commission on Civil Rights, 1, 72,
    146-56
U.S. Servicemen's riots, 21-22, 50, 146,
    166-73

Valdez, Luis, 101
Vásquez, Tiburcio, 18, 77-79, 89
Vigil, Diego, 88-89
vigilantes (vigilantism), 51, 53-55, 59,
    62-64, 66-68, 71, 110

Webb, Walter Prescott, 3, 31, 67, 71, 75,
    96, 239n.

zoot-suiters
    and juvenile delinquency, 183
    as part of jitterbug "dance cult," 183
    as target of symbolic annihilation,
        172-73
    negative attitudes toward in Anglo
        community, 17, 21, 163-67
    negative attitudes toward in Mexican
        community, 184-85
    negative attitudes toward in press, 21,
        156-57, 159, 166, 169-71, 175,
        188
    violence directed at, 50, 166-73
    See also pachuco; U.S. Servicemen's
        riots
zoot-suit riots. See U.S. Servicemen's riots